The United Nations and Sustainable Development Goals

"This book encompasses all the facets for the development of- and ingredients required for- sustainability, which include science, technology, education, health, social and environmental factors. It is a must-read!"

—Professor Emmanuel Glakpe, *Howard University, United States*

"Bold, innovative, and ultimately groundbreaking. It provokes and yet offers creative solution to the recurring challenges of the Sustainable Development Goals initiative. It generates new debates and offers a clear, succinct, and brilliant body of knowledge."

—Dr. Michael Onyebuchi Eze, *Leiden University, The Netherlands*

"Unique for its focus on practical matters and for spotlighting the obstacles in the way of SDGs achievement in some developing nations, it provides the opportunity to listen to the voice from the Global South on the global agenda for sustainability."

—Dr. Xavier Moyet, *University of Leeds and University of Kent, United Kingdom*

"An exceedingly relevant text in facilitating implementation and realisation of the SDGs in developing countries. It is a book for research, and for policy makers, bureaucrats and civil society activists."

—Professor Umaru Pate, *Vice-Chancellor, Federal University Kashere, Nigeria*

"Providing a lucid account of the type of future the Global South must build, and offering refreshing insights into the substantive role global actors must consider in shaping that future, the text is thus a must-read for those seeking knowledge on development from interdisciplinary and globalist viewpoints."

—Dr. Paschal Anosike, *Director, Centre for African Entrepreneurship and Leadership, University of Wolverhampton, United Kingdom*

"An excellent read! The chapters cover many aspects of sustainability, which is of paramount importance to the world."

—Professor Satish Vasu Kailas, *Indian Institute of Science, Bangalore, India*

"A compelling narrative detailing the work of the UN on sustainability via the SDGs, and which postulates critical areas where the organisation's future role and activities can be more impactful. I wholeheartedly recommend this book."

—Professor Nnamdi Nwulu, *University of Johannesburg, South Africa*

"The Chapters put together in this book, which cover the various themes of the UN are worth reading, for awareness and the journey ahead."

—Professor Tien-Chien Jen, *University of Johannesburg, South Africa*

"The chapters focus on the perspectives and impact of the UN Agenda broadly and particularly on the African continent. The text is compelling."

—Professor Akindele G. Odeshi, *University of Saskatchewan, Canada*

Sheriff Folarin · Esther Akinlabi ·
Aderemi Atayero
Editors

The United Nations and Sustainable Development Goals

palgrave
macmillan

Editors
Sheriff Folarin
Covenant University
Ota, Ogun State, Nigeria

Aderemi Atayero
Covenant University
Ota, Ogun State, Nigeria

Esther Akinlabi
Department of Mechanical
Engineering Science
University of Johannesburg
Johannesburg, South Africa

Pan African University Life and Earth
Sciences Institute
Ibadan, Nigeria

ISBN 978-3-030-95970-8 ISBN 978-3-030-95971-5 (eBook)
https://doi.org/10.1007/978-3-030-95971-5

This Palgrave Macmillan imprint is published by the registered company Springer Nature Switzerland AG
The registered company address is: Gewerbestrasse 11, 6330 Cham, Switzerland

Papers from United Nations at 75 International/Virtual Conference, October 22–24, 2020, Covenant University, Ota, Ogun State, Nigeria. Conference was jointly organized by Covenant University & United Nations Information Centre-Nigeria.

To all the heroes of the COVID-19 pandemic, and to the memory of over one million victims globally, whose exit was never foretold.

Foreword by David Oyedepo

Mr. Secretary-General, distinguished ladies and gentlemen, I congratulate you on the occasion of the 75th Anniversary of the United Nations. In the history of international organizations, from the period of Westphalia in Middle Age Europe, to the nineteenth century, when nations began to attempt the forging of interstate blocs, the United Nations has been the greatest success story.

First, the UN is the only organization that has lived up to 75 years, making it the oldest surviving global body and with a record of accomplishments. Created in 1945, the UN is an offspring of the League of Nations, which failed to prevent the Second World War or solve the myriad of problems that bogged her down. The height of failure of the League was its inability to stop the superpower rivalry and control over the League, which cascaded into one of the worst conflicts in human history.

The UN that came into existence was thus positioned to correct the obvious lapses of the League and pursue the following goals:

- To maintain global peace and security
- To develop friendly relations among nations
- To achieve international cooperation
- To be a centre for harmonizing the actions of nations
- To prevent and resolve conflict and to minimize savagery of war

Accomplishing the goals in the last 75 years has come with its costs. As a close observer of trends, and in view of the enormous global challenges, one can posit that the UN has spent a considerable part of its existence contending with issues more than pursuing lofty goals. Some of the seemingly interminable global crises the organization has battled with include:

- A difficult post-Second World War reconstruction
- The protracted Cold War which institutionalized superpower conflict
- A nuclear arms race that made the world a global arms dump
- Intra-state conflicts caused by struggles for self-determination
- Leadership meltdown in nations leading to coups, political instability, civil wars and regional conflicts
- Human and drug trafficking
- Poverty and global health pandemics such as SARS, Ebola, COVID-19, etc.
- New threats to global peace, such as global, regional and local terrorism; climate change; global financial crisis; refugee crisis and the phenomenon of Internally Displaced Persons; cyber insecurity and growing cases of international financial crimes; and of course
- Superpower rivalry, inequality among nations, use of UN by great powers to achieve national goals and not being able to make super powers account for their excesses.

The good news is that, against all the odds, the UN is still a success story. If not for anything, the organization has been ingenious in preventing the outbreak of a Third World War. However, beyond this, there are other monumental achievements, including:

- Initiating and successfully engendering conflict resolution and peacekeeping in all regions of the world
- Combating climate change and health pandemics through innovative ideas, movements, specialized agencies and international agreements or treaties and protocols
- The Millennium Development Goals (MDGs) and Sustainable Development Goals (SDGs) initiatives whose Vision 2030 is aimed at resolving most of the global problems from the roots. The SDGs

represent a milestone in the integrated framework initiated by the UN to enhance human development.

A system that came into existence in 1945 cannot expect to do things differently or being able to face twenty-first-century problems if it remains what it was 75 years ago. UN is due for reforms. For this to happen and to achieve other goals, the UN would have to make the following internal reforms:

- Restructure the UN Security Council, in line with the reality of contemporary international relations
- Position herself for the inevitable challenges of the twenty-first-century international diplomacy, where digitization is fast outpacing shuttle diplomacy and where power is becoming redefined and diffused
- The UN must become more de-politicized in her administrative operations and deliberately create a culture of inclusiveness in policy process and implementation so that member-states can regard themselves as equal partners
- The UN must become more democratized in her structure, giving more room to the rising powers and emerging economies, especially from the global South to exercise their influence in leadership
- The international community has the responsibility to strengthen existing multilateral institutions of which the UN is the best model to meet these inevitable challenges.

Mr. Secretary-General, distinguished Ladies and Gentlemen, we will need a new wine in a new wineskin (as against the old wine in a new wineskin) for a UN we want for our generations after us to be birthed. There will be a need to transform the United Nations and offload the excesses that have tied her down.

We want to see a UN that will stand up against superpowers when their actions endanger the very essence of human existence. We wish to see a UN that will present a common platform where race, colour, ethnicity and region will have no basis in the scheme of things. We seek a United

Nations that will have an African nation given a permanent seat in the Security Council.

A world of equals and with equal opportunities. This is the future we want.

Dr. David Oyedepo
Chancellor
Covenant University
Ota, Ogun State, Nigeria

Foreword by Antonio Gueterres

The 75th anniversary of the United Nations falls in the middle of a global pandemic. Our founding mission is more critical than ever:

- To promote human dignity
- Protect human rights
- Respect international law
- And save humanity from war

When the pandemic hit, I called for a global ceasefire. In our world today, we have one common enemy: COVID-19. Now is the time for a stepped-up push for peace to achieve a global ceasefire. The clock is ticking. We must also make peace with our planet. The climate emergency threatens life itself. We must mobilize the whole world to reach carbon neutrality—net zero emissions of greenhouse gases by 2050. A growing number of countries and companies have already pledged to meet this goal.

Around the world, we must do more to end human suffering from poverty, inequality, hunger and hatred—and fight discrimination on the basis of race, religion, gender or any other distinction. The months of the pandemic have seen a horrific rise in violence against women and girls. We must build on progress. A remarkable global collaboration is underway for a safe, affordable and accessible COVID-19 vaccine for all.

The Sustainable Development Goals give us an inspiring blueprint for recovering better.

We face colossal challenges. With global solidarity and cooperation, we can overcome them. That is what the United Nations is all about. On this anniversary, I ask people everywhere to join together. The United Nations not only stands with you… The United Nations belongs to you and is you: "We the Peoples". Together, let us uphold the enduring values of the United Nations Charter. Let us build on our advances across the decades. Let us realize our shared vision of a better world for all.

Antonio Gueterres
Secretary-General, United Nations

Acknowledgement

Special thanks to God for the book initiative and for making the planning and execution of the UN75 International/Virtual Conference, from which papers for this book are generated, successful. Gratitude goes to the United Nations System, which through the United Nations Information Centre (UNIC) in Nigeria, extended the hosting right of such a big UN anniversary event to Covenant University. And gratitude also goes to the Chancellor, Dr. David Oyedepo, then-Acting Vice-Chancellor, Professor Akan Williams and the entire university management for accepting to host the conference and coordinate the publication of this book.

Specific mention must be made of Professor AAA Atayero, the fourth substantive Vice-Chancellor of Covenant University, who from October 2019 and September 2020 towards the end of his tenure, embraced the initiative and tenaciously drove the execution of the two (conference and book) projects. Others worthy of mention are UNIC Country Director, Mr. Ronald Kayanja and his team; Conference Chair and lead editor, Professor Sheriff Folarin and his team of dedicated organizers; Professor Esther Akinlabi of the University of Ibadan, who stood in gap from the time she was on sabbatical at Covenant, in the negotiations with Palgrave Macmillan; and Balaji Varadharaju and the entire Palgrave Macmillan team that handled this book project. In addition, many thanks to Dr. Olusola Ogunnubi of University of Kwa-Zulu Natal, South Africa and Carleton University, Canada, for painstakingly going through the manuscript to vet and make inputs.

Statement of Peer Review

As corresponding editor of the book project, I hereby certify that we have adhered to the double-blind peer review process to safeguard good scientific practice in publishing. I affirm the following:

- All articles were subjected to peer review first by the conference scientific committee and second by in-house for a book publication. The publisher furthered this review process internationally and independently on two separate occasions.
- Reviews were conducted by expert referees, who were requested to provide unbiased and constructive comments aimed, where necessary, at improving the work. They were asked to advise on publishability of each of the chapters.
- The editors took all reasonable steps to ensure that the quality of the materials published and their decision to accept or reject a paper for publication was based only on the merits of the papers and the relevance to the theme.

Sheriff.

Professor Sheriff Folarin, Ph.D.
Conference Chair, UN75 International Conference
Department of Political Science and International Relations
Covenant University
Ota, Ogun State, Nigeria
For: The Editors

Contents

Editors and Contributors

About the Editors

Sheriff Folarin is a professor of international relations at Covenant University and currently a visiting scholar in Political Science Department and William P. Hobby Centre for Public Service of Texas State University, United States. A two-time departmental chair, he was also the pioneer head of international programmes/collaborations at Covenant University. He is a 2007 fellow of the Study of the United States Institutes (SUSI) and visiting fellow of the Walker Institute of International and Area Studies of the University of South Carolina. Among other awards, he is also a 2013 host-fellow of Carnegie African Diaspora Fellowship Programme, and a member since 2019 of the United Nations Office on Drugs and Crimes group of scholars. Folarin is a mentor of faculty of the Ife Institute of Advanced Studies and a three-time visiting professor in the University of Rwanda Center for Security Studies and Command and Staff College, where he teaches the senior officer corps of the military across African states enrolled in the Master in Security Studies programme. He is also a founding member of the Classroom Beyond Borders Partners' Institute, which took him to Ithaca College, New York, three times as a collaborative scholar. Folarin is author of Visibility and Relevance in International Politics, and a co-author of Religion and Global Politics. He has over seventy articles published in peer-reviewed journals, books, and conference proceedings. He has also presented keynotes at several international conferences, served as chair/member of over forty thesis committees in Nigeria and overseas, producing three scores and ten of PhDs in the process and has earned other numerous academic awards, honors and recognition.

Esther Akinlabi is a professor of mechanical engineering at the University of Ibadan; she currently serves as the Director of the Pan African University for Life and Earth Sciences Institute (PAULESI), Ibadan, Nigeria. The PAU is a continental initiative of the AUC. Before now, she was professor at the Department of Mechanical Engineering Science, Faculty of Engineering and the Built Environment, University of Johannesburg. Her research interest is in the field of modern and advanced manufacturing processes—Friction stir welding and additive manufacturing, among other areas. She is a recipient of several research grants and has received many awards of recognition to her credit. She is a member of the prestigious South African Young Academy of Science and registered with the Engineering Council of South Africa.

Aderemi Atayero is a professor of Communication Engineering and immediate past vice-chancellor of Covenant University. He is a 2013 Carnegie African Diaspora Fellowship Programme scholar. A multiple award-winning vice-chancellor and scholar, he led Covenant to the top ten universities in Africa and the number one academic institution in West Africa and Nigeria in the Time Higher Education rankings for two consecutive years, the first time the institution has ever risen to that position. It was in his time as vice-chancellor that Covenant earned the respect as a leader in the transformation of African higher education, for which he also won an international award. Professor Atayero is recognized for contemporary multidisciplinary academic research across wireless/mobile communications, Internet of Things (loT) and smart cities and cyber-physical systems. He is a senior research fellow of the International Association of Research Scholars and Administrators, and a fellow of the Science Association of Nigeria (FSAN).

Contributors

Adedoyin Abinusawa Department of Chemical Engineering, Covenant University, Ota, Ogun, Nigeria

Mercy Adebayo Department of Sociology, Covenant University, Ota, Nigeria

Olujide Adekeye Department of Psychology, Covenant University, Ota, Nigeria

Janet Adeleke Lagos, Nigeria

Adewale Adeniyi Department of Civil Engineering, College of Engineering, Covenant University, Ota, Nigeria

Christiana Adetunde Department of Sociology, Covenant University, Ota, Nigeria

Adedeji Afolabi Department of Building Technology, Covenant University, Ota, Ogun State, Nigeria

Esther Ajiboye Department of Languages and General Studies, Covenant University, Ota, Nigeria

Esther Akinlabi Department of Mechanical Engineering, University of Johannesburg, Johannesburg, South Africa;
Pan African University Institute for Life and Earth Sciences (PAULESI), Ibadan, Nigeria

Isaac Akinwumi Department of Civil Engineering, Covenant University, Ota, Nigeria

Victor Akpan Department of Civil Engineering, Covenant University, Ota, Nigeria

Isaac Iorhen Akuva Department of Political Science, Federal University Dutsin-Ma, Dutsin-Ma, Katsina State, Nigeria

Oladapo Alagbe Department of Computer and Information Sciences, Covenant University, Ota, Nigeria

Moses Saa-Aondo Andza Department of Political Science, Federal University Dutsin-Ma, Dutsin-Ma, Katsina State, Nigeria

Aderemi Atayero Department of Electrical and Information Engineering, Covenant University, Ota, Ogun State, Nigeria

Adetomiwa Atayero Department of Political Science and International Relations, Covenant University, Ota, Ogun State, Nigeria

Clemson Ayegbusi Babcock University, Ilisan-Remo, Ogun State, Nigeria

Olaniyi Ayodele Departement of International Relations, Coveant University, Ota, Nigeria

Ibukun Balogun Department of Sociology, Covenant University, Ota, Nigeria

Daniel Bassey Department of Civil Engineering, Covenant University, Ota, Nigeria

Lily Chimuanya Department of Languages and General Studies, Covenant University, Ota, Nigeria

Moses Duruji Covenant University, Ota, Ogun State, Nigeria

Eghosa Ekhaese Department of Architecture, Covenant University, Ota, Ogun State, Nigeria

Francis Elehinafe Chemical Engineering Department, Covenant University, Ota, Nigeria

Emmanuel Fagbenle Department of Civil Engineering, Covenant University, Ota, Nigeria

Oluwafunke Folarin Department of Leadership Studies, North Carolina A&T State University, Greensboro, NC, USA

Sheriff Folarin Department of Political Science and International Relations, Covenant University, Ota, Ogun State, Nigeria;
Department of Political Science, Texas State University, San Marcos, USA

Tayo George Department of Sociology, Covenant University, Ota, Nigeria;
Lagos, Nigeria

Abiodun Gesinde Department of Psychology, Covenant University, Ota, Ogun, Nigeria

Enoch M. Ibitogbe Department of Civil Engineering, Landmark University, Omu-Aran, Nigeria

Samuel Ibok Department of Political Science and International Relations, Covenant University, Ota, Ogun State, Nigeria

Joshua Ighalo Department of Civil Engineering, College of Engineering, Covenant University, Ota, Nigeria

Felix Ishola Mechanical Engineering Department, Covenant University, Ota, Nigeria

Jide Jimoh School of Communication, Lagos State University, Lagos, Nigeria

Asim K. Karmakar Department of Economics, School of Professional Studies, Netaji Subhas Open University, Nadia, India

Oluwatobi Kolawole Department of Chemical Engineering, Covenant University, Ota, Ogun, Nigeria

Justin Lazarus Department of Civil Engineering, Covenant University, Ota, Nigeria

Angela Mamudu Chemical Engineering Department, Covenant University, Ota, Nigeria

Sovik Mukherjee St. Xavier's University, Kolkata, India

Ben Ngene Department of Civil Engineering, Covenant University, Ota, Nigeria;
Department of Civil Engineering, Michael Okpara University of Agriculture, Umudike, Nigeria

Gift Nnamani Department of Banking and Finance, Covenant University, Ota, Nigeria

Oyinlola Obanla Department of Chemical Engineering, Covenant University, Ota, Ogun, Nigeria

Jonathan Odukoya Department of Psychology, Covenant University, Ota, Ogun, Nigeria

Isaac Odun-Ayo Department of Computer and Information Sciences, Covenant University, Ota, Nigeria

Olatokunbo Ofuyatan Department of Civil Engineering, College of Engineering, Covenant University, Ota, Nigeria

Gideon Ogunduyile Chemical Engineering Department, Covenant University, Ota, Nigeria

Oluseyi Ogunnowo Department of Poltical Science and International Relations, Covenant University, Ota, Nigeria

Rapheal Ojelabi Department of Building Technology, Covenant University, Ota, Ogun State, Nigeria

Modupe Ojewumi Department of Chemical Engineering, Covenant University, Ota, Ogun, Nigeria

Emeka Okoro Petroleum Engineering Department, Covenant University, Ota, Nigeria

Lawrence Okoye Covenant University, Ota, Ogun State, Nigeria

Olusolami Okunlola Department of Psychology, Covenant University, Ota, Ogun, Nigeria

Olawole Olanipekun Department of Chemical Engineering, UNILAG Akoka, Lagos, Nigeria

Faith Olanrewaju Department of Poltical Science and International Relations, Covenant University, Ota, Nigeria

Olawale Olonade Department of Sociology, Covenant University, Ota, Nigeria

David Olukanni Department of Civil Engineering, College of Engineering, Covenant University, Ota, Nigeria

John Oluwafemi Department of Civil Engineering, College of Engineering, Covenant University, Ota, Nigeria

Olanrenwaju Oluwole Department of Architecture, Covenant University, Ota, Ogun State, Nigeria

Oluwasegun Omidiora Department of Languages and General Studies, Covenant University, Ota, Nigeria

Kester Onor Covenant University, Ota, Ogun State, Nigeria

Lai Oso School of Communication, Lagos State University, Lagos, Nigeria

Mercy Ozoya Department of Sociology, Covenant University, Ota, Nigeria

Oluseyi Soremekun United Nations Information Office, Lagos, Nigeria

Oluwakemi Udoh Department of Political Science and International Relations, Covenant University, Ota, Ogun State, Nigeria

List of Figures

List of Tables

CHAPTER 1

Introduction

Sheriff Folarin, Esther Akinlabi, and Aderemi Atayero

United Nations and Sustainable Development Goals, is a book commemorative of the seventy-five years of existence of United Nations (UN). It is partly a product of the only international academic conference in Africa

S. Folarin (✉)
Department of Political Science and International Relations, Covenant University, Ota, Ogun State, Nigeria
e-mail: sheriff.folarin@covenantuniversity.edu.ng; jrj191@txstate.edu

Department of Political Science, Texas State University, San Marcos, USA

E. Akinlabi
Department of Mechanical Engineering Science, University of Johannesburg, Johannesburg, South Africa
e-mail: etakinlabi@uj.ac.za

Pan African University Life and Earth Sciences Institute, Ibadan, Nigeria

A. Atayero
Department of Electrical and Information Engineering, Covenant University, Ota, Ogun State, Nigeria
e-mail: atayero@cu.edu.ng

S. Folarin et al. (eds.), *The United Nations and Sustainable Development Goals*, https://doi.org/10.1007/978-3-030-95971-5_1

organised to celebrate UN's 75th anniversary. The conference was co-organised by Covenant University and the United Nations Information Centre in Nigeria. Some of the chapters are selected from the Covenant-African Development Issues (C-ICADI) conference of 2020. From the pool of papers submitted for the academic meetings, nineteen, which bore direct relevance to the theme were picked and subjected to peer review. The final set of selected papers are put together, which constitute this twenty-five-chapter book.

Focusing on the theme of the anniversary, 'The Future We Want, the UN We Need: Reaffirming our Collective Commitment to Multilateralism', most of the chapters dwell on a wide range of topics that mirror the UN, global system, human society and issues of world concern in a multidisciplinary, transdisciplinary and interdisciplinary way. The focus of the book is not so much of dwelling on the past of the international organisation, as it is of charting a new course for the world through the lens of multilateralism.

However, the enterprise does not attempt to discount the modest achievements and some grim experiences of the past, which set the platform for peeping into and taking control of the future as some of the chapters have done. The future is uncertain; hence, concrete steps have to be taken to give a direction to the course of the future. Ideas rule the world. Like social constructivists, who argue that the global system is not merely driven by quest for material gains, the configuration of the world today is a product of the constructs of prolific mind- from the Congress of Vienna which created a 'Concert of Europe', to the Hague Conferences of the nineteenth century, League of Nations and now United Nations. Constructivism argues that the most important aspect of international relations is social, not material—the world exists only as an intersubjective awareness among people; the world system is thus constituted by ideas, not by material forces. Put differently, the international system is a human invention or creation not of a physical or material kind but of a purely intellectual and ideational kind (Theys, 2018).

The global narrative is a mixed bag of vicissitudes and the United Nations has been at the centre of them. The organisation was established in 1945, to foster global peace and security, provide platforms for the development of friendly relations among nations, achieve international cooperation and be the hub for harmonisation of the actions of governments and other international legal personalities in the world. For many decades of its existence, the UN has worked assiduously to fulfil these roles and achieve these objectives. Specifically, in the last decade, the organisation made remarkable contributions to global peace, global growth, health, education and diffusion of science and technology.

However, as the organisation continues to contend with, and manage the plethora of global and human challenges, even in its 75 years of existence, it is also apparent that the world is increasingly at risk of facing the impact of technological change accompanied by economic and political conflagrations, climate crisis, religious extremism and terrorism. Today, the world faces a global health pandemic that threatens the very existence of humanity. The novel coronavirus (COVID-19) was unanticipated in 2020, so there was little or no preparation for it. The disease, now in its fourth wave globally, with the Omicron variant that is more deadly because of its rapidity of spread has, as of November 2021, infected a total number 270 million and killed 5.3 million people, all within two years (*New York Times*, 2021). This kind of global tragedy, like several other ones, is an existential threat to development and sustainability locally and internationally. And yet, the world is only nine years away from the 2030 Agenda for Sustainable Development.

The UNSDGs are seventeen. These are in the order of priority, No Poverty, Zero Hunger, Good Health and Wellbeing. Others are Quality Education, Gender Equality, Clean Water and Sanitation, Affordable and Clean Energy, Decent Work and Economic Growth; Industry, Innovation and Infrastructure. The rest are Reduced Inequalities, Sustainable Cities and Communities, Responsible Consumption and Production, Climate Action, Life Below Water, Life on Land; Peace, Justice and Institutions; and Partnerships for the Goals (United Nations, 2015).

The 2030 SDGs were adopted by all member-states of the UN in 2015, to provide a framework for peace and prosperity for the world. It succeeded the Millennium Development Goals (MDGs) which were adopted in 2000 to perform a similar role of the SDGs. The MDGs were however not as far-reaching as the SDGs and few nations only were able to meet the target. Majority of the UN member-states lagged far behind (United Nations, 2015). It was not that the MDGs were not good enough. Some of these goals were eradication of poverty and hunger, achieving universal primary education, promoting gender equality and women empowerment, reduction of child mortality, improvement of maternal health, environmental sustainability and development of partnership for development. While they were solid goals in terms of the needs of humanity, most nations of the world did not have the capacity or enabling environment to achieve the millennium goals. Fifteen years later, the SDGs were articulated and outlined to be more comprehensive and give room for possibilities of meeting many of the goals.

Hence, as the world approaches the set timeline to attain the SDGs, it becomes imperative to pause, ponder on and consider some essential questions, and hard-hitting conversations that arise as the UN system and stakeholders look ahead into the future. Is there a collective future we want? Are we futures-literate? Why do we need a futures-literate United Nations? What kind of United Nations do we need in the future we want? Is the effort to re-skill individuals essential? Should we re-skill individuals for the future we see or for the future we want? What morphological models exist for the individual, organisation or economies we want in the future?

It is these questions and more that constitute the focus of this book. The chapters are submissions from scholars, students, professionals from around the world and international public servants. Issues are addressed from individual, organisational, state, national, regional or global perspectives, but with the view to illuminating the global impact of these diverse perspectives. The book provided a common platform for scholars and others to engage and share their research and have interdisciplinary and multidisciplinary dialogues on topical issues and concerns facing the world.

The book has three sections, each addressing various human, cultural, health, environmental, scientific and technological concerns of the present and future. The first two sections address country-specific issues relating to development and sustainability. These sections focus on concerns in Nigeria and Africa, as they are some of the most challenged in meeting SDGs in view of their plethora of struggles politically, economically and security problems that endanger sustainable development. Yet, there are also innovations in this region, which could enhance sustainability, which some chapters examine.

While the second section pays particular attention to Africa, it also addresses global development issues and sustainability. The chapters examine and discuss the searing challenges for the world and United Nations in the present and future. They are—but not limited to—terrorism, global climate change, fake news syndrome, peace and security.

The third section commits to health, science and technological discourses and presentation of findings of groundbreaking empirical researches. The chapters in this section examine and discuss how scientific and technological innovations are an extension of sustainability on the one hand, and how these aid in preservation of human, environmental and health development.

Generally, the book explores issues ranging from sustainability, to industrial development. Also, it focuses on future role of machines, responsible science and the future of learning. From such atomistic concerns to human challenges such as migration, ethnicity, xenophobia, insurgency and diplomacy, the book captures the essence of life. There are appendices, in which keynote and lead papers at the UN75 International Conference (October 22–24, 2020) are presented.

It is hoped that the book will expand the dialogue on the future desirable for the UN and international community as well as provide a good framework for research on UN and global issues in the twentieth and twenty-first century. This book is and will be an all-time research database. It will be resourceful for academics/educators, governments, non-governmental and advocacy organisations, professionals, students, journalists, scientists, engineers, profit and non-profit-based organisations, among others. It is expected to serve as an addition to the understanding of the purpose, value and workings of the United Nations on the one hand; and the understanding of the global system on the other. The complexities, complications, challenges and dynamics of the global system are presented in such a manner that those searching for answers from all fields of human endeavour can find this source-material as the databank to fill the gaps required.

References

New York Times. (2021). Coronavirus in the United States: Latest map and case count. Retrieved February 2, 2021 from https://www.nytimes.com/interactive/2020/us/coronavirus-us-cases.html

Theys, S. (2018). *Introducing constructivism in international relations theory*. E-International Relations. Retrieved January 28, 2021 from https://www.e-ir.info/2018/02/23/introducing-constructivism-in-international-relations-theory

United Nations. (2015). *The 17 goals*. Department of Economic and Social Affairs. Retrieved February 2, 2021 from https://sdgs.un.org/goals

PART I

Country-Specific Human Development Issues and Sustainability

CHAPTER 2

African Elite and Human Security in Africa: Examining SDG-8

Kester Onor, Lawrence Okoye, and Moses Duruji

Background

Various factors are responsible for the deplorable human security situation in Africa (Omoniyi, 2018). The immediate causes of human insecurity in Africa include dictatorial regimes, poverty, state weakness or fragility, injustice, exclusion and discrimination. Others include political instability, ethno-religious rivalries and electoral violence (Langenhove, 2004). Beyond the immediate pathologies mentioned above, various historical factors account for these perennial disorders. The great cataclysms of Western colonialism, imperialism and neo-colonial interventions and the subsequent misrule by post-colonial political leaders are fundamental factors that are impeding the human security situation in Africa (Langenhove, 2004). However, this paper will critically examine the role played by the African elites in exacerbating the human security situation in the continent.

K. Onor (✉) · L. Okoye · M. Duruji
Covenant University, Ota, Ogun State, Nigeria
e-mail: kester.onor@covenantuniversity.edu.ng

S. Folarin et al. (eds.), *The United Nations and Sustainable Development Goals*, https://doi.org/10.1007/978-3-030-95971-5_2

The African Predicament

The African continent has been most unfortunate in human development and this is not unrelated to its checkered history of slavery and colonization. The contact of Africa with Europe stunted the organic and natural development of African societies who were forcefully incorporated into global capitalism as producers of primary goods (Ajayi, 2011).

Even, though most African countries got their independence from European colonialism over six decades ago, most of the countries in the continent are still struggling with the issue of underdevelopment (Kalu, 2018). The nature of the state which African leaders inherited from their European colonial masters, was a state designed to oppress the people and exploit their resources (Terreblanche, 2011).

The desire of the European powers to sustain a neo-colonial contraption that protects their economic interest in Africa gave rise to the pseudo-political system where accession to power is through manipulation and brigandage (Duruji et al., 2015). This system has created situations in Africa where leadership is alienated from the vast citizenry.

The outcome of this situation is the backwardness, underdevelopment, poverty, insecurity, misery, disease and wanton socio-political crisis that continues to beset the continent. The situation has also continued to produce underinvestment in infrastructure. Physical infrastructure across much of the continent that will create the environment for economic take-off remains a huge challenge to productivity (Park et al., 2020).

Sustainable Development Goal 8 and Human Security in Africa

The United Nations seventeen new goals referred to Sustainable Development Goals which replaced the Millennium Development Goal in 2015, were all cast to make the world a living place that is better for all and sustainable for the coming generations.

Goal 8 of SDG aims at promoting full and productive employment and decent work. The targeted outcome includes ensuring that sustained per capita economic growth in accordance with national circumstances. It also aims at achieving higher levels of economic productivity through a diversified technological upgrading and innovation that bring high-value-added and labour-intensive sectors that provide means of livelihood for the masses. It also aims at promoting development-oriented policies that support productive activities, create decent jobs and encourage entrepreneurship, creativity and innovation that will spur the formalization and growth of micro, small and medium enterprises. It also aims at improving global resource efficiency in consumption, production and endeavours that will decouple economic growth from environmental degradation (Olu-Owolabi et al., 2020).

The achievement of SDG Goal 8 relates to human security in the sense that human security addresses sustainable peace by recognizing the social, economic and political grievances that are often the root causes of conflict and societal violence.

The realization of SDG Goal 8 would ensure freedom from pervasive threats to people's rights and safety of their lives. As such taking concrete steps to realize the lofty goals of SDG Goal 8 will produce ~~a~~ positive human security of the people that translates to freedom from fear and freedom from want. Human security therefore becomes an approach for United Nations Member States to identify and address widespread and cross-cutting challenges to the survival, livelihood and dignity of their people.

The Elite in Africa

Fundamentally, all governments have elites at the head. Elites are viewed as essential elements of the political and social life of the country and in every country, the stability of the nation and its regime seems to depend in large measure on the way in which the elites are organized and fit with the other sectors. There are qualities, which constitute the hallmark of competent groups. These qualities are essential for national development. Essentially, elite's formation is legitimated by their identification with the most pervasive goals in society. That is, elites ideally are an embodiment of national consensus. Elite therefore is a nexus of need fulfilment that binds situational demands and group membership. Thus, the failure and success of national development depend on elite's effectiveness in knitting together political influence so that it responds to functional demand on the system. By personalizing national values and giving a relentless drive to development, ideally, elites energize the productive capacity of the society. Indeed, the quality of a nation's elites and the image, which they project to the world, constitutes an important source of power.

A small group of educated Africans spearheaded the agitations for Africa's independence. These groups of individuals were united in their struggle against colonialists. However, subsequent developments show that they merely united because they had common enemies. As soon as the Europeans left, this unity collapsed. Each leading nationalist wanted to achieve power using the people of his tribe as the base. This shows that what African nationalist elites took as the unity of purpose was only an illusion.

The indigenous elites were nurtured by the political culture of the colonial state and had been accustomed to identifying the state as the only purveyor of financial resources and favour. Instead of changing colonial institutions, laws and values for the better, African ruling elites and leaders entrenched deeply compromised governance systems (Adetiloye et al., 2017). The newly independent governments were often highly centralized and strongly dominated by one political leader and his political, ethnic or regional faction. Post-independence governments reposed enormous powers in the hands of their 'founding fathers' (Ake cited in Sawyer, 2004, p. 3). The dominant structural make-up of post-independence governments has meant that they can seamlessly fit into a centralized political culture very much like the colonial administration. New African leaders saw state power as an instrument of domination that did not require the consent of those subject to it (Bandoura, 1995). At independence, elite groups adopted the maximalist state structure where the state is expected to play a fundamental role in the political and economic life of their countries. Hence, many post-colonial states in Africa assumed a leading and wide-ranging interventionist role with a large public sector. Pitcher (2002, p. 17) notes that 'states were expected to be the mechanism that would hasten economic and social development; they would be responsible for making their countries modern. They would bankroll large, technologically sophisticated industrial projects and mechanize agriculture'.

As the political centre was broadened, it generated increased agitation and demands by various ethnic nationalities for self-rule. Ethnic elites rejected indirect rule as an insufficient form of political representation and demanded privileged access to the highest echelons of the central government to credibly guarantee their security and a fair share of state spoils (Roessler, 2011, p. 304). These ruling classes found themselves in a sociological and economic situation, not of their own historical making. They have been placed in the positions they hold as a result of the departure of the metropolitan servants of a colonial empire who were merely Europeans working within the matrix of colonial empire, all sharing the same culture and traditions with their homologues in the European headquarters.

The bureaucratic class that was nurtured during the colonial era was naturally promoted as the new instrument of exploitation as the era of neo-colonialism took hold. This was the genesis of Africa's comprador bourgeoisie. The unskilled indigenous communities that were impoverished by colonial policies had significant holdings in the private sector. Very few grassroots cadres, which formed part of the liberation movements, had professional careers outside the struggle. At independence, many were simply appointed to posts for which they had little aptitude, experience or skills to perform. Such a situation fuelled corruption as newly acquired state bureaucracy, military, judiciary, nationalized private industries were often seen as the 'spoils' of victory and the reward for the struggle of independence. The whole process became opaque and unaccountable with 'struggle aristocracies' dishing out patronage—jobs, government tenders and newly nationalized private companies to their political allies, ethnic group(s) or regional interests.

The Role of African Elites in the Contemporary Human Security Situation

Giving jobs to members of the same faction, ethnic group or region meant the idea of merit-based appointments was all too often thrown out of the window. This also meant that even if the newly empowered independence movement launched economic development programmes to transform the colonial economy, such reforms were likely to have minimal impact, given that unqualified 'cronies' were managing key public institutions, and that scarce resources were being diverted to allies, family and friends. Liberation aristocracy loyalists increasingly occupied appointments to the key institutions that scrutinize as well as hold rulers to account—the judiciary, the police and the media. These institutions already corrupt under colonialism, continued to be perverted by a new set of management cadres who were unlikely to hold the rulers, through whose patronage they served, to account. In many countries, this continues to be the case. Those who held junior ranks in the colonial hierarchy but had little skills and education found it difficult to make a decent living in the post-colonial society. They too were forced to seek out, by corrupt means, the patronage of leaders that had control over the distribution of the 'spoils'. Almost the only jobs available in the newly independent country were in government or, the newly nationalized media, banks, schools, universities, etc. Remunerated employment depended on 'clearance' from the liberation movement leaders or the ruling group. In most cases, those critical of the incumbent regimes or their policies were likely to be excluded from work in the public and private sectors (Burton, 1997).

African post-colonial governing elites were confronted with the challenge of how (under conditions of low economic development) to establish and maintain control of diverse and geographically dispersed societies, in the absence of strong political institutions or a unifying national ideology. In order to mitigate this colonial legacy, governing elites initially built ethnically inclusive governments in which appointees from rival ethnic groups played a role similar to that played by tribal chiefs during colonialism, acting as intermediaries between regime and society, to facilitate the transfer of local information and mobilize support for the regime (Rothchild and Foley cited in Roessler, 2011, p. 303).

The ethnic power-sharing formula and the elite accommodation boosted the legitimacy of leaders of independent countries as national figures and strengthened their societal control through the institution of ethnic brokerage. The ethnic power holders were compensated with influence at the highest levels of government and access to state resources, which they amassed with impunity and subsequently, employed and financed their own patronage networks and mobilized societal support for the regime (Van de Walle, 2009, p. 6). Thus, many post-colonial African states relied on the promise of development and their ability to work towards meeting the important needs of all citizens. The legitimacy of their governments was incumbent on ameliorating these needs. Unable to fulfil their pre-independence promises, the post-independence regime became increasingly authoritarian to sustain their positions and legitimacy (ibid.).

However, as development initiatives failed, it quickened recourse to repression as regime maintenance became the most important preoccupation of African post-colonial governments. Ake (1996) notes that democracy is not a significant item on Africa's post-independence governance agenda. Rather, political practice became entrenched in accordance to which the access to state resources and personal enrichment went hand-in-hand. Due to their weak material resource base, post-colonial governing elites used state power for their personal aggrandizement and wealth accumulation in order to wield influence over followers and competitors, thereby placing high premium on power which consequently made politics a violent zero-sum game resulting in discord amongst the component parts of the states by politicizing ethnicity and religion. Politics thus degenerated into a life-and-death struggle over private access to (limited) public resources. Moreover, the traditional leaders who had been left aside during the process of independence, along with marginalized ethnic nationalities of the newly independent states felt disadvantaged and disenchanted by lopsided power distribution. They put increasing pressure on post-independence elites to live up to their promises of improved conditions of life and equitable distribution of resources and power (Chazan et al., 1999). Given the inability of many African governments to meet the social and economic needs of their people, the citizens became disillusioned with governments that could not provide basic social and economic services, such as jobs, education and adequate health-care. These rulers created 'atmosphere[s] of perpetual musical chairs' by their frequent reshuffling of ministers in and out of the government. Though costly in terms of government efficiency and productivity, 'revolving door' appointments can be an effective political tool, as it prevents clients from amassing too much power within their respective ministries.

Moreover, it expands the size of the ruling coalition whilst minimizing disaffection if the ruler can credibly convince clients that the revolving door to power always remains open, providing those who have been replaced with an incentive to stay in the ruler's favour in hopes of a possible future appointment, rather than defecting and joining the opposition (Chazan et al., 1999, p. 52).

Cilliers (2004, p. 34) notes that Africa's post-independence leaders appeared to be more concerned with staying in power, and building an economic base for themselves, than in the economic and social development of the citizens. In the process, leaders were virtually deified for their commitment to the struggle for independence, and spent their later years embroiled in an undignified fight for political power at the expense of their countries. Often, African leaders appeared distracted by the benefits of office since 'power also brought with it many opportunities for attaining wealth in an African context of extreme scarcity and poverty as well as limited private accumulation'. Since most other avenues to wealth were restricted, with the larger private enterprises being in non-African hands, political power and the benefits associated with state control became the focus of intense struggle. Thus, 'Patronage politics has been integral to post-colonial efforts to maintain political control in poor, ethnically diverse peasant societies. Yet, although valuable in helping to consolidate ruling coalitions, the dynamics of patronage relations have proved economically highly damaging' (Beekers & Van Gool, 2012, p. 11).

In conclusion, the human security situation in many African states was undermined due to patronage politics of African elites that empowered minorities economically and increasingly impoverished the masses in a continent rich in natural resources and development potential. The inability of post-colonial governments to meet the legitimate needs of their citizens degenerated into violence and exacerbated deep-seated ethnic animosities. The governing elites responded to this threat by adopting the strategy of ethnic exclusion to safeguard their grips on power, even at the cost of forfeiting societal control and risking civil war (Horowitz, 1985, p. 471). This condition created room for military intervention in African politics.

Conclusion

The continent of Africa is one place that continues to experience the challenges of human insecurity. The irresponsible African ruling class has not been able to mitigate these due to the alienation from the masses. The lack of visionary and self-centred leadership in most parts of Africa, highly corrupt and unwilling to reform the African state is what gives rise to the many challenges of conflict, war, poverty and disease. The African elites slowness in realizing that it is in its own interest to carry the mass of the people along in the governance of the African space, made it difficult for a workable programme that would have addressed the human security in Africa.

The United Nations SDG Goal 8 provides an avenue for tackling the challenges of human insecurity in the continent and the commitment of contemporary African leaders and elites raises hope. As the entire global community celebrates the 75th anniversary of the United Nation, African elites should use the renewed opportunity to improve the human security in the continent by implementing policies and programmes that realizes the lofty goals of SDG Goal 8.

References:

Adetiloye, K. A., Taiwo, J. N., & Duruji, M. M. (2017). *Market risk instrument and portfolio inflows in African frontier economies in contribution to economics*. Springer.

Ajayi, T. (2011). Africa's incorporation into the world capitalist system: The substantive features and issue. *International Journal of Economic Develoment Research and Investment, 2*(3), 103.

Ake, C. (1996). *Democracy and development in Africa*. The Brookings Institution.

Bandoura, D. (1995). Etat et securite en Afrique. *Politique Africaine, 61*, 39–54.

Beekers, D. T., & Van Gool, S. M. (2012). *From patronage to neopatrimonialism: Postcolonial governance in Sub-Sahara Africa and beyond*.

Burton, J. (1997). *Violence experienced: The source of conflict violence and crime and their prevention*. Manchester University Press.

Chazan, N. L., Mortner, P., RothChild, R. A., & Stedman, D. (1999). *Politics and society in contemporary Africa*. Lynn Rienner Publisher.

Cilliers, J. (2004). *Human security in Africa. A conceptual framework for review. A monograph for African human security initiative*. Pretoria. http://www.africanreview.org

Duruji, M. C., Ayo, S., & Oni, A. (2015). *Making a case for e-voting proceeding of the European Conference on e-government ECEG*, 100–106.

Horowitz, D. (1985). *Ethnic groups in conflict*. University of California Press.

Kalu, K. (2018). Explaining Africa's underdevelopment. In *Foreign aid and the future of Africa. African histories and modernities*. Palgrave Macmillan. https://doi.org/10.1007/978-3-319-78987-3_9

Langenhove, L. V. (2004). *Regionalising human security in Africa*. United Nations University—CRIS Occassional Paper Series 0-2004/8.

Olu-Owolabi, F. E., Gberevbie, D. E., & Abasilim, U. O. (2020). Ethics of democracy development in Africa: A philosophical foundation. *African Identities, 5*, 1–12.

Omoniyi, B. B. (2018). An examination of the causes of poverty on economic growth in Nigeria'. *Africa's Public Service Delivery and Performance Review, 6*(1), a175. https://doi.org/10.4102/apsdpr.v6i1.175

Park, C. Y., Villafuerte, J., & Abiad, A. (2020). *An updated assessment of the economic impact of COVID-19* (No. 133). Asian Development Bank.

Pitcher, M. A. (2002). *Transforming Mozambique—The politics of privatization, 1975–2000*. University Press.

Roessler, P. (2011). The enemy within: Personal rule, coups, and civil war in Africa. *World Politics, 63*(2), 300–346.

Sawyer, A. (2004). Violent conflicts and governance challenges in West Africa: The case of the Mano River basin area. *The Journal of Modern African Studies, 42*(3), 437–463.

Terreblanche, S. (2011) *The exploitation of Africa and Africans by the Western World since 1500 A bids eyeview*. Paper read at the uBuntu Conference at the Law Faculty of the University of Pretoria, August 2–4.

Van de Walle, N. (2009). *The democratization of political clientelism in sub-Saharan Africa*. Paper presented at the Democracy and Development in the Middle East Conference in honor of John Waterburg. Princeton University, April 2–3.

CHAPTER 3

Rail Transport in Nigeria: Sustenance-Bound Prospects

Daniel Bassey, Ben Ngene, Isaac Akinwumi, Victor Akpan, Enoch M. Ibitogbe, and Gift Nnamani

Introduction

Over the decades, the Nigerian inland transportation sector has developed in three phases of overdependence. Firstly, the phase of inland water transportation overdependence between the pre-colonial era and 1900, secondly, the period of development and dependence on the

D. Bassey (✉) · B. Ngene · I. Akinwumi · V. Akpan
Department of Civil Engineering, Covenant University, Ota, Nigeria
e-mail: daniel.bassey@stu.cu.edu.ng

I. Akinwumi
e-mail: isaac.akinwumi@covenantuniversity.edu.ng

V. Akpan
e-mail: victor.akpan@stu.cu.edu.ng

B. Ngene
Department of Civil Engineering, Michael Okpara University of Agriculture, Umudike, Nigeria

S. Folarin et al. (eds.), *The United Nations and Sustainable Development Goals*, https://doi.org/10.1007/978-3-030-95971-5_3

railway systems between 1898 and the 1960s, and presently, the phase of road transport dominance (Tolofari & Gubbins, 1984). Over 80% of the railway infrastructure available in Nigeria today was built within the second phase by the British colonial administration to aid with the movement of agricultural commodities and coal during exportation operations (Ayoola, 2016). As of the late 1960s, agricultural products accounted for over 40% of all freight traffic on the railways, agricultural turnouts later declined from about 863,821 tons per year to about 355,691 tons per year with the discovery and exploitation of crude petroleum (Oshin, 1991).

The Nigerian railway network is currently managed by the Nigerian Railway Corporation (NRC). It is majorly composed of single-tracked narrow-gauged (1067 mm) ballasted tracks of over 3505 km in total length and 662 km of standard-gauged (1435 mm) ballasted tracks (Abuja–Kaduna, Itakpe–Ajaokuta–Warri, and Lagos–Ibadan) (NRC, 2019). It constitutes over 1600 curves of degrees ranging from 4° to 10° and maximum vertical grade of 2% along segments (Adesanya, 2010; Ayoola, 2016). The network was primarily designed to connect the major production centres (agriculture and colliery) through highly populated regions to the southern ports. Thus, providing for the movement of long-haul freight and passenger traffic in either direction (Oshin, 1991).

To keep pace with the rising mobility demands accompanying population and economic growth; while boosting productivity, the rejuvenation of the Nigerian railway system has, in recent years, gained priority. Several railway network expansion and rehabilitation projects commenced within the last decade, including the phased completion of the Lagos-Ibadan and Abuja-Kaduna lines, the upgrade of the Lagos-Kano line to standard gauge, the commencement of the Ibadan-Osogbo-Ilorin, and the Itakpe-Warri line, amongst others (Chen, 2018). The objective of this paper is to elucidate the past and contemporary challenges that have hampered

---

E. M. Ibitogbe
Department of Civil Engineering, Landmark University, Omu-Aran, Nigeria
e-mail: ibitogbe.enoch@lmu.edu.ng

G. Nnamani
Department of Banking and Finance, Covenant University, Ota, Nigeria
e-mail: gift.nnamanipgs@stu.cu.edu.ng

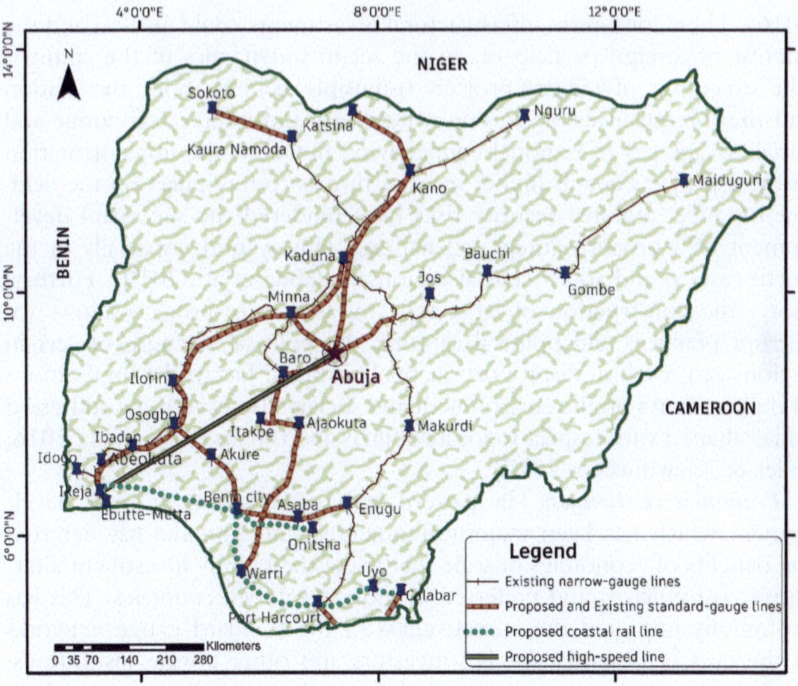

Fig. 3.1 Nigeria railway network: existing and proposed

the growth of the Nigerian railway sector, and further present prospects to promote the sustainable development of Nigeria railways in line with Goals 8, 9, 11, and 16 of the sustainable development goals established by the United Nations. Figure 3.1 shows the Nigerian railway network, and it indicates the existing lines and the proposed lines.

Discussions

Current Security, Social, and Economic Challenges

Considering the long-ranging durations of railway projects, the involvement of foreign investors in Nigeria's railway infrastructure development has been hampered due to instabilities in governmental policies and the issues of insurgence in certain conflict regions of the country (Toogood,

2016). These long-term infrastructural investments could also expand the interest of foreign participants in the security dynamics of the country. The execution of railway projects ostensibly benefits both the Nation and the foreign investors through the direct and indirect economic and social advantages of regional connectivity; however, the implementation of these projects entails higher security threats to foreigners on the field. For instance, regional security risks have hindered the successful development of a properly integrated national railway grid, especially in the north-eastern and south coastal regions (Adebiyi et al., 2019). Furthermore, the construction of large-scale infrastructure projects allows for corrupt practices and political capture; the political strength of certain regions can result in disproportionate allocations. Lastly, the implications of these railways on the environment and society also need to be addressed and evaluated with respect to local conflicts and threats (Song et al., 2016; Tuler & Kaewunruen, 2017).

Economic challenges: The pattern of Nigeria railway network development which has been majorly fragmented and sporadic has deterred the benefits of economies of scale that make the railway investment alternative cost-efficient and preferred in most developed countries. This has profoundly impacted the attractiveness of the standard gauge networks in the eyes of potential foreign investors and other private institutions; this increases doubts over the profitability and sustained viability of these progressively sprawling rail lines (Abioye et al., 2016; Babatunde, 2020). Another essential concern remains on how the administration plan on servicing these loans: the likelihood that these routes will recuperate their initial costs via user fares is meagre, and the values of commodities have imposed high strains on governmental budgets and the capacity to fund new railway projects (Abioye, 2016; Tovar, 2019). Furthermore, major foreign actors such as Chinese firms gain contracts in Nigeria via the help of China's Exim Bank modus operandi. However, this model results in issues of moral hazard since its state-owned firms push fiscally unprofitable projects with the finances of the Chinese government (Chen, 2018).

Regional politics and corruption: the political impositions on railway assets remains a lasting limitation to the development of networks. Over time, political corruption has contributed massively to both the rapid deterioration of the railway system and the patchy evolution of its recovery (Locatelli et al., 2017). Several ruined rehabilitation projects and the standardisation of the north-eastern rail line were beset by allegations of corrupt practices under the past governments, and corruption definitely plays a role in railway infrastructure contracted costs. A broader issue is the absence of continuity in policies regarding railway development. The western route alone has been overseen by seven different governments, resulting in inconsistencies in execution plan across governments, and even amid the government and foreign investors (Chen, 2018).

The spatiality of railway assets is particularly susceptible to political alterations. An instance is seen with the planned linkage of the western route to Sokoto (north-west), indicating the political reputation the sultanate imposes on impending elections and disregarding the fiscal advantages of linking the regions. There is always a tendency for railway routes to drift with each government, to accentuate presidential states and hometowns. As economic constrictions demand the phased segmentation of rail lines, politics will dictate the priority of each segment (Bönner, 2020). The governments' decision to fund the segment between Kano and Kaduna has been assumed to indicate the predominance of the interest of the north in the political elite. Similarly, of the highly anticipated coastal lines, the eastern line to connect Calabar and Port Harcourt is planned to be first constructed rather than lines on the west coasts from Lagos. This generally illustrates the political prominence of Rivers state, and not any fiscal-related rationale, which could promote the expansion of the existing networks (Chen, 2018). Politics in the development of Nigeria railways have been a cause of complaint to the burgeoning pro-Biafrans in the south-eastern regions: although the planned coastal route is hyped as valuable to the fiscal growth of the southern regions, the Igbo-dominated states are considered neglected in the recent railway plans; hence, criticisms to the recently planned developments is strong. Funding is yet to be secured for the development of the eastern trunk lines since it is not covered in the standard gauge upgrade plans (Taiwo-Hassan, 2017). Marginalisation perceptions in separatist clusters of the south-south and south-east are further fuelled by these exclusions, growing the risk of railway projects being possible flash-points for militant groups intending to pressurise the government.

Insurgency: Recently, the Buhari-led administration claim to have efficaciously reduced the impact of the Boko Haram insurgents in the north-east region and regained control over Maiduguri, Borno state capital, yet civilians still suffer periodic acts of terrorism. Presently, there exist no planned railway lines in the north-east funded by the government or foreign investors, and the risk of insurgence has largely dissuaded any development plan for railways in Borno (Asenime, 2020). The final phase of the rehabilitation of the eastern trunk route from Enugu to Maiduguri, undertaken by a Nigerian company since 2011, was reported to be abandoned due to Boko Haram attacks (Chen, 2018). Companies (e.g. the CCECC®) have indicated a lack of interest in further rehabilitating any segments in the region. In spite of the necessity and the peace-generating potential, the development of railway infrastructure offers, the north-eastern regions of the country remain in a perplexing situation. As such, until the issues of insurgency are completely controlled, the likelihood of foreign investors patronising railway infrastructure projects in the region is zilch. Meanwhile, with the cessation of the amnesty initiative in the Niger-Delta regions, a renaissance of militancy on infrastructure can occur: though these threats have been majorly beset on the oil and gas sector, new railway projects and the entry of foreign construction workers could pose highly vulnerable targets (Abodunrin, 2019; Ogbu, 2017; Omokhoa & Ikelegbe, 2016).

Local security and abductions: With the high rates of unemployment and poverty in Nigeria and particularly, the Niger-Delta and south-eastern regions, new railway construction projects could attract further security threats such as the abduction of workers (Bello & Jamilu, 2017; Saheed, 2016). The abduction of foreigners, especially in the oil and construction sectors, has influenced the readiness and capacity of foreign firms to execute projects. For instance, Julius Berger®, was earlier made to withdraw and demobilise from the rehabilitation of the central trunk, compelling the Ministry of Transportation to contract CCECC for the completion of the work (Albert et al., 2020; Onuoha & Okolie-Osemene, 2019). This is owing to the fact that Chinese firms make lesser security demands compared to American and European firms (who reportedly demand armoured trucks throughout project execution). The resulting security costs exacerbate the total project costs since permanent security details are required for the site yards, tracks, and personnel.

Environmental and Societal issues: The environmental and social impacts of railway construction is also of high importance at the local level, especially with the case of land ownerships and appropriations. The rapid and successful completion of the Abuja-Kaduna railway line was majorly possible because it is a one-track route; it was less cost-intensive to build, and the governments' right-of-way ownership within and around Abuja annulled the appropriation requirements (Song et al., 2016; Tuler & Kaewunruen, 2017). The planned standard-gauge line from Lagos to Kano will align with the current narrow-gauge line to mitigate this environmental problem. However, the planned coastal segments may be highly challenging. In the case of brownfields, lands privately owned will demand appropriations and fiscal compensations, making it a highly political challenge. Land rights issues also impose substantial challenges to the linkage of ports to towns: port linkages to major economic hubs such as Port Harcourt, Lagos, and Warri remain undeveloped even with the rapid rates of urbanisation and industrialisation. This involves large movements of people, thereby complicating the process of compensation, which further creates opportunities for rent-seeking, locally (Chen, 2018). This circumstance could be a fundamental limitation in planning and developing future coastal railway routes. Federal and state governments are majorly responsible for addressing these challenges; however, foreign actors face material and reputational threats since they would most like be held accountable by locals if environmental and social requirements are not achieved.

Economic and Social Prospects of Strategic Railway Development

Though railway development poses many threats as aforementioned if not properly managed, several benefits and opportunities can be achieved with a properly integrated and strategic development of railway systems. The inherent prospects of railways over roadways are in the economy of scale they can afford: railways operate at much higher speeds, are more efficient over long distances, and require less frequent maintenance, making them the inland transport alternative with the highest profitability index for both passenger and freight movements, thereby promoting trade (Dalibi et al., 2020).

Linking the extensively robust commercial hubs and ports in the coastal regions of Nigeria to the largely undeveloped but resource-abundant inland regions would have apparent advantages. This would reduce the cost of on-land transportation, which has been a major challenge to both the manufacturing and the agricultural sectors: thereby improving the competitiveness of Nigerian-owned businesses against importations and theoretically encourage the trade and exportation of Nigerian products (Dalibi & Bello, 2017). The provision of new state-of-the-art rolling stock and terminals could also attract tourism, investment, and migration to newly developed regions. The possibilities of a constructive spill-over effect on complementary sectors such as construction materials and steel industries operating in upstream supply chains are high with strategic railway developments, as this increases the demand for retail and facilities, and consequently, promoting employment (Obiakor, 2016). A high-speed central trunk rail line can boost the outputs of the mining and agricultural industries in the north-central regions. Similarly, the planned upgrade of the rail line from Lagos to Kano would be advantageous to the northern pastoral farmers and leather manufacturers, currently incurring high overheads from high costs of inland transportation (Chen, 2018).

Reduced transportation costs likewise, endorses regional integration in areas whereby road roadways are typically congested, inadequately maintained, and unsafe, with the ease of migration and mobility, at societal levels. The implications of this improved mobility would largely promote social integration amidst ethnicities, language groups, and regions. Prequel to the decline of Nigeria railways, colonial railways aided in connecting rural settlements to commercial centres and stimulated rural–urban immigration (Bayane et al., 2020). Development of new railways can reduce the current tensions of segregation of the populace with respect to religious differences and geopolitical zonation by providing economic and cultural integration, and offering safety and affordability in transportation for migrants in search of greener pastures. These prospects are already seen with the Abuja to Kaduna route completed, with a rapidly increasing demand, not attributed to its efficiency alone, but for the improved security compared to the roadways (Bayane & Yanjun, 2020).

In the Niger-Delta regions, where monetary complaints and notions of corruption have over time been a major cause of local conflicts and militancy threatening foreign investors, the economic benefits in terms of opportunities that a coastal rail route offers can facilitate conflict resolution and post-conflict renovation efforts. Proper railway systems can attract investors from sectors other than oil and gas to these regions, thereby encouraging healthier agglomeration across industries (Evans & Kelikume, 2019; Ighodaro, 2018).

Employment has already been generated with the ongoing railway projects within the country (Bayane & Yanjun, 2020). In contrast with common beliefs of foreign contractors importing labourers, companies such as Julius Berger® and CCECC® adopt guidelines that mandate a one-to-ten ratio of imported to Nigerian workers. CCECC® reported that in constructing the Abuja to Kaduna railway line, about 4000 local jobs were created, and presently, about 500 locals are engaged in the management and operations of the line (Chen, 2018). Moreover, the inadequacy in technology in the country demands for sustained inclusion of foreign contractors in the running and maintenance of the tracks and rolling stocks (Chen, 2018; Kerr, 2018). Many foreign actors have also actively conducted training programmes and provided technological centres to develop Nigerian engineers in areas such as modules on railway communication and signal systems, and track maintenance (Alade, 2020). Nonetheless, the effective transfer of skill and technology demands a systematic and long-term investment into the capacity building of Nigerians, which would involve a sustained mutual relationship between the government and the foreign actors.

Policy-Based Recommendations for Railway Sustenance

Having highlighted the limitations and prospects of the railway sector, certain policy-based alternatives are recommended in this section to further promote successful implementation.

Improved financing model: The model of funding currently adopted by the Ministry of Transportation, through the NRC requires improvements via multiple sources, including public–private partnerships (PPP) and internal revenue generation via commerce. The recently enacted Railway Act has allowed for concessionary models in the operations and resuscitation of Nigeria railways; however, improved financing for both rolling stocks and locomotives, improved functionality of maintenance facilities and terminals must be put in place. The enacted concessionary model does not necessarily imply that the NRC should completely relinquish its monopoly to private actors; rather, it necessitates productive collaborations to achieve financial efficiency in sustainably managing Nigeria railways. Furthermore, the government can establish novel fiscal policies to incentivise the railway sector and attract investors. The Central Bank of Nigeria can also, ensure that loans are granted to private investors with highly viable plans to develop the railway sector.

Adoption of a special purpose entity: A Special Purpose Vehicle (SPV) should be established by the Ministry of Transportation to oversee the PPPs between the government and contracted foreign investors with a proven track record of past developments of sustainable railway solutions in other countries. The established SPV must ensure the continuity of the agreement even with newly elected administrations. The funding plan can be similar to that of the Presidential Power Initiative (PPI) between the Ministry of Finance, Ministry of Power, and Siemens which entails: 85% from a consortium of banks, guaranteed by the German government through the Euler Hermes credit insurance firm; and 15% from the federal government counterpart funding. This agreement employed a moratorium of 2–3 years and a payback period of 10–12 years, at concessionary interest rates (Odutola, 2020). However, this should be adjusted to fit railway development requirements. The foreign private investor will work alongside quality-assured local companies. Thereby creating employment opportunities and improving the economy at large. Just like the PPI that will operate in different phases, the railway initiative should operate in phases across the six geopolitical zones in order to ensure sustainability in the railway transportation system.

Strict adherence to the 2015 Railway Act: The 1955 Railway Act guided the NRC for six decades. With several situational variations over the years, the necessity for amendments became inherent. The government, in 2015, enacted the long-awaited Railway Act that recognised the need for PPP in the sustainable development of the railway system. However strict monitoring and regulatory measures must be put in place to ensure that all actors inclusive adhere strictly to the stipulated requirements to completely extricate corruption and promote transparency in establishing railway concessions and in the implementation of projects.

Development of Intra-city commuter railway services: Besides the National trunk railways being developed by the federal government through the NRC, state governments should also be encouraged to develop intra-city railway infrastructure (metros) across individual states. Highly populated cities like Lagos, Ibadan, Kano, Port Harcourt, Abuja, and Kaduna can be profitably served by several forms of railway infrastructure (tramways, mono-rails, funiculars, light metros, and other regional commuter railways). This will consequently reduce the overdependence on-road transportation, thereby plummeting traffic congestions and associated environmental and social impacts.

Railway technological capacity building: In the strive towards sustainable railway developments, local capacity building, as well as industrialisation in the fabrication and assemblage of railway equipment such as rolling stock and locomotives, is highly indispensable. In the 1980s, the NRC made plans to develop manufacturing plants for railway equipment in Kaduna state, in collaboration with a South Korean company, Daewoo®. The NRC's Diesel facility situated in Enugu state similarly met standards for diesel-based locomotive design and production, based on General Electric® technical and fiscal requirements (Kerr, 2018). This approach does not only have the potential of creating multiple jobs. Rather, it could significantly conserve funds that would have been employed in the procurement and importation of locomotives, while expanding trade in railway equipment parts and lessening the down-time of railway equipment.

Conclusion

This study presented a review on the phased development of Nigeria railways to elucidate the past and contemporary challenges that have hampered the growth of the sector, and further present prospects to promote the sustainable development of Nigeria railways. The study revealed that the railway sector has endured substantial negligence in previous years, regardless of the massive opportunities and benefits attainable from its proper integration and functionality. Undeniably, the past abandonment and the issues of corruption and insurgency largely deterred the attractiveness of the sector to foreign investors. Furthermore, the desertion of the railways has been consequential to the rising demands, costs, and terrible conditions of the country's roadway transport mode. However, these can be aptly managed if the recommended policy-based alternatives are taken into account. As such, the Nation must now be highly invested than ever to tackle the emerging challenges, with the full capacity of the government. Most importantly, the acceleration of executory actions is required if the condition of the sector is to be timely and effectively revigorated.

References

Abioye, O. (2016). *Privatisation of the Nigerian Railway Corporation: An evaluation of critical choices*. Cardiff Metropolitan University. https://repository.cardiffmet.ac.uk/handle/10369/7860

Abioye, O., Shubber, K., & Koenigsberger, J. (2016). Evaluating the role and impact of railway transport in the Nigerian economy, options and choices: Case of Nigerian Railway Corporation. *AshEse Journal of Economics, 2*(4), 103–113.

Abodunrin, O. (2019). Resurgence of militancy and the challenges of sustainable peace and development in the Niger Delta. *Covenant University Journal of Politics and International Affairs, 7*(1). http://107.180.69.44/index.php/cujpia/article/view/1632

Adebiyi, J. O., Sanni, G. A., & Oyetunji, A. K. (2019). Assessment of political risk factors influencing the corporate performance of multinationals construction companies in northeastern Nigeria. *Global Journal of Business, Economics and Management: Current Issues*, *9*(2), 63–75. https://doi.org/10.18844/gjbem.v9i2.4232

Adesanya, A. (2010). Bringing the Nigerian Railways back to track: Challenges and options. *Monthly NISER Seminar Series*, 0–20.

Alade, T. A. (2020). *Innovation adaptation in urban light-rail transport* [Erasmus University Rotterdam]. https://repub.eur.nl/pub/126120/Taslim-Alade-Phd-embargo-version.pdf

Albert, I. O., Danjibo, N., & Albert, O. (2020). Back to the past: Evolution of kidnapping and hostage taking in the Niger Delta, Nigeria. *Beijing Law Review*, *11*(01), 211–226. https://doi.org/10.4236/blr.2020.111015

Asenime, C. (2020). Evaluating the potential impact of the east-west rail service on the socio-economic output of communities along its corridor. *Journal of Advances in Economics and Finance*, *5*(2), 23–29. https://doi.org/10.22606/jaef.2020.52002

Ayoola, T. A. (2016). Establishment of the Nigerian Railway Corporation. *Journal of Retracing Africa*, *3*(1), 21–42.

Babatunde, A. I. (2020). Efficiency of railway transport as a sustainable mode of transport in Nigeria: A study of rail mass transit in Lagos and its environs. *SSRN Electronic Journal*. https://doi.org/10.2139/ssrn.3576072

Bayane, B. M., Yanjun, Q., & Bekhzad, Y. (2020). A review and analysis of railway transportation system in the economic community of West African States: Towards the development of sustainable regional goal. *Global Journal of Engineering and Technology Advances*, *2*(2), 011–022. https://doi.org/10.30574/gjeta.2020.2.2.0004

Bayane, B., & Yanjun, Q. (2020). Past, present and future development of West African railways. *Journal of Sustainable Development of Transport and Logistics*, *5*(1), 103–114. https://doi.org/10.14254/jsdtl.2020.5-1.10

Bello, I., & Jamilu, I. M. (2017). An analysis of the causes and consequences of kidnapping in Nigeria. *African Research Review*, *11*(4), 134. https://doi.org/10.4314/afrrev.v11i4.11

Bönner, A. (2020). *Nigeria: An archaeology of political corruption* [Berliner Wissenschafts-Verlag]. http://medien.bwv-verlag.de/9783830539216_p.pdf

Chen, Y. (2018). China's role in Nigerian Railway development and implications for security and development. In *United States Institute of Peace: Special Report* (Issue 423). www.usip.org

Dalibi, S. G., & Bello, S. B. (2017). *Socio-economic impacts of Chinese government financed infrastructural development projects in Nigeria*, 579–588. https://doi.org/10.2991/febm-17.2017.78

Dalibi, S. G., Feng, J. C., Abubakar, S. G., Kumo, H. A., Danja, I. I., Mukhtar, A. A., & Inuwa, L. U. (2020). Socio-economic performances of mega construction projects (MCPs) in the light of sustainable development of Nigeria's built environment. *IOP Conference Series: Earth and Environmental Science, 495*(1), 012046. https://doi.org/10.1088/1755-1315/495/1/012046

Evans, O., & Kelikume, I. (2019). The impact of poverty, unemployment, inequality, corruption and poor governance on Niger Delta Militancy, Boko Haram Terrorism and Fulani Herdsmen attacks in Nigeria. *International Journal of Management, Economics and Social Sciences, 8*(2), 58–80. https://doi.org/10.32327/ijmess/8.2.2019.5

Ighodaro, C. A. (2018). Foreign direct investment-led industrialisation in Nigeria: Lessons from Chinese industrialisation. *Uongozi Journal of Management and Development Dynamics, 28*(2). https://doi.org/10.2234/UONGOZI.V28I2.31

Kerr, I. J. (2018). The transfer of Railway technologies and Afro-Asian labor processes within the British Empire. *HoST—Journal of History of Science and Technology, 12*(1), 31–74. https://doi.org/10.2478/host-2018-0003

Locatelli, G., Mariani, G., Sainati, T., & Greco, M. (2017). Corruption in public projects and megaprojects: There is an elephant in the room! *International Journal of Project Management, 35*(3), 252–268. https://doi.org/10.1016/j.ijproman.2016.09.010

Nigerian Railway Corporation. (2019). *About NRC..... – Nigerian Railway Corporation*. https://nrc.gov.ng/home-2/about-nrc/

Obiakor, N. J. (2016). British colonial economic policies and infrastructure in Nigeria: The rail transport example, 1898–1960. *IGWEBUIKE: An African Journal of Arts and Humanities, 2*(3), 2504–9038. http://igwebuikejournals.com/pdfcreated/2.3.2.pdf

Odutola, A. (2020, July). *UPDATED: FG approves N8.64 billion for Phase 1 of Presidential Power Initiative | Nairametrics*. https://nairametrics.com/2020/07/29/just-in-fg-approves-phase-1-of-presidential-power-initiative-funding/

Ogbu, S. U. (2017). Amnesty as a tool in the negotiation to end insurgency in the Niger Delta. *Global Journal of Political Science and Administration, 5*(2), 1–22. https://www.academia.edu/download/55329373/Amnesty-as-a-Tool-in-the-Negotiation-to-end-Insurgency-in-the-Niger-Delta.pdf

Omokhoa, E., & Ikelegbe, A. (2016). Amnesty programme in Nigeria: The impact and challenges in post conflict Niger Delta, region. *IOSR Journal of Humanities and Social Science, 21*(4), 7–62. https://doi.org/10.9790/0837-2104076265

Onuoha, F. C., & Okolie-Osemene, J. (2019). The evolving threat of kidnapping for ransom in Nigeria. In *Internal security management in Nigeria* (pp. 233–258). Springer Singapore. https://doi.org/10.1007/978-981-13-8215-4_12

Oshin, O. (1991). Road transport and the declining fortunes of the Nigerian Railway, 1901–1950. *Journal of Transport History, 12*(1), 11–36. https://doi.org/10.1177/002252669101200102

Saheed, O. B. (2016). Kidnapping in pre-and post-amnesty Niger Delta, Nigeria. *International Journal of Peace and Conflict Studies (IJPCS), 3*(2), 2354–1598. http://rcmss.com/2017/IJPCS/Kidnapping-in-Pre-and-Post-Amnesty-Niger-Delta-Nigeria.pdf

Song, M., Zhang, G., Zeng, W., Liu, J., & Fang, K. (2016). Railway transportation and environmental efficiency in China. *Transportation Research Part d: Transport and Environment, 48*, 488–498. https://doi.org/10.1016/j.trd.2015.07.003

Taiwo-Hassan, A. (2017). *Amaechi denies excluding eastern region from new rail projects | Premium Times Nigeria*. https://www.premiumtimesng.com/regional/ssouth-east/231672-amaechi-denies-excluding-eastern-region-from-new-rail-projects.html

Tolofari, S. R., & Gubbins, E. J. (1984). Nigerian railways: Problems and prospects. *Transportation Planning and Technology, 8*(4), 225–235. https://doi.org/10.1080/03081068408717255

Toogood, K. (2016). Understanding the emerging relationship between China and Africa: The case of Nigeria. *Stimson Center*, 1–10. www.jstor.org/stable/resrep10795

Tovar, A. (2019). Chinese infrastructure investments in Africa: A case study of the Addis Ababa-Djibouti Railway in Ethiopia and Djibouti and the Abuja-Kaduna Rail Line in Nigeria. *Senior Theses*. https://research.library.fordham.edu/international_senior/25

Tuler, M. V., & Kaewunruen, S. (2017). Life cycle analysis of mitigation methodologies for railway rolling noise and groundbourne vibration. *Journal of Environmental Management, 191*, 75–82. https://doi.org/10.1016/j.jenvman.2016.12.075

CHAPTER 4

Designing for Security in Church Architecture Against Insurgency in Northern Nigeria

Eghosa Ekhaese and Olanrenwaju Oluwole

Introduction

Over the years, the government of Nigeria has not been able to control the violence and destruction of lives and property by terrorists. This is as a result of the overwhelming nature of attacks and new strategies the terrorist group use in carrying out their attacks. Yet, the most dreaded terrorist organization responsible for most attacks in Nigeria is known as Jama'atu Ahlis-Sunnah Lidda Awati Wal. Jihad popularly known as Boko Haram (Olusola & Marcus, 2014). The result of frequent attacks on public and religious buildings in Nigeria by individuals believed to be in radical Islamic sects has resulted in Insurgency. Therefore, the resultant effect is a decline in peace and stability in the country. Insurgency is the premeditated intention of a person or group of people to carry out violent

E. Ekhaese (✉) · O. Oluwole
Department of Architecture, Covenant University, Ota, Ogun State, Nigeria
e-mail: noel.ekhaese@covenantuniversity.edu.ng

S. Folarin et al. (eds.), *The United Nations and Sustainable Development Goals*, https://doi.org/10.1007/978-3-030-95971-5_4

attacks on an individual or a group of people who are usually unarmed and harmless (Sampson & Onuoha, 2013). These attacks are more prevalent in the Northern region of the Federal Republic of Nigeria. The expectations are always on the government to tackle the insurgency but Nigerians are not aware that there are measures to be implemented in the design of public facilities to protect users against the impact of possible attacks on such buildings. Since Nigeria resumed democracy in 1999, the country has experienced different ethno-religious crises. However, Boko Haram has been a turbulent sect in Nigeria since 2009 (Eme & Onyishi, 2014). Their activities have resulted in a series of death, abduction and displacement of Nigerians in tens of thousands. Apart from Boko Haram attacks, Churches have witnessed several attacks from ethno-religious crises especially in states such as Plateau, Kaduna and Kano state (RRT, 2005). Nigeria has experienced a rise in terrorist attacks over the years and this can be reflected in the rise in the national budget allotted for security (Ushe, 2012). In the year 2011, out of 177 countries, Nigeria ranked 14th out of 177 nations ranked by multiple factors in the Fund for Peace (FFP) Failed State Index as shown in Table 4.1.

The Church architecture by some standard is supposed to be regarded as safe spaces. Conversely, terror attacks on churches are easily carried out

Table 4.1 Attacked churches and casualties

S/N	*Date of attack*	*State*	*Location of attack*	*Impact*
1	25th December, 2011	NIGER	Christmas Day Bombing in Madalla Christ Apostolic Church was attacked	50 people killed
2	6th January, 2012	ADAMAWA	and Igbo people were also killed in Mubi	37 people killed
3	8th April, 2012	KADUNA	In the same state Easter Day Church	38 people killed
4	17th June, 2012	KADUNA	Bombing Multiple attacks on churches	12 people killed and 80 injured
5	7th August, 2012	KOGI	Deeper Life Church attack	19 people killed

*Source*Adedayo et al. (2017)

as a result of the open access policy of many churches, hence making them easily targeted by terrorists (Hammer, 2008). Still, the government has not been silent about terror attacks. Although their strategies to tackle terrorism may not be regarded as sufficient, Nigeria government has made progress in installing surveillance facilities in some parts of the country (Azazi, 2011). With the above occurrences, the need for extra effort to secure church architecture cannot be overemphasized. It might be impossible to prevent occurrences or casualties, but the amount of loss of lives and properties can be minimised, if the right security architecture can be put in place. Therefore the goal of security may be achieved with the design phase of the project (Fennely, 2013). It is against this background that the study is adopting and implementing physical security measures in church building premises at the design, construction and renovation stage. A systematic literature review was adopted to analyse similar research so as to situate this study in the current perspective.

Literature Review

According to Afolabi (2016), Boko Haram is an Islamic sect that first emerged in the early 2000s. They are known to attack properties owned by the government and most especially religious institutions. Their major aim is to get the country to abolish western culture and uphold traditional Islamic culture. Over two decades ago, some radical Islamic youths worshipped in Alhaji Muhammadu Ndimi Mosque in Maiduguri. In the year 2002, there was a division amongst the radical Islamic youths as a result of corruption. The divided group then decided to withdraw from the city of Maiduguri to a community at the outskirts of Maiduguri based on the principles of Islam. In the year 2003, they got into a conflict with the police because of communal fishing rights in a local pond which led to the death of many of the members as a result of a shootout (Zartman & Faure, 2011). The survivals then returned to Maiduguri and grew to establish branches of their mosque in neighbouring states without disturbance from the authorities. The survival group was named Boko Haram in Hausa which means "Western Education is forbidden" (Kwaja, 2011). Boko Haram went ahead to accommodate more members by making provisions for the homeless and jobless in Nigeria. This enabled them to grow their membership and breed more Islamic fighters with funding from foreigners and prominent Nigerians. After a series of attacks on innocent Nigerians by the Boko Haram sect, the police after their investigation went on a rampage at the Boko Haram mosque displacing the terrorist and eliminating some suspected members of the sect (Dudouet, 2010). This deadly terrorist group later launched itself as an international terrorist group when it started bombing delicate places and buildings owned by government authorities and religious buildings. Examples of such attacks were carried out at the National Police Headquarters, and the United Nations building in Abuja (Walker, 2012). Nigerian states affected by Boko Haram insurgency include Yobe, Taraba, Plateau, Kogi, Kano, Kaduna Gombe, Borno, Bauchi and Adamawa states (The Law Library of Congress, 2014).

Eme et al. (2018) argued that the Fulani people are known as nomadic people who move from one place to another with their cattle in search of greener pasture. However, in the process of looking for a greener pasture for their cattle when migrating from one place to another, they enter into well-cultivated crop farms and allow their cattle to graze on the crops of the farmers. The reaction of farmers to Fulani herdsmen has resulted in societal conflicts. This has led to the attack of defenceless communities which in turn result in the loss of numerous lives and properties.

Moulaye (2006) described Security as a concept that is concerned with the safety and survival of individuals, a group of people and citizens of a country or state. Some people believe that it is the sole responsibility of the government to provide security for territories but some others believe that security is achieved by the interdependence of efforts from individuals and institutions (Zabadi, 2005). Security in buildings does not only involve keeping out people who may pose as a threat, it also involves protecting building occupants. A building that can be regarded as safe possesses measures that limit the impact of hazards on the building. A building regarded to be safe has a design balance of physical, technical and operational principles to achieve safety in a given location (Othman, 2005). Security is a state whereby people and properties are prevented from the risk of being harmed, attacked, stolen or destroyed entirely. However, security is misunderstood as one cannot touch security but feel secure according to Carey (2000). Therefore, if security is a feeling, then it is a feeling of safety from a form of threat or the other. Responsibility of security should not only rest on the government, but private and corporate organizations should be made to implement security strategies in the premises of their organizations in order to control security.

Gillick (2002) agreed that building security could be separated into levels. This will make it easier to achieve the goal of designing for security. However, the levels of security according to Becker (2004) are expected to commence from the building interior extending to the external part of the facility. The first zone is the building interior. A security cubicle should exist in which everyone gaining access into the church building is scanned using heavy metal and weapon detectors. It could also include alarm systems, automatic lock systems, CCTV cameras as well as guard tours. This will prevent threats from gaining easy access into the worship area in churches. The second zone is the perimeter of the church building. This includes reinforcing and hardening the external wall of the building and introducing landscape to control movement around the building structure. The third zone has to do with using elements of a building to protect a building's ground. The fourth zone has to do with protecting walkways around the building including building services as well as barriers and car parks. The fifth zone is related to parking areas. Vehicles can be scanned for weapons in this zone and a vehicle identification system could also be implemented. The sixth zone depends on the government and society. It is to create a synergy between the building facility state security operatives and emergency services such as ambulances and firefighters (Shafii, 2005).

Becker (2000), claimed that security is needed because of potential threats to life and property. However, depending on the location of people that need to be secured, there is something known as warranted fear and unwarranted fear. Actual threats are associated with warranted fear and unwarranted fear emerges as a result of our individual imagination. Acts of terrorism might not be regular, but injuries of a terror attack leave a lasting impact on victims or their families. Most terror attacks are carried out with explosives or guns and in some cases, fire set intentionally. Terrorists now operate in innovative ways which catch security operatives unawares. Therefore, advanced intelligence is regarded as the best security measure, however it is important to note that physical barriers and weapon detectors are still effective in countering security threats. According to Carpenter (1999, November 30), there were 400 cases of foiled terrorist attacks on US embassies in 1998 as a result of security surveillance in the embassies. According to Joint Operations Group (2018), the following are possible ways by which terrorist attacks can be carried out in church buildings: Vehicle-borne improvised explosive device; Attack by armed assailants; Chemical and biological attacks; Improvised explosive device; and Unauthorized entry.

Rupp (2018) believe that church buildings in Northern Nigerian region have been hit severely in recent years by bandits. Before now, security in church environments was about locking the doors, but no it involves more than that to keep the environment safe on service and non-service days. Although the church is expected to be a peaceful environment. The church is to provide security in case of attacks based on a variety of factors such as the church size, church location, violence history in the church vicinity and the type of members that worship in the church. Possible reasons why a church needs to be secured are in case a banditry group decides to attack the church during a service or plant explosives in the church premises before a service. Also, security should be considered in case the fire spreads out of control, a protest occurs outside the church during a service. Another factor that should affect the design for security is if there is a medical emergency or an accident occurs in the church premises. However, security measures implemented in the design of the building will be effective when people are involved in ensuring that the security system put in place is functional. This will include the pastorate, ushering department, security personnel and other necessary service units.

Materials and Method

This research adopted the qualitative research method (Ekpendu & Filibus, 2019). A systematic exploratory-descriptive and contextual approach were presented to observe, explain, interpret, analyse and discuss designing for security in church architecture against insurgency in northern Nigeria. The study used an in-depth interview guide and observation schedules as the instruments for the collection of data. A total of 15 participants was interviewed to elicit the required information for an effective and efficient security design on church buildings against insurgence. The interviewees are experts drawn for 5 building professionals (3 architects, 2 civil engineers), 5 security experts (1 criminologist, 2 electrical and 2 computer engineers) and 5 church owners and founders. The study has adopted the implementations of this security measure at the design stage, construction stage and renovation stage. Vigilance cannot be overestimated in church buildings and this can be enforced by hiring security personnel. This is highly cost-effective; hence it is advisable to accommodate innovative strategies at the building design stage in order to reduce life cycle cost on the church facility.

Result and Discussions

The church in Northern Nigeria has experienced an ugly decade as a lot of churches have been attacked by Boko Haram. The mainstream of the attacks were bomb attacks while some were sporadic shootings. Religious buildings and environments are symbols of peace therefore previous designs do not accommodate comprehensive security strategies as they were not needed. However, it is expected that the design of buildings evolves to cater to the users of tall buildings and security is an urgent need for all churches in Northern Nigeria. Therefore, if comprehensive security measures are implemented in the design of religious buildings, then it is expected that fatality from such attacks will be reduced to the minimum.

From interviews with religious leaders, it was gathered that they have different perspectives in which the issue of insurgency in the nation can be controlled. Cardinal John Onaiyekan who is the Arch Bishop of Abuja stated that "*amnesty is the best solution to curb insurgency as 80% of the terrorist fighters do not share the ideology of the terrorist group, they are only fighting because they have no choice*". This may be a good step to end insurgency, the government has made efforts to initiate amnesty talks with the insurgents but the terrorist organization still carry out attacks even after some terrorist surrendered to the Nigerian Military. In February 2020, a suspected suicide bomber attempted an attack during a Sunday worship service at Living Faith Church Sabo in Kaduna. The chief security officer in the person of Mr. Ekpeyong stated that "*it was discovered that the suspect was acting strange and he was being monitored with the CCTV camera installed around the church*". This means that if there was no CCTV camera system installed or the people monitoring the CCTV camera system were not vigilant enough, if the suspect succeeded in triggering the improvised explosive device it would have led to the loss of life and caused many others to be injured. This shows that security measures put in place could either reduce or prevent the loss of lives and properties in church buildings. In an interview with Ola Olanrewaju, the lead minister of Worship Centre in Kaduna, he stated that "*clerics focus on preaching peace and expect the government to provide security, while we are waiting for the government to work on the security, we cannot allow the flock of Christ to keep perishing in the north all because they came to church. As a body of Christ we need to upgrade physical security measures within our church buildings and if possible hire armed security operative to guard the church premises during worship services*".

This shows that the majority of clerics focus on the government to provide security and condemn the activities of terrorists. Some of them have improved security measures in their premises by using bomb detectors to search worshippers when it is time for service and this will require a lot of manpower. Therefore, to reduce the need for manpower, physical security measures architecturally could be used to control security around church buildings.

Physical Security Control Measures

Physical security measures are instrumental in reducing the risk and impact of attacks on the facility. These measures may be implemented passively or actively (Homeland Security, 2010). The passive security measure is a permanent measure that includes measures put on-site and the building structure. This combines engineering and architectural ideas to implement improved security which will help to eliminate security threats by vehicle bombs and improvised explosive devices. Passive security measures that can be applied in buildings include bollards, concrete planter's fences, stand-off zone distance and trees. All these should be put in place at the design inception stage (Security Design Manual, 2007). More openings in buildings have also been recommended in order to ensure visibility from the building to the surrounding. Hence this can be implemented in the administrative section of the church facility as it is not advisable to implement it in the worship area as it is meant to be reinforced in case of possible attacks (Talbot & Jakeman, 2011) (Plate 4.1).

Physical Security Considerations for Church Buildings

Physical security strategies implemented will not discourage terrorists from attacking the buildings, however, it could help prevent attacks from being a serious disaster that would have claimed more casualty if these strategies are not implemented in the design of the building (Brown, 1999).

Plate 4.1 Showing a plant acting as a passive fence and a landscape element (*Source* Glenwood [2016])

Access: Accessing church buildings should be limited to entrances where checkpoint facilities are implemented.

Daylighting: Achieving daylighting is usually done using windows, however in order to limit openings in buildings that can be accessible to terror attacks daylighting could be achieved by using interior atriums.

Landscaping: Landscaping techniques applied in the church facility can be used to control the movement of people, hence directing them to where security checks can be carried out.

Structural Design: The major worship space which is usually the major focus of a terror attack should be reinforced so as to limit the impact of a terror attack when possible terrorists are restricted from access as a result of security strategies put in place.

Siting: Siting includes landscaping, circulation paths and setbacks. All these factors when properly planned can prevent unwanted movement and control circulation within the church premises.

Building Materials: Building material decisions help in achieving the desired strength for the building in order to resist a terror attack, protect lives and reduce casualties during a terror attack.

Parking: Worshippers bring their vehicles to church and there are times when terrorists disguise themselves as worshippers with a car bomb attached to the vehicle. Therefore, it is advised for car parks to be sited away from the worship area of the premises. Also restrictions to parking should be made so that church officials could park close to the worship area if needed. The following measures can be implemented into parking areas: There should be different parking zones in the premises for church officials based on their assignment and a public parking zone as well. Only inspected vehicles should be sited in the stand-off zones. However adequate setback should be maintained between the building and car park and structural hardening may be required where the setback is not adequate. This should be done in order to minimize the effect of potential vehicle bombs (Adedayo et al., 2017). Circulation around car parking areas should be defined in such a way that monitoring and control are promoted.

Conclusion

Insurgency in Nigeria is rising by the day. There are numerous cases of banditry attacks on innocent Nigerians such as kidnapping, armed robbery and terrorism attacks. However, Boko Haram is an Islamic Fundamental sect that stood out in unleashing mayhem on the innocent citizens of Nigeria. The aim is to abolish Western culture and create a country governed by Sharia law. Since 2011 this is this terrorist group has been involved in planting explosives in public places and churches in the Northern region of Nigeria. Apart from religious buildings, they have been involved in attacking school buildings which have made a lot of Nigerians lose their loved ones.

References

Adedayo, O., Ailoyafen, D., & Adebayo, O. (2017). Landscaping for passive security and adaptation to climate in church environment, Niger State, Nigeria. *Nigerian Journal of Technology, 13*, 7–17.

Afolabi, O. (2016). Religious violence and national security in Nigeria, 1999–2011. *International Affairs and Global Strategy, 15*, 23–31.

Azazi, A. (2011). *Responding to the emerging trend of terrorism in Nigeria*. 5th Policing Executive Forum Conference Proceedings Organized by CLEEN Foundation. Lagos.

Becker, G. (2000, November 30). Balancing security and openess. *GSA public buildings*. US General Services Administration and the US Department of State.

Becker, S. M. (2004). Emergency communication and information issues in terrorist events involving radioactive materials. *Biosecurity and Bioterrorism: Biodefense Strategy, Practice, and Science, 2*(3), 195–207.

Brown, J. (1999, November 30). Balancing security and openness. *GSA public buildings*. Washington, DC, USA: US General Services.

Carey, R. (2000). *The contemporary nature of security. Issues in international relation*. Routledge.

Carpenter, D. (1999, November 30). Balancing security and openess. *GSA Public buildings service*. US General Services Administration and the US Department of State.

Dudouet, V. (2010). *Meditating pece with proscribed armed groups*. UNO Publication.

Ekpendu, I., & Filibus, Z. (2019). Biblical response to religio-ethnic crisis: Study of Kafanchan crisis in Nigeria. *Journal of Education and Human Development, 11*, 99–113.

Eme, O., & Onyishi, T. (2014). Boko Haram and security challenges in Nigeria. *Kuwait Chapter of Arabian Journal of Business and Management Review, 23*, 1–18.

Eme, O., Ugwu, C., & Onuigbo, R. (2018). *Economic effect of Fulani Herdsmen Farmers Clashes in Nigeria*. Science Arena Publications. Specialty Journal of Politics.

Fennely, L. (2013). *Protective Barriers*. www.sciencedirect.com/science/article/pii/B9780124158924000055

Gillick, T. (2002). Designing a concentric appproach to security. *Real Estate Weekly*, USA.

Hammer, R. (2008). Does your church need a security guard? *Church Law and Tax Report, 10*, 1–12.

Homeland Security. (2010). *Department of homeland security, guarding against terrorism and ensuring transportation security*. https://www.dhs.gov/xlibrary/assets/9-11commission-update-report-7-22-10.pdf

Joint Operations Group. (2018). *Guidelines for enhancing building security in Singapore*. Ministry of Home Affairs.

Kwaja, C. (2011). Nigeria's pernicious drivers of ethno-religious conflict. *Africa Security Brief, 11*, 1–8.

Moulaye, Z. (2006). Democratic governance of security in Mali; A sustainable development challenges. *Abuja: Friedich Ebert Stiffing*, 17–18.

Olusola, A., & Marcus, B. (2014). Security problems in Nigeria: A challenge to Christian Women Associations. *Academic Research International, 23*, 413–420.

Othman, M. (2005). Enhancing safety and security in high-rise building through suatainable design. *Council on Tall Buildings and Urban Habitat, 10*, 1–12.

RRT. (2005). *RRT research response*. Australia: Reugee Review Tribunal.

Rupp. (2018, October 10). Church safety and security—An alliance approach. *Pistol in the Pulpit*, 1–6.

Sampson, I., & Onuoha, F. (2013). Forcing the horse to drink or making it realise its thrist? Understanding the enactment of ati-terrorism legislation (ATL). *Perspectives on Terrorism, 3*, 3–4.

Security Design Manual. (2007). Physical security design manual for VA facilities. *Life Safety Protected Facilities*. Washington, DC, USA: Department of Veterans Affairs.

Shafii, F. (2005). Enhancing safety and security in high-rise building through sustainable design. *ctbuh.org/papers* (pp. 1–12). CTBUH 2005 7th.

Talbot, J., & Jakeman, M. (2011). *Security risk management body of knowledge*. http://books.google.com/books?id=5xAhp9B1264C&pg=PT73.

The Law Library of Congress. (2014). *Nigeria: Boko Haram*. Report for the U.S. Department of Justice, 1–11.

Ushe, M. (2012). Religious conflicts and education in Nigeria: Implications for national security. *International Journal of Educational Research and Development, 15*, 011–022.

Walker, A. (2012). *What is Boko Haram?* UNO Publication.

Zabadi, S. (2005). *Understanding security and security sector dynamics baltimore*. John Hopkins University Press.

Zartman, W., & Faure, G. (2011). *Engaging extremist*. John Hopkins University Press.

CHAPTER 5

Revisiting the Nigerian Undergraduate English Curriculum for Global Relevance and Sustainability: The Future We Want

Lily Chimuanya, Esther Ajiboye, and Oluwasegun Omidiora

Introduction

While the discourses on curriculum development in tertiary institutions vary, they are generally centred on step-by-step holistic processes geared towards positively improving the courses offered by tertiary institutions. "Curriculum development involves the selection of educational objectives, selection of content and learning experiences, organisation of content and learning experiences, and the evaluation of learning outcomes" (Akpochafo & Filhop, 2006, p. 494). More often than not, these processes are necessitated by societal innovations, technological development, globalisation and internationalisation, which tertiary institutions are expected to acknowledge. Essentially then, when we theorise

L. Chimuanya (✉) · E. Ajiboye · O. Omidiora
Department of Languages and General Studies, Covenant University, Ota, Nigeria
e-mail: lily.chimuanya@covenantuniversity.edu.ng

S. Folarin et al. (eds.), *The United Nations and Sustainable Development Goals*, https://doi.org/10.1007/978-3-030-95971-5_5

the concept of curriculum development, we are exploring a totality of deliberate efforts made towards the creation of an instructional guide that is in sync with social realities in terms of knowledge production and knowledge distribution/communication. As such, curricula should be results-oriented as well as process-based for them to be relevant in the knowledge economy. In coherently realising students' learning outcomes, then, curriculum developers understand that frameworks have to be put in place.

In recent times, scholars have made efforts at theorising "21st Century Learning." Their studies emphasise a curriculum that is "sufficiently responsive to a complex, globalised world in which skills, critical thinking, adaptability, and creativity will be more important than knowledge per se" (McPhail & Rata, 2016, p. 54). Also, the United Nations identifies quality education as a core goal in realising sustainable development globally. It is, therefore, important that every member state of the United Nations strives towards attaining quality education. This study focuses on the quality of the BA English curriculum in Nigeria and its ability to match up with global requirements for sustainable development.

Several studies (e.g. Amadioha, 2016; Nakpodia, 2010; Oluniyi & Akinyeye, 2013) have examined curriculum development at pre-tertiary levels in Nigeria. However, there are not many studies that have examined tertiary education curriculum development in Nigeria, in particular, in the humanities. While Edegbo (2011) focused on library and information science curriculum in Nigerian universities, Akpochafo and Filho (2006) provided an overview of barriers to curriculum implementation in Nigerian universities. In this study, we question the adequacy of the BA English curriculum in Nigeria. We attempt to foreground the need for humanities' curriculum in Nigeria, specifically, the Bachelor of Arts (BA) in English programme, to embrace a more integrated framework that responds to actual societal needs in the Industry 4.0 revolution.

University Curriculum Development Initiatives in Nigeria: Past and Present

When the first indigenous Nigerian university, University of Nigeria, was established in Nigeria in 1955, it was to serve as a bedrock of raising a veritable crop of leaders and workforce who would respond to Nigeria's needs and problems. The Nigerian university curriculum was anchored on this objective, and this was further elaborated in the Nigerian Policy on

Education (2013) which states that the objectives of the Nigerian tertiary educational system are premised on teaching, research, and development. In an even simpler description, Obanya (2002) succinctly describes generic skills that students are expected to learn in the university system, namely: analytical strength, communicative skills, problem-solving skills, team spirit, creativity, versatility, lifelong learning skills, and Information Technology (IT) skills.

As vibrant communities and prosperous society are built on the foundation of a robust education system (Tabish & Nabil, 2013), the Nigerian government has, over the years, paid attention to higher education development in Nigeria. However, these efforts require optimisation, as fewer resources are now being allocated to the education sector (Solanke & Olatunji, 2015). The Nigerian Universities Commission (NUC), the umbrella body responsible for university curriculum development and quality assurance in Nigeria, was mandated in Decree 16 of 1985 (amended in Decree 48 of 1988) to set the minimum academic standards (MAS) for programmes run in Nigerian universities. The first MAS was approved in 1989. Since then, the NUC has stipulated the structure and contents of specific courses for each university undergraduate and graduate programme. Every accredited university is mandated to abide by the curriculum provisions of this regulatory body.

In 2001, in a bid to make the MAS more relevant to contemporary societal needs, the NUC commenced processes to ensure that Nigerian universities' curricula are responsive to technological advancements and globalisation. Subsequently, the NUC conducted a needs assessment survey of labour market for Nigerian graduates. They also hosted workshops for academic experts and vice-chancellors with the aim to revise the MAS, to make it more outcome-based rather than sketchy and prescriptive. This brought about the evolution of the MAS into a new document, the Benchmark Minimum Academic Standards (BMAS) published in 2007. The BMAS combined the NUC's Benchmark Style Statements with the MAS and among other things, stipulated compulsory, required, and elective courses for each programme. It also specifies the minimum credit requirements for each programme; most four-year bachelor's programmes in Nigerian universities require between 120 and 160 credit unit weightings. Importantly, the BMAS merger was considered necessary to enhance flexibility and innovation in curriculum development as well as institutional autonomy across university programmes (Okorojie, 2007, 2014).

This means that universities can introduce additional courses, which are relevant to their respective university goals, to their curricula.

In 2005, to promote the development of entrepreneurs who would function in local and global markets, the NUC introduced new curricula which focused on entrepreneurial education and development for all Nigerian university students. It further mandated that all universities should establish entrepreneurship centres for the reinforcement of entrepreneurial education. The NUC has continued to offer more initiatives to ensure that the Nigerian university curriculum stays relevant in the contemporary world.

The BMAS has since been reviewed, and a draft version was circulated in 2015, however, a comprehensive review of the Nigerian university curriculum is ongoing as academics and professionals regularly reviewed the provisions of the existing curricula. As at 2020, the NUC noted that they were in the final stage of a comprehensive review of the Nigerian university curriculum ("Review of the university curriculum," 2020).

The Idea of a World-Class University Curriculum

World-Class University (WCU) is a catchphrase that describes the process of creating and acquiring advanced knowledge for a globally competitive capacity in higher education. (Salmi, 2009, p. 3). Universities that have attained a world-class status are usually marked by cutting-edge research, knowledge transformation, employable graduates and the application of modern technology (Ahmed, 2015), geared towards the development of a nation's global knowledge competitiveness. This assertion resonates with Levinson et al.'s (2006) submission on the three key functions of great universities, vis-à-vis quality education delivery, knowledge dissemination and social services. To this end, an aspiring world-class institution emphasises excellent instructional activities which are prioritised in its curriculum.

Therefore, a World-Class University curriculum is one born out of conceptually focused research, where education planners investigate students' experiences of the courses they take. The information derived from such inquiry guides teachers to refine the pedagogy environment. The need for rich sources of evidence to guide course development is also underscored. This will focus on discovering the relevance of the proposed courses students are to take, and identify industries in which they are required. Stakeholders, that is, students, teacher, education planners and the likely industries that would engage the students also need to engage in stimulating discussions. This would help evaluate the skills the students require in specific courses (Tabish & Nabil, 2013). A World-Class University is also characterised by observational learning, which has proven over time to be a very effective strategy, hence field trips and internship programmes should be compulsory features in the curriculum.

One of the dividends of globalisation and advancement in internet technology is collaboration. Global skills cannot be learned within the confines of a classroom without recourse to global classrooms (Chimuanya & Awonuga, 2020), either via the internet or exchange studies. A World-Class University curriculum, therefore, takes cognisance of an active student engagement that incorporates global issues and perspectives into pedagogy.

As the world changes and globalisation accelerates, with new technologies revolutionising the way we communicate and share information, tutoring needs to underscore these changes. With the expectations of young people rising for quality education and decent jobs, tertiary institutions are confronted with the new challenges of equity, quality and relevance (Tabish & Nabil, 2013). It is, therefore, expedient for academic institutions to transform to meet the challenges of the present era—where the goal of every World-Class University is to equip each student with the opportunities to improve in knowledge, know-how, wisdom, and character (Tabish & Nabil, 2013). One primary capacity in which higher institutions must think reform to meet this global task is in the area of curriculum development.

Relevance and Curriculum Development

The 2030 Agenda for sustainable development has heralded new global parameters for development. The agenda opens up new opportunities to reinvent efforts towards advancement, with a focus on sustainability. Although education is directly related to SDG 4, it is at the core of the actualisation of all the 17 Sustainable Development Goals (SDGs). Education cuts across the entire SDG agenda which are grouped under the three broad dimensions of economic, environmental and social solutions. In 2015, the importance of education for building resilience and empowering learners was reiterated in the 19th Conference of Commonwealth Education Ministers (CCEM) in the Bahamas. The principal goal of the

Conference was to have Commonwealth citizens positively participate in the socio-economic development of their communities, with one of the outcomes being the launch of a curriculum framework for the SDGs. The framework was to enhance the development of life skill-sets and (Osman et al., 2017). Therefore, since education is at the centre of actualising the SDGs, there is a dire need to revisit school curriculums, especially those of the disciplines in tertiary institutions, and in particular, the Nigerian undergraduate English curriculum. Beyond developing a high level of communicative competence, which is at the core of the philosophy that guides the English programme, what other competencies do graduates in the discipline required to navigate the complex 4.0 industries? With evolutions in internet technologies changing the ways communication takes place, and with the near disappearance of the print media, how equipped is the Nigerian graduate of English in dealing with a programming and AI globe? Will the current English curriculum provide sustainable relevance for a graduate by 2030? These questions call for resituating the BA English curriculum to serve the future needs of both the graduate and the Nigerian communities.

Through its teaching, research and community service roles in building the workforce and transfer knowledge that is needed in industry and other domains in the country, every nation sees her tertiary education as a viable tool for development (Nweke & Nwoye, 2016). For instance, in Nigeria, the National Policy on Education, through its recent reforms in the educational system, highlighted the goals of General Studies in tertiary education (National Universities Commission 2007). A principal aim in the highlight is to develop individual and societal survival skills. This is the broad goal of every education endeavours, and indeed the reason for the crucial place of education among the SDGs.

This study proposes the re-evaluation of the sustainable capacity of the BA in English programme using expert-derived assessment tools. The most suitable for a single discipline is the Sustainability Tool for Assessing University Curricula Holistically (STAUNCH). STAUNCH explores the available syllabus and course descriptions as a data set built on 37 sustainability topics across the three broad SDG dimensions—economic, environmental, and social solutions. This method has been successfully used in universities across Europe (Caeiro et al., 2013) and in assessing the Engineering curricula in two Nigerian universities (Akeel et al., 2019). STAUNCH will match the course contents of the English programme against sustainability topics to evaluate their relevance.

The Nigerian Undergraduate English Curriculum: An Overview

The National University Commission, through the amended Decree (Act) No. 48 of 1988 is charged with the responsibility of prescribing the minimum criteria for all disciplines in Nigerian universities. Thus, in 1989, the Minimum Academic Standards (MAS) was developed by the commission but was later revised in 2001 to become the Benchmark Minimum Academic Standards (BMAS) that clearly defines the expected outcomes for learners (NUC, 2007).

Situated under the Faculty of Arts, English Language which comprises Language and Literature in English is a programme of study after which a degree of Bachelor of Arts (BA) is awarded. The underlying philosophy of the English programme stipulates language proficiency for use in the available administrative job opportunities for graduates. Similarly, the objectives of the discipline are summed up under three themes: communicative competence, variety differentiation and skill acquisition.

The NUC benchmark learning outcomes for BA English are distributed across specific knowledge domains that cater for all levels of linguistic description. These include: subject knowledge, language skills, linguist knowledge, and sociolinguistic knowledge.

Using Covenant University as a case study, the units required for graduation in the BA English programme is presented in Table 5.1.

Table 5.1 shows the distribution of the Units required to earn a BA degree in English. Observe that while the compulsory courses make up more than half of the total Unit requirement with 65.2%, electives comprise 8.7% and 0% industry training is required. This distribution

Table 5.1 Covenant University graduation requirements

Level	*100/%*	*200/%*	*300/%*	*400/%*	*Total/%*
Compulsory courses	22/52.4	23/58.9	32/80	28/70	105/65.2
electives	4/9.5	4/10.3		6/15	14/8.7
Industrial training (SIWES)					0/0
College course	2/4.8	2/5.1	2/5	2/5	8/4.9
University courses	4/9.5	4/10.3	4/10	4/10	16/9.9
NUC courses	10/23.8	6/15.4	2/5		18/11.2
Total	42/100	39/100	40/100	40/90	161/100

shows a clear gap in the English curriculum especially if the aim is to equip graduate with sustainable relevant skills that would enable them perform competitively in an evolving job market. An examination of the emerging opportunities for English graduates shows the need to expand the present curriculum to accommodate relevant future skill sets for survival. A good place to begin would be to create industry experience and allowance for cross-disciplinary electives.

Therefore, in response to the twenty-first-century skill requirements for a graduate of English, this paper proposes a review of the objectives for which the BA English degree is hosted in Nigerian universities. The reason is that the present categories of students who apply to study English are Millenials who mostly have English as their chronological first language (Dada, 2007). As a result, they already have substantial Standard English competence required to delve into more specific aspects of new knowledge like building interdisciplinary digital language and sustainability capacity from the outset of their study. Succinctly, the scope of the curriculum needs to be expanded to accommodate more industry-relevant and challenging issues which correspond to students' needs.

Emerging Global Opportunities for Graduates of BA (English)

The BA English curriculum is currently divided into the study of language, that is, linguistics and literature, and "provides advanced problem-solving skills that are critical to many professions" (St John & Wooden, 2005, p.82), and therefore, holds inherent value for graduates. However, there is still much more that can be done to improve the curriculum to earn it a better competitive advantage and utility. Ruggeri (2019) notes that "for many students, future earnings have become a 'litmus test' for deciding between different universities and subjects to specialise in." While there are no available statistics or empirical reports for the trend in Nigeria, in other climes, it has become apparent that recipients of English major degrees are on the decline, globally. St John and Wooden (2005) report that, over the years, humanities graduates have less earning power and lower employment rates in comparison to graduates in STEM and other applied disciplines.

Besides the fact that the current age is that of the Internet of Things (IoT), it is also the industry 4.0 age; that is, an age driven by technological innovations. This means that there are emerging career opportunities that are largely technologically driven; in fact, software and data are the currency of the industry 4.0 revolution. If graduates of English seek relevance in the industry 4.0 era, then, they need to be open to new opportunities in computational linguistics, forensic linguistics, corpus linguistics and digital humanities. Smith and Shum in Feloni (2018) categorically state that:

> ...skilling-up for an AI-powered world involves more than science, technology, engineering, and math. As computers behave more like humans, the social sciences and humanities will become even more important. Languages, art, history, economics, ethics, philosophy, psychology and human development courses can teach critical, philosophical and ethics-based skills that will be instrumental in the development and management of AI solutions.

Although codes, algorithms, and binary numbers are central to software, data, and artificial intelligence (AI), language is still very relevant. For instance, in geo-tagging, voice recognition, dictionary compilation and word processing, language processing, language learning applications, corpora building, sentiment analysis, fraud detection, among others. There is always the need to incorporate the human (empathic, context-sensitive) element into AI. As such, computational linguistics comes to the fore; hence, English majors can specialise as compilers; lexicographers; programmers; data scientists; text analysts; to mention a few.

Since there are vast opportunities available to graduates of English, the Nigerian BA. English curriculum requires an upscaling to match up to contemporary demands in the global economy. It should lay more emphasis on sustainable relevance; the practical aspects of the BA. English programme, rather than theory alone.

Reinventing a Sustainable Curriculum for the Degree We Want

Studies have evaluated the inclusion of sustainability concepts in existing disciplines in the social and natural sciences (Iyer-Reniga & Andamon, 2012; Segalas et al., 2008) with findings showing that Arts and Humanities have been given little attention in this inclusion. Sustainability explicitly aims to integrate economic, environmental and social dimensions in any field (Clark, 2007). Therefore, embedding the principles of sustainability in the BA English curriculum will involve developing an inter- and transdisciplinary problem-based curriculum. Applying sustainability to the curriculum can also be achieved by a multidisciplinary approach that allows the sharing of faculty and courses across disciplines. Whichever model of entrenching sustainability is used, it would result in variation in the programme structure, design and content (O'Byrne et al., 2015). However, in an attempt to connect with the natural and social science, and incorporate the interconnectedness of economic, environmental and social issues, there is a consensus on the core concepts that a sustainable curriculum should address as well as different learning models for achieving them (Anderson et al., 2008). It is stipulated that while core courses should constitute the majority of the programme curricula in various disciplines, there should be a balance between them and sustainability courses like climate change, renewable energy, water etc. This will enable graduates to fully engage in sustainable problem-solving and discourse on the broader community (O'Byrne et al., 2015).

A starting point for the BA in English curriculum is to capture and articulate aspects of sustainability the programme intends to explore in its philosophy, with an explicit description of the motivations for their selection. Due to time and space constraints, and the features of sustainability courses, their inclusion would be most valuable in Arts and Humanities as elective courses. The end is to enable graduates to engage with both local context and international community needs in a cross-disciplinary participatory production of scientific knowledge (Yarima et al., 2012).

Conclusion

This study, necessitated by the urgent need to incorporate relevantly, sustainability disciplines and insights, calls for a revision of the BA in English curriculum of the Nigerian university system. Since education is a fundamental index in the actualisation of the UN 17 SDGs, we argue for a sustainable World-Class University model, matched with a curriculum that would enable graduates of English make value-laden contributions and interact with diverse disciplines, cultures and beliefs. An exploration of twenty-first-century global opportunities for graduates of English also reveals the need to upscale the curriculum to equip graduates with requisite IoT and industry 4.0 skills that will facilitate their competitive advantage in the new world. The study concludes with recommendations that would guide the proposed curriculum review.

Recommendations

Although the NUC has attempted to consider the SDGs in the crafting of all course contents, extra efforts need to be effected in Arts and Humanities programmes. There should be a more deliberate effort to integrate relevant international issues and perspectives into the curriculum. For instance, the language of science and technology should explore themes around climate change, renewable energy, green life, water, etc. while every final year project should identify with any of the 17 SDGs. Besides, particular emphasis should be given to applied linguistics courses like computational linguistics, forensic linguistics, and peace linguistics. Changes in the ways communication take place, using new language forms also calls for the study of New Media English varieties. Also, using STAUNCH, universities should assess the English syllabi and course descriptions for relevance.

The concept of sustainable interdisciplinary studies should be introduced to undergraduate students of English; this is an industry 4.0 requirement. To this end, the curriculum should provide opportunities for the student to pick elective courses from Social Sciences, Engineering and Pure Sciences, different from the General Studies (GSTs). This will be with the objective of not only making them aware of the interconnectedness of issues in STEM and the Social Sciences which would make them think beyond their discipline but also ensuring that the students carry out collaborative projects with peers in those disciplines. Such projects may be assessed as a prerequisite for moving on to the final year.

Communication runs through every life endeavour, coupled with the fact that English, with its prestigious global status, is the language of transactions in all disciplines. Thus, the exploration of specialised language corpus by undergraduates should necessitate cross-disciplinary internship and field trips as a prerequisite for graduation. This will facilitate the innovation that the BMAS seeks to achieve in Arts and Humanities curricula.

References

Ahmed, H. O. K. (2015). Strategic approach for developing world-class universities in Egypt. *Journal of Education and Practice, 6*(5), 125–145.

Akeel, U., Bell, S. J., & Mitchell, J. E. (2019). Assessing the sustainability content of the Nigerian engineering curriculum. *International Journal of*

Sustainability in Higher Education. https://www.researchgate.net/publication/333495476_Assessing_the_sustainability_content_of_the_Nigerian_engineering_curriculum. Accessed August 6, 2020.

Akpochafo, W. P., & Filho, W. L. (2006). An overview of the barriers to curriculum implementation in Nigerian universities. *International Journal of Continuing Engineering Education and Life-Long Learning, 16*(6), 493–501.

Amadioha, S. (2016). Curriculum development practices in Nigeria: Definition, aims and a brief history of the comparative education and adaptation centre (CESAC). *Australian Journal of Arts and Science Research, 21*(2), 87–94.

Anderson, K., Burns, M., Bursztyn, M., Douglas, A. H., Laudati, A., Matus, K., & McNie, E. (2008). *The Ruffolo curriculum on sustainability science: 2008 Edition* (CID Graduate Student and Research Fellow Working Paper No. 32). Center for International Development at Harvard University, December 2008

Caeiro, S., et al. (2013). *Sustainability assessment tools in higher education institutions: Mapping trends and good practices around the world*. Springer International Publishing. https://doi.org/10.1007/978-3-319-02375-5

Chimuanya, L. & Awonuga, C. (2020). *Pedagogical implication of the use of English in Nigeria*. 12th International Conference of Education and New Learning (EDULEARN, 20), 6th–8th July, 2020, Spain (Conference Proceedings).

Clark, W. C. (2007). Sustainability science: A room of its own. *Proceedings of the National Academy of Sciences of the United States of America (PNAS), 104*, 1737–1738.

Dada, S. A. (2007). *Language contact and language conflict: The case of Yoruba-English bilinguals* (Kansas Working Papers in Linguistics, 29, pp. 85–113). http://hdl.handle.net/1808/1789

Edegbo, W. O. (2011). Curriculum development in library and information science education in Nigerian universities: issues and prospects. *Library Philosophy and Practice*, 1. http://citeseerx.ist.psu.edu/viewdoc/download?doi=10.1.1.473.9470&rep=rep1&type=pdf

Federal Republic of Nigeria. (2007). *National Policy on Education* (4th ed.). NERDC Press.

Federal Government of Nigeria, FGN. (2013). *National Policy on Education*. Federal Ministry of Information.

Feloni, R. (2018, January 21). *Microsoft's president says liberal arts majors are necessary for the future of tech*. https://www.businessinsider.com/microsoft-president-says-tech-needs-liberal-arts-majors-2018-1

Iyer-Raniga, U., & Andamon M. (2012). *Sustainability education in the engineering and built environment curriculum: The case for the Asia-Pacific ICERI2012 proceedings*. http://www.ias.unu.edu/prospernet/wp-content/uploads/2012/09/Iyer-Raniga_Andamon_Paper_id_730_25456_Final.pdf

Levinson, H. M., Jeong, D. W., & Ou, D. (2006). *What is world class university?* http://www.tc.columbia.edu/centers/coce/pdf_files/c12.pdf

McPhail, G., & Rata, E. (2016). Comparing curriculum types: 'Powerful knowledge' and '21st century learning.' *New Zealand Journal of Educational Studies, 51*(1), 53–68.

Nakpodia, E. D. (2010). Culture and curriculum development in Nigerian schools. *African Journal of History and Culture, 2*(1), 001–009.

National Universities Commission. (2007). *Benchmark minimum academic standard for undergraduate programmes in Nigerian universities*, pp. 55–68.

NUC. (2020, January 25). Review of university curriculum in final stage—NUC. *The Nation*. https://thenationonlineng.net/review-of-university-curriculum-in-final-stage-nuc/

Nweke, C. C., & Nwoye, C. D. (2016). Higher education and general studies in Nigeria: A philosophical investigation. *Mgbakoigba: Journal of African Studies, 6*(1).

O'Byrne, D., Dripps, W., & Nicholas, K. A. (2015). Teaching and learning sustainability: An assessment of the curriculum content and structure of sustainability degree programs in higher education. *Sustainability Science, 10*, 43–59. https://doi.org/10.1007/s11625-014-0251-y

Obanya, P. (2002). *Revitalizing education in Africa*. Stirling-Horden Publishers.

Okorojie, J. (2007). Preface. In *Benchmark minimum academic standards for undergraduate programmes in Nigerian universities*. National Universities Commission.

Okorojie, J. (2014). Preface. In *Benchmark minimum academic standards for undergraduate programmes in Nigerian universities* (Draft). National Universities Commission.

Oluniyi, O., & Akinyeye, C. O. (2013). Curriculum development in Nigeria; historical perspectives. *Journal of Educational and Social Research, 3*(1), 73–73.

Osman, A., Ladhani, S., Findlater, E., & McKay, V. (2017). *Curriculum framework for the sustainability development goals*. Commonwealth Secretariat.

Ruggeri, A. (2019). *Why 'worthless' humanities degrees may set you up for life*. https://www.bbc.com/worklife/article/20190401-why-worthless-humanities-degrees-may-set-you-up-for-life

Salmi, J. (2009). *The challenge of establishing world-class universities*. The World Bank.

Segalàs, J., Ferrer-Balas, D., & Mulder, K. (2008). Conceptual maps: Measuring learning processes of engineering students concerning sustainable development. *European Journal of Engineering Education, 33*, 297–306. https://doi.org/10.1080/03043790802088616

Solanke, O. & Olatunji, L. (2015). Resource allocation in higher education: A case study of selected polytechncs in Nigeria. *International Proceedings of Ecconomics Development and Research IPEDR (83).* Singapore: IACSIT Press.
St John, E. P., & Wooden, O. S. (2005). Humanities pathways: A framework for assessing post-baccalaureate opportunities for humanities graduates. In M. Richardson (Ed.), *Tracking changes in the humanities* (pp. 81–112). American Academy of Arts and Sciences.
Tabish, S. A., & Nabil, S. (2013). Towards establishing world-class universities. International *Journal of Science and Research (IJSR), 4*(1), 614–633.
Yarime, M., Trencher, G., Mino, T., Scholz, R. W., Olsson, L., Ness, B., Frantzeskaki, N., & Rotmans, J. (2012). Establishing sustainability science in higher education institutions: Towards an integration of academic development, institutionalisation, and stakeholder collaborations. *Sustainability Science, 7*(1),101–113.

CHAPTER 6

The Future We Want: Countering Fake News and Hate Speech in the Democratic Process in Nigeria

Lai Oso, Oluseyi Soremekun, and Jide Jimoh

Introduction

Among other contestations in journalism, the twin concepts of fake news and hate speech rank high owing to the enablement provided by the internet. For one, the speed with which the internet enables the media to manufacture, process and disseminate information in this digital age has become dizzying. Secondly, the easy access it has given to hitherto

This study was supported by UNESCO's International Programme for the Development of Communication (IPDC) through Media Awareness and Information for all Networks MAIN

L. Oso (✉) · J. Jimoh
School of Communication, Lagos State University, Lagos, Nigeria

O. Soremekun
United Nations Information Office, Lagos, Nigeria

S. Folarin et al. (eds.), *The United Nations and Sustainable Development Goals*, https://doi.org/10.1007/978-3-030-95971-5_6

unrecognised participants in information production and dissemination has broken boundaries of professional and ethical gates leading to a flurry of unprocessed information flow. Confronted by the consequences of the situation, society has also responded through studies by scholars and voices of concerned citizens to the emerging realities. It is within the need for continuous critical assessment of the situation and finding lasting solutions that this study is situated. With the rise of right-wing extremism worldwide and the somewhat disruptive and vituperative discourse that attended the 2016 US elections that produced Donald Trump as president, interest has heightened on the use of fake news and hate speeches as instruments of political contestations. In Nigeria, the 2015 and 2019 general elections have also witnessed the upsurge in the use of fake news and hate speeches. A clear understanding of the pattern of use and implications and countermeasures have become even more imperative. Thus, this study focuses on the 2019 elections in Nigeria by apprehending fake news and hate speeches in the run-up to, during and after the election with a view to providing a road map for countering the malodorous effects on the polity.

Fake News

United Nations Educational and Scientific Organization (UNESCO) as part of its global initiative for excellence in journalism education, released a handbook in which it notes that "fake news" has no straight forward or commonly-understood meaning because "news means verifiable information in the public interest, and information that does not meet these standards does not deserve the label of news. In this sense then, 'fake news' is an oxymoron which lends itself to undermining the credibility of information which does indeed meet the threshold of verifiability and public interest-i.e. real news" (Ireton & Posseti, 2018).

UNESCO further stressed that to better understand cases involving exploitative manipulation of the language and conventions of news genres, "this publication treats these acts of fraud for what they are- as a particular category of phoney information within increasingly diverse forms of disinformation, including in entertainment formats like visual memes" (Ireton & Posseti, 2018, p. 7). From the statements above the publication would seem to prefer the use of disinformation and misinformation for the phenomenon. Indeed, it describes misinformation as misleading information created or disseminated without manipulative or malicious intent noting that "both are problems for society but disinformation is particularly dangerous because it is frequently organised, well resourced, and reinforced by automated technology".

Nevertheless, a common thread in the various definitions is the intention to deceive the audience to achieve selfish aims. The real intention of the creator and disseminators of fake news and its synonyms—disinformation campaigns, cyber propaganda, cognitive hacking and information warfare is the manipulation of public opinion to affect the real world in the attempt of manufacturing consent. There could also be a motivation for financial gains. For those Okaiyeto and Badmus refer to as "Bloggerprenuer", the financial gains of the cyberspace has been the only motivation for the burgeoning blogosphere in Nigeria (Okaiyeto & Badmus, 2019, p. 206). They noted that fake news has been used to lure traffic to many blogs by many bloggerpreneurs. Many bloggers and social media influencers are linked to individual politicians, political parties, ethnic and religious groups both for political and commercial reasons (see Hitchen et al., 2019, p. 21 for example). As Wasserrman and Madrid-Moroles have argued these two motivations, political and financial gains "bear resemblance to public relations or 'spin' and propaganda respectively, although, fake news may encompass both" (2009, p. 108). Perhaps to avoid the definitional conundrum, Claire Wardle, focused her intervention on providing a taxonomy of fake news to take care of various manifestations of the phenomenon. Wardle (2017) classifies fake news into seven categories:

1. False connection (where headlines, visuals or captions do not support content);
2. False context (genuine content shared with false contextual information);
3. Manipulated content (genuine imagery/information manipulated to deceive);
4. Misleading content (misleading use of information to frame an issue or individual);
5. Imposter content (genuine sources are impersonated);
6. Fabricated content (100% false, designed to deceive and harm); and
7. Satire/parody (with potential to fool but no intention to cause harm)".

The typology of fake news listed by Wardle has been adopted and incorporated into the content categories used in this study.

Hate Speech

Even more difficult to define is the concept of hate speech. Hate speech is not a recent phenomenon but like fake news, has been enhanced by the coming of the internet and the attendant democratisation of the means of information gathering and dissemination through the social media. In response to the prevalence of hate speech in the political discourse in Nigeria, government has, among other responses, proposed to legislate against hate speech and amidst strident criticism proposed the death penalty for certain categories of hate speech. Yet, neither government nor the society has reached an agreement on what constitutes hate speech. Can there be legislation against a phenomenon that has not been properly defined? As CITAD (2018, p. 1) notes, "there is the danger that given lack of clarity of what hate speech means across actors, that hate speech narrative could be used to either stifle freedom of speech or silence criticism of government, including political opposition".

In another publication, CITAD (2017) had adopted the definition by Benesch who proposed the term "dangerous speech" as that segment of hate speech that has the propensity to catalyse violence. Thus, CITAD operationalised hate speech to be speech that:

1. Insults people for their religion;
2. Abuses people for their ethnic or linguistic affiliations;
3. Expresses contempt against people because of their place of origin;
4. Disparages or intimidates women or girls because of their gender;
5. Condones discriminatory assertions against people living with disability;
6. Abuses or desecrates symbols of cultural or religious practices;
7. Denigrates or otherwise ridicules traditional or cultural institutions of other people (CITAD, 2017, p. 3).

Thus, the test for hate speech should consider the content and context of use. Specifically, it must meet certain standards. The following test, developed by the Ethical Journalism Network (EJN) and based on international standards, highlights questions in the gathering, preparation and dissemination of news and helps place what is said and who is saying it in context:

1. Status of the Speaker
   - How might their position influence their motives?
   - Should they even be listened to or just ignored?
2. Reach of the Speech
   - How far is the speech travelling?
   - Is there a pattern of behaviour?
3. Goals of the Speech
   - How does it benefit the speaker and their interests?
   - Is it deliberately intended to cause harm to others?
4. The Content Itself
   - Is the speech dangerous?
   - Could it incite violence towards others
5. Surrounding Climate – Social/Economic/Political
   - Who might be negatively affected?
   - Is there a history of conflict or discrimination? (https://ethicaljournalismnetwork.org).

Given that a precise and universal definition of hate speech may not be feasible, the set of standards for its determination provides a better route in interrogating the concepts of hate speech and fake news and that has been applied in this study.

The Nigerian Social Media Landscape

The ethnic and religious polarisation existing in Nigeria and evident in the Mass Media has been carried over to the internet and social media. While noting some of the problems of blogosphere particularly the lack of journalistic skills and ethical standards, Ayankojo asks the question, what about its very critical and debasing language of communicator? (Ayankojo, 2014, p. 2).

Like the mainstream media, the landscape of the social media in Nigeria is quite extensive. According to the Nigerian Communications Commission (NCC), by the end of August 2020, internet users have reached 149.7 million while broadband penetration remained 43.3%. As of December 2019, there were more than 27 million Nigerians on Facebook. This is followed by Twitter users whose figure has been growing while WhatsApp hosting of many groups is also very popular.

Social media has been defined as "a collection of internet websites services and practices that support collaboration, community building, participation and sharing" (Otieno and Matoke 2014). Facebook as of March 2018 had 28 million users in Nigeria (CITAD, 2017, p. 22).

Politicians have increasingly turned to the social media to enhance their visibility and communication with the electorates especially the younger generation. In the campaign leading to the 2011 General Elections in Nigeria, Goodluck Jonathan, the presidential candidate of the People's Democratic Party (PDP) relied heavily on Facebook, culminating into the publication of a book, *My Friends and I*, celebrating the perceived success of his interaction on the social media platform and the subsequent elections in 2015. 2019 witnessed even more politicians across parties making use of social media.

It is no surprise then that the battle to win followers and sway them from the opposition was increasingly sought on social media platforms.

Objectives of the Study

The general objective of this study is to find out the influence of fake news and hate speech in the 2019 elections in Nigeria hence the specific objectives are:

1. To establish the extent of fake news and hate speech in the 2019 general elections in Nigeria.
2. To determine the extent of fake news and hate speech in Nigerian social media
3. To find out dominant issues in fake news and hate speech
4. To analyse the probable implications of fake news and hate speech on the outcome of the 2019 elections.

Theoretical Background

Many theories popular in media and communication studies suggest themselves for this research. Three main ones immediately come to mind: Technological determinism, media effect and audience/reception theories and the theory of public sphere. This study considers the theory of public sphere most relevant to this study.

Theory of Public Sphere

The theory basically relates to the role of the media in a democracy. The public sphere is a neutral autonomous space where people come together to deliberate "based on reason, logic and persuasive augmentation – what Habermas describes as rational –critical debate – rather than the rank or status of individual speakers, provides the basis for political discussion". The theory foregrounds the importance of the media in providing a discursive space for citizens to debate political issues so that the citizens can be well informed in making political decisions and choices.

Methodology

Content Analysis

The method used in this study is content analysis supported by In-Depth Interview (IDI) of major social media influencers. According to Berelson (1952, p. 14) content analysis is the "research technique for the objective, systematic and quantitative description of the manifest content of communication". IDI has been described as "a one-person-at-a-time, unstructured but not aimless conversation between the researcher or an interviewer and a respondent". IDI is particularly helpful in interrogating the "why" of issues observed from content analysis since the unstructured nature allows for in-depth questioning and analysis.

A 16-item coding schedule was designed to obtain information from social media sites on the issue of fake news and hate speech. Also, an interview guide containing 18 questions was also designed and administered to selected social media influencers and administrators of popular social media sites. The study is based on content analysis of social media content and interview with social media influencers. The choice of social media is due to the fact that they are now becoming the major social discourse platform especially among the youth. Social media have greatly widened the public sphere and enhance higher level of public engagement and participation hitherto neglected and/or marginalised social segment of the populace.

The kind of professional restraint (gatekeeping) we find in the mainstream media is largely absent on social media platforms.

Findings, Conclusion and Recommendations

General Findings

The combination of content analysis and in-depth interviews, yielded some interesting findings that shed light on the nature of the problem at hand and provided a basis for the conclusions and recommendations that follow.

Objective One:

The extent of fake news and hate speech in the 2019 general elections in Nigeria.

A total of 103 stories were found to be either fake news or hate speech in the various social media studied. As depicted in table one below, out of the 103 items analysed for fake news and hate speech, 57 (55.3%) were fake news and 45 (43,7%) were hate speeches. The study found more hate news than hate speeches within the study period. This may not indicate the prevalence of hate speech over fake news generally but it is an indication of the high level of prevalence of both in the 2019 general election in Nigeria. Interestingly, the study also found one story that is both a hate speech and fake news. This lethal combination highlights the need to pay more attention to both phenomena in the political and other spheres of the polity. Thus, the study found that there is high prevalence of fake news and hate speech in the 2019 Elections in Nigeria.

The situation above is also corroborated by findings from the in-depth interviews of social media influencers and administrators. One of them Mr Dele Dele-Olukoju, Founder of Memes United, a Facebook Closed Group (8,164 members) in response to the prevalence said. "At least twice weekly, I received social media contents that I considered hateful or fake. It was that bad. And it is continuing even after the elections".

Another respondent, Biodun Kuye, an administrator of Ogun State Polytechnic WhatsApp group added, "Yes, I am aware of fake news and hate speech circulating in Nigeria. In the run up to the last general elections, I received several media content that I considered hate speech or fake news especially through the social media".

Ms Suzan Ade CokerFounder, RantHQ on Facebook (Over 1.2 million members) also said:

> It was generally through the social media...Facebook, Twitter, Whatsapp, Instagram...but the traditional media is regulated and people who run traditional media are trained. So because of their training they wouldn't do such things. It was rampant only on the social media.

The statistics from content analysis and views from in-depth interviews agree on the high prevalence of fake news and hate speech in the pre, during and after the 2019 General Elections in Nigeria.

Objective Two:

Extent and sources of fake news and hate speech in Nigerian social media.

It is also of interest to this study to find the media mostly used for the dissemination of fake news and hate speech in the 2019 elections in Nigeria. Online news platforms have the highest with 36 counts (35%). Twitter takes the second position with 33 representing 33% of the total. This is a pointer to the increasing popularity of the social medium of Twitter in the discourse of political issues in Nigeria. Facebook comes a distant third with 10 (9.7%) and blogs with 8 counts (7.8%). Thus online news platforms, Twitter and blogs are the most significant social media used to disseminate fake and hate speeches. Other media such as WhatsApp was also used but because of its end to end encryption it is more difficult to track by non-members of the group. Nevertheless, the hate speech and fake news tracked on other platforms are also shared by members in the WhatsApp group rapidly.

Views from the interviews also corroborate the statistics above. Dele-Olukoju said, *"I cannot remember receiving any hate speech or fake news through the traditional media of radio, television and newspapers. It was more of a social media problem"*.

Kuye added:

> During the elections, hate speech and fake news got into my social media space most frequently. As frequent as 4 times in a week. Even up till now, you still get some forwarded fake news.

So, between social media and traditional media the prevalence is more on social media and this is explained by Suzan Ade Coker, "the traditional media is regulated and people who run traditional media are trained. It was rampant only on the social media".

Objective Three:

Dominant issues in fake news and hate speech.

> We also found that politics dominated the type of issues/focus of discourse on fake news and hate speech with 73(72.3%) followed by electoral issues with 15 (14.9%). Others are religion 6.8%, economy 5.0% and the military 1.0%.

The in-depth interview also yielded some interesting views. Suzan Ade Coker, a social media influencer opined: "They are about many things: religion, politics, tribe. Politics is the most, though. Political issues take the lead in hate speech and fake news".

Dele-Olukoju said: "The issue surrounding president Buhari's certificate was political. Even all hate speech/ fake news on personality issues during the elections period, were politically motivated".

Kuye added,

> Most hate speech and fake news I have heard and received were about Buhari, about APC, about PDP, about Atiku.

The dominant issues were political, even when discussing ethnicity, religion and other divisive issues they were used as instruments for political advantage.

Objective Four:

Probable implications of fake news and hate speech on the outcome of the 2019 elections.

After determining the presence, extent and dominant issues, it would be interesting to find out the implications for the 2019 elections in

Nigeria especially whether it influenced the outcome of the election, an objective of this study. This was largely determined through in-depth interviews of social media influencers and administrators.

Putting the influence in context, Kuye averred,

> From experience and discussion with friends and associates, so many people believed the hate speech and fake news, and they would argue with you that it is true. But I believe that their views did not affect the outcome of the elections because, most of the people on the social media were not registered voters.They did not have voters.

His point was that if it did, Buhari would not have won. Olukoju corroborated that line of thought, saying:

> We need to realise the social media penetration. Social media is popular in the urban area. Influencers, opinion leaders, role models, etc. are the ones who dictate in the areas that are not metropolitan. There are places where people don't have phones in this country, talk less of smart phones. A lot of people don't have FB accounts. In Lagos, Abuja, PH, you can say yes…but there are several other states, penetration is not as far-reaching as in the cities. So, if you look at the number of people voting and compare it with the penetration of the social media, we find a shortfall. Everybody has one thing or the other that influenced people in voting, but for social media, I am not sure it influenced the outcome of the elections.

In line with the debate on media effects, a third respondent was hesitant in determining the influence of social media on the electoral outcome, "I am not sure really. I think it is Yes and No. Because there were times that people reported cases of violence in some areas and people could not go out to vote because of that. I know during the Osun State elections, some people informed me that there was violence…that they didn't go out to vote because of reports of violence". Ade Coker concluded.

What may not be in doubt from the literature on fake news and hate speech is the negative effect it has on the polity and the need for media literacy training to counter them.

Timing/Period

This study also sought to determine the period with the highest amount of fake news and hate speeches. For this purpose, the study was delineated into three phases—before, during and after the election. The findings show that the period before election features the highest with 49 (48.0%). It declined to 17 (16%) during the election and rose again after the election to 36 (35.3%). The pre-election high score is explained by the fact that that is the height of campaigns by the various contenders for positions. It also points to the need to target any intervention early in the election season.

The category of statement/speech dominates with 78 (75.7%) followed by publication or report with 10 (19.4%), 3(2.9%) with no source indicated and press conference 1.9%

Medium of Expression

The medium of expression dominating the communication of fake news and hate speech in this study is editorial matter with 86 (83.5%). Editorial matters are made up of news stories, features, opinions as against video 6.8%, picture 4.9%, audio 1% and others 1%. From the above, the written word dominates.

Summary of Findings

- This study found a high prevalence of both fake news and hate speech in the run-up to, during and after the 2019 elections in Nigeria.
- It also found that the social media such as Twitter, Facebook and WhatsApp and online news platform were used for most of the fake news and hate speech.
- The dominant issues revolved around politics but ethnicity and religion were weaponised for political ends.
- A vast number of people believed the messages from social media but interviewees are of the opinion that such messages might not have significantly affected the outcomes of the elections.
- The most critical segments of youth in the social media may not have exercised their franchise.
- False contents were the most popular means of spreading fake news.

- The pre-election period witnessed a spike in both fake news and hate speech.
- Editorial matter as against pictures, videos and audio were the most popular means of disseminating fake news and hate speech.
- Members of the public through comments were the highest disseminators of fake news and hate speech.
- A high majority of both fake news and hate speech emanated from the male gender in Nigeria.

Recommendations

To counter the advent of fake news and hate speech in Nigeria and stem the surge and its damaging impact on the polity, as documented by this study, the following recommendations are worthy of consideration:

i. Establish a fake news/hate speech observatory to monitor and log incidents of fake news and hate speech for the attention of the authorities.
ii. The UN in Nigeria in collaboration with the Nigerian Government should adopt, and adapt the United Nations global "Verified" campaign on fake news.
iii. Create a "Fact-Check" platform that is accessible to the public.
iv. Media and Informational Literacy (MIL) needs to be strengthened through aggressive outreach to Secondary Schools and Universities
v. Training of Politicians (Party Executives and Candidates) on the fake news and hate speech and the implications on peace and security of the nation
vi. Training of digital media producers on media ethics and national development
vii. Promote self-regulation among digital media producers
viii. Awareness raising on rights (political, cultural, social, religious) of individuals and groups
ix. Continuous training of journalists on conflict-sensitive reporting with emphasis on respect for diversity

References

Ayankojo, K. (2014). Blogs as alternative to mainstream media. In L. Oso, R. Olatunji, & N. Owens-Ibie (Eds.), *Journalism and media in Nigeria*. University Press.

Bernard, B. (1952). *Content analysis in communication research*. The Free Press.

Boyd-Barrett, O. (2002). *Theory in media*.

CITAD. (2017). *Faith and language as domains of hate speech mobilization in Nigeria: 2017 annual hate speech report*. CITAD.

CITAD (2018). *Annual report*. CITAD.

Hall, S. (1986). Media power and class power. In J. Curran, J. Ecclestone, G. Oakley, & A. Rechadson (Eds.). *Bending reality*. Plato Press.

Hitchen, J., Hassan, I., Fisher, J., & Cheeseman, N. (2019). *Whatsapp and Nigeria's 2019 election: Mobilizing the people, protecting the vote*. Centre for Democracy & Development and University of Brimingham.

Howley, K. (2007). Community media and the public sphere. In E. Devereux (Ed.), *Media studies: Key issues and debates*. Sage.

Internet World Stats. https://www.internetworldstats.com/stats1.htm retrieved on 27 September 2020.

Ireton, C., & Posseti, J. (Eds.). (2018). *Journalism, fake news and disinformation: Handbook for journalism education and training*. UNESCO.

Jimoh, J. (2017). Gender sensitivity in the coverage of conflict situations. In U. A. Pate & L. Oso (Eds.), *Multiculturalism, diversity and reporting conflict in Nigeria*. Evans Brothers Nigeria Publishers Limited.

Jonathan, G. (2010). *My friends and I: Conversations on policy and governance via Facebook*. GDP Associates Ltd.

Okaiyeto, S. A., & Badmus, R. I. (2019). Fake news, social media and the consolidation of the Nigeria's democratic culture. In N. Owens-Ibie, M. Oji, & J. Ogwezi (Eds.), *Fake news and hate speech narrative of political instability*. University Press.

Oremus, W. (2017). *Facebook has stopped saying 'fake news'*. Accessed 20 December 2019. http://www.slate.com/blogs/future_tense/2017/08/08/facebook_has_stopped_saying_fakenews_is_false_news_any_better.html

Oso, L. (n.d.). *The emerging trend of fake and false news: Challenges of gate keeping*. Paper presented at Newspaper Proprietors Association of Nigeria's (NPAN).

Owens Ibie, N. (2019). Stoking political instability: An introduction. In N. Owens-Ibie, M. Oji & J. Ogwezzy (Eds.), *Fake news and hate speech: Narratives of political instability*. Canada University Press.

Newbold, C. (2019). Research. In O. Boyd-Barrett & H. Van 'Den Buck (Eds.), *The media book*. Arnold.

Nigerian Communications Commission (NCC). https://www.ncc.gov.ng/statistics-reports/industry-overview#view-graphs-tables-6. Retrieved on 6 October 2020.

Scammell, M., & Semetko, H. (2000). *Media, journalism and democracy*. Dartmouth Publishing.

Verjee, A., Kwaja, C., & Onubogu, O. (2018). *Nigeria's 2019 elections: Change, continuity and the risk to peace, Special report 429*. United States Institute for Peace.

Wardle, C. (2017). *Fake news: It's complicated*. Accessed 19 December 2019. https://firstdraftnews.com/fake-newscomplicated

Wasserrman, H., & Madrid-Morales, D. (2009). An exploratory study of "fake news" and the media trust in Kenya, Nigeria and South Africa. *African Journalism Studies*, *40*(1), 107–123.

Williams, A. (2014). *The nature of national narratives: The press and the evolution of modern media in Nigeria*. Canada University Press.

CHAPTER 7

Environmental Impact Assessment (EIA) in Actualizing SDGs: Lessons from Community Development in Ogun State, Nigeria

David Olukanni, Justin Lazarus, and Emmanuel Fagbenle

Introduction

The development of land and its various environmental resources are some of the most important factors that characterize communities and cities. The key aspects of urbanization, industrialization and other related economic developments involve the establishment of infrastructures such as road construction, dam and electric power plant construction, etc. Despite the importance of these infrastructures, their execution usually come with some negative effects on the environment (air, water, plants and animals). As such the importance of EIA (Environmental Impact Assessment) as a legislative and scientific instrument for quality assurance,

D. Olukanni (✉) · J. Lazarus · E. Fagbenle
Department of Civil Engineering, Covenant University, Ota, Nigeria
e-mail: david.olukanni@covenantuniversity.edu.ng

S. Folarin et al. (eds.), *The United Nations and Sustainable Development Goals*, https://doi.org/10.1007/978-3-030-95971-5_7

protection and decision making in project development cannot be overlooked. This was the beginning of National Environmental Protection Agency (NEPA) of 1969 in the US of which other European countries began to emulate and later spread down to developing economies including Nigeria though with variations in the mode of operation (Wood, 2000).

Environmental Impact Assessment (EIA)

The act whereby a planned project is assessed to see if it would impend environmental components (i.e. the biological, physical, social and economic) and subsequent preventive measures are designed to reduce the impacts known as an EIA (Lawrence, 2003). Wood, 2000 described EIA as the most effective idea of the twentieth century being implemented in over 100 nations. The concept of Environmental Impact Assessment allows decision-makers the opportunity to know the effects of project operational activity and determine its continuity or termination. It ensures that the potential problems are foreseen and addressed early in the planning and design stages of the project. It serves as a scientific tool for predicting, assessing and description of the aftermath of a project on the physical and living environment (Glasson et al., 2012; Morris & Therivel, 2001). This can be seen as a big step towards the practice of sustainable development. EIA is usually undertaken in a systematic manner that includes screening, scoping, description of environment, public consultation, prediction and evaluation of impacts, mitigation and monitoring of impacts, presentation, documentation, review and decision making (Echefu & Akpofure, 2002; Ogunba, 2004).

In Nigeria there are three independent EIA systems: Petroleum Act of 1969, EIA Decree 86 of 1992 and Town and Country Planning Decree 88 of 1992. However, reports show that analysts have found the nation's EIA regulatory structure and practise faulty among other things by not including people in the Environmental Impact Assessment processes, notwithstanding the statutory provisions (Eromosele, 2015). It is worthy to note that though the EIA is set up as a tool to enhance clarity for sound decision making, in most instances, developmental projects are approved regardless. The EIA statement covers a brief description of the project, description of the existing environment, possible project impact, mitigation and security steps and consideration of alternatives. Hence, the goal of EIA should not be seen as just a tool for making better decisions, but as an appraisal tool for improving the overall project lifecycle with a keen consideration of the environmental impacts for meeting the objectives of SDGs.

Concept of Sustainable Development Goals (SDGs)

The current global vision, SDGs brings into perspective the need to protect every aspect of human life and the environment where they live. These goals are very important and must be upheld by the government, researchers and all relevant stakeholders. In addition, promoting sustainable urban development in all forms of engineering projects would guarantee and sustain a complete baseline for overall project planning and implementation. Also, since sustainable development of an unconventional infrastructure as it is the case globally, touches several facets of life including social, economic, environmental and cultural aspects (Chang & Lin, 2018), designing green environmental index evaluation system would help to avert environmental consequences of land development, lessen loss to life and assuage impending maintenance and management costs. Therefore, this review aims to examine the role of EIA in achieving sustainable development goals when applied to Ogun state community development. The concepts of this report are to: Examine how well the scoping phase of the EIA was conducted for World Bank community development project in Ogun state and to arrive at a satisfactory report; Examine the impact assessment of Ewekoro Cement plant on its physical environment and the implicating health challenges on the Residents; Examine the various theoretical approaches to a good EIA practice, taking a look at the legislative provision for EIA in the study area and procedural framework in Nigeria; Study the empirical data and the final EIA report of the case study to confirm the adherence to these guidelines that would influence the attainment of some SDGs.

EIA of Ogun State World Bank Community-Based Development Project

The Ogun State community development project came through the approved World Bank Community-based Urban Development Project in which the state was a beneficiary among other seven Nigerian states. Based on the condition of infrastructure, two communities (Ijeun

Irunbe/Ago-Oka Community and Owu/Gbagura Community) were chosen for the project. However, as part of the requirements of the World Bank, before any project commencement, an EIA study was mandatory in the area (Ogun State Government, 2001). Therefore, the stepwise process carried out to ascertain the benefits or impacts of the project was examined.

Legal and Administrative Policy Framework Requirements

One of the most important requirements of EIA studies is that they are to be conducted under the structure of both local and global environmental standards (Ogun State Government, 2001). These regulations and guidelines to EIA Studies include those specified by indigenous and international organizations such as that of Federal Environmental Protection Agency (FEPA) and World Bank's International Bank for Reconstruction and Development (IBRD), respectively, which formed the bedrock on which the EIA study was carried out. Under the FEPA Procedures as indicated in UNEP EIA Training Manual (Echefu & Akpofure, 2002), the proponent was required to notify FEPA in writing about any proposed project with the following procedures:

i. Screening (i.e. agency required to conduct an Initial Environmental Examination (IEE) and apportion the project into groups depending on the size, scope, length, frequency and threats).
ii. Scoping; this is where the proponent is required to provide Terms of Reference (TOR) for the proposed EIA study.
iii. Implementation of the EIA study; this includes making a final draft and an EIA report, and
iv. Review Process, Approval and Certification.

In addition, the following guidelines were considered; the 1992 Urban and Regional Planning Decree 88, World Bank guidelines on environmental assessment, 1994 edition of Ogun State Environmental Protection Agency and international conventions on environmental matters. The requirements/specifications of each of the legal frameworks were reviewed in detail for the EIA study (Ogun State Government, 2001). The requirements of section 33 of Urban and Regional Planning Decree

No 88 (1992) states that; at the time of submitting application for development, a developer must provide to an appropriate authority a detailed environmental impact statement for any of the following categories of projects: (a) residential land development in excess of 2 hectares (b) building or expanding a factory or constructing an office of over four floors or 5,000 square metres of a permissible space or (c) permission for ~~a~~ major recreational development.

The Environment Impact Analysis Process

Purpose of the EIA

The report established that an EIA study was required to achieve the following:

i. Find out the available biological, geographic, physical and socio-economic conditions of the chosen locations.
ii. Ascertain the possible impacts (positive and negative) that may result from the installation and running of the proposed project.
iii. Recommend ways for mitigating/controlling the extent and manage implication of the identified impacts.
iv. incorporate the views, opinions and objectives of all stakeholders into the local and international environmental guidelines, standards and conventions pertinent to the proposed project activities for the final project design in accordance with EIA report (Ogunba, 2004).

This stage of the EIA study is to assist in predicting the impact of upgrading project in the two communities at all levels (i.e. the pre-construction, construction, operation and maintenance) and to suggest mitigation actions where applicable. At the same time, this criterion was established in line with the regulatory requirements of the Federal Environmental Protection Agency (FEPA), Urban and Regional Planning Laws and the Ogun State Environmental Protection Agency (OGEPA) at the time of the study.

Justification of the Project

Ogun State is one of the main industrial hubs of Nigeria. As such, there is a need to find solutions to the continuous failure/lack of infrastructure in the selected communities that make the extended major portion of Abeokuta (Ogun state capital). In addition, these were somewhat suburban communities that lacked adequate electricity, portable water supply and other social facilities. Moreover, the roads are winding, narrow and uncoordinated. All these challenges attracted the attention of the state government in collaboration with the World Bank to provide an urgent upgrading solution to the communities. The project which was focused on improving the crumbling urban centres would help to boost economic growth, upturn literacy level, decrease health hazard and reduce insecurity within and outside the regions. In addition, the success of the project would guarantee a more conducive, convenient and comfortable environment for the inhabitants of the communities.

Consultation/Public Participation

Before any project is carried out, relevant stakeholders involvement (e.g. community leaders) by way of direct or indirect participatory consultation is paramount to completing an EIA study (REMA, 2008). As such, consultation and meetings with the key stakeholders (i.e. the Oba's, chiefs, youths and other relevant community leaders) is very instructive. This is necessary to identify and involve all stakeholders and to discuss suitable alleviation methods for any identified adverse impacts. More importantly, it is to ensure that the proponent maintains consistency with the policy of the government to uphold an effective, accurate and friendly relationship with the shareholders so as to keep them constantly up-to-date with all development undertakings in the communities (Ogun State Government, 2001).

Collection of Data

The data collection for the EIA study process covered both the existing condition of the place and the proposed upgrading plan. The data was collected from primary sources and secondary sources. While the primary data involved interviews of the community residents and preliminary survey on climate, socio-economic, and land use data, the secondary data was from the relevant literature to complement the information collected from the field.

Assessment of the Impacts

Impact analysis are usually done in accordance with the environmental and social impact assessment (ESIA) report through the various phases of the project as described below:

i. The pre-construction phase
ii. The construction phase
iii. The operation phase and
iv. The commissioning phase

The impact intensity as well as the probability of its occurrence based on the OGEPA standards includes;

Anticipated Socio-Economic Benefits

i. Increased earning to local labourers from vegetation clearing and site preparation
ii. Provision of social amenities like potable water supply, electricity and asphalt road

Potential Negative Impacts

i. The use of energy and non-renewable resources
ii. Depletion of ecosystem resources and potential soil and water pollutio
iii. Emissions to air (in particular dust); discharge of effluent/wastewater to the aquatic environment and potential water pollution etc., especially during the road construction rehabilitation process.

Mitigation of Environmental and Social Impacts Measures

The control of identified adverse impacts was conducted in stages considering prevention, reduction and elimination in order to enhance the beneficial impacts.

Mitigation Measures during Pre-Construction

i. There was no displacement of residents, hence no resettlement action plan was made.
ii. There was need to develop and implement stakeholder engagement plan for each phase of the project including the involvement of HSE personnel during operations.
iii. Development and Implementation of H&S management plan to protect every worker involved in construction activities.

Measures during the Operations/Execution Phase

i. Two major negative impacts were identified at this stage; suspended particles (air pollution and vibrations (noise pollution). They were verified to be temporal and would cease after the project, however, their nose masks, ear buds and other protective kits were provided.
ii. To prevent traffic, only taxis, private cars and utility vehicles were permitted to use the roads at controlled speed levels. Also, speed breakers, road signs and zebra should be constructed along schools roads to enable easy and safe passage for students/children.

Environmental Management Plan (EMP)

Specific Environmental Management Plans for all phases of the project was designed to promote health, safety and security of members of the public that are direct and indirect beneficiary. These management plans as required by the legal frameworks (Echefu & Akpofure, 2002; Ogunba, 2004) includes:

i. Waste Management Plan
ii. Vegetation Management Plan
iii. Physical Cultural Resources Management Plan and
iv. Emergency Management Plans

Training and Performance Monitoring Plans

The training of all operating staff is necessary to enhance technical know-how and to guarantee competence. The operating staff must fully understand the emergency response plan's procedures and each worker must understand the warning and intervention procedures in the event of an emergency (Transmission Company of Nigeria [TCN], 2018). Performance monitoring is to be carried out to ensure that the required EMP activities are being implemented and that the desired targets and outcomes are being achieved and assess the strengths and weaknesses of the EMP's and mitigation plans (TCN, 2018).

Ewekoro Cement Factory

Ewekoro is one of the villages along the Sango–Ifo–Abeokuta expressway. Ewekoro bordering Papalanto in the west, Abeokuta in the east and various villages along the northern and southern axes. The climate is no different from those of the neighbouring towns and villages like Ifo, Ilaro, Sagamu and others. The siting of the West African Portland Cement Company (WAPCO) in this area has changed the town's economic sphere. Although top-notch limestone has been found in this settlement since the colonial period, mining and quarrying did not begin until the early 70s when mine and export attempts were made. However, the company was established as a follow-up to the first and second National development plans with Lafarge of France being the main technical partner. Since then, the company has been privatized. Figure 7.1 shows the location of the study area on the Nigerian map.

Impact of Ewekoro Cement Plant on the Natural Environment

Limestone extraction in Ewekoro has led to the conversion of agricultural land to quarry sites. The types of house on the site are mainly the makeshifts, built for use on no long-term basis. The houses are used primarily as shops and stores for factory products. These houses were built without any planning regulations and thus could pose health risks for the occupants. Deforestation is a very important impact of the quarry. This simply means losing the vegetation cover required by the need to move equipment to the site, removing the topsoil, stemming explosives

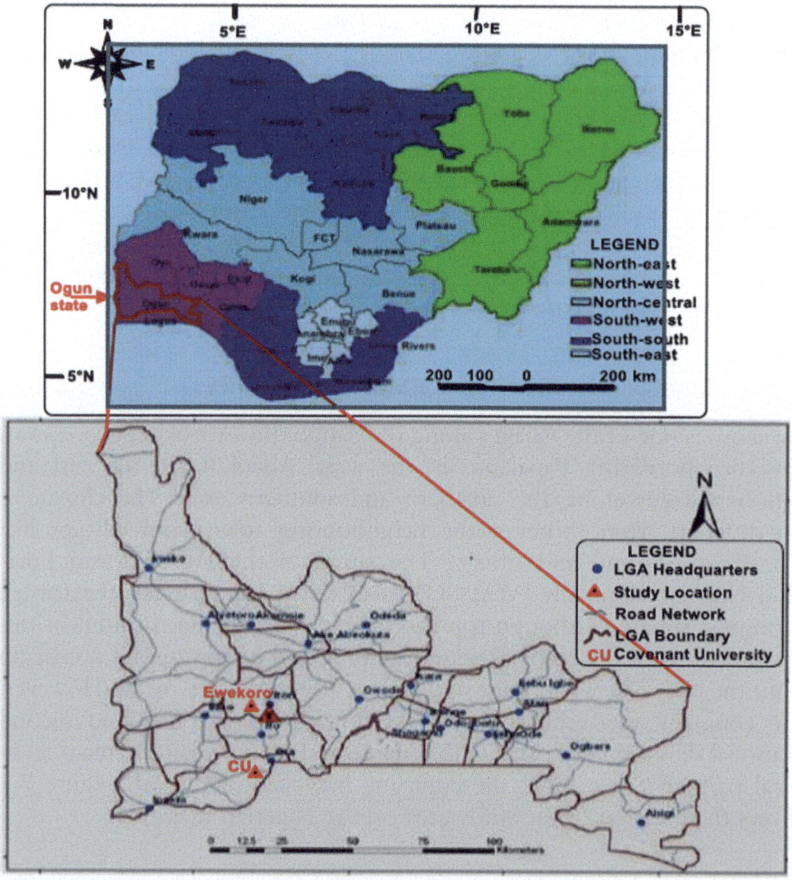

Fig. 7.1 Zonal map of Nigeria revealing the study locations in Ogun state

and removing blasted calcareous stones. These impacts are usually minimized by appropriate mitigating steps such as reclaiming of the mined areas using new overburden products, and afforestation policy requiring planting of varieties of trees with ornamental qualities that can maintain the soil structure well and could well cover the exposed land (Ilalokhoin et al., 2013). Limestone mining in Ewekoro had led to many farmland and settlements being converted into quarry sites. The types of house on the site are predominantly the type of makeshift constructed for use on no permanent basis. The few landowners on the site of the factory are resident on-site to participate in the cement business and no longer do farming.

Studies revealed that the West Africa Portland cement made efforts to resettle the landowners in the estate that was built very near the factory. Since this approach was not acceptable to the community, the gradual takeover of the old farm site took place. Farmers had been removed from the site while the quarry was being used and the cutting/felling of the trees began, resulting in a huge expanse of land exposed to Environmental degradation. The lake that was formed as a result of calcareous blasting and water release from the accumulation of Limestone could serve as habitat for freshwater fish, but this has not been established (Yusuf & Duru, 2014). The ammonium compound washed into the lake from its primary source (explosive materials) can be used as manure and can promote the growth of plankton, algae and improve the lake's liming and fish cultivation (Lameed & Ayodele, 2010). The prospect of having an excessive quantity of the ammonium compound washed into the lake, however, can pose a serious risk to the life of aquatic animals. Apart from this, the level of vibration and noise from earthmovers in quarries are to be kept under control to fall at least within the limit permitted by the Federal Environmental Protection Agency (FEPA). Using vibrogram, these factors are monitored while keeping the vibration level below 50 mm per second, and the noise below 120 dB (decibel). Table 7.1 shows the associated diseases with the siting of the factory in this location.

Many workers are exposed to crystalline silica including those in high-risk settings. Empirical research shows that while most workers are

Table 7.1 Diseases associated with the factory

Disease	*Frequency*	*Percentage*
Asthma	34	19.77
Heart disease	19	11.05
Skin cancer	24	13.95
Diarrhea	9	5.23
No disease	56	32.56
No response	30	17.44
Total	172	100

*Source*Aribigbola et al. (2012)

covered, the neighbouring inhabitants are exposed to the dust during the period of processing.

Chemical spillage is another major effect of the operation. This comes from outlets such as main and secondary crushers, mobile plant workshops and sites, oil drum and tank sites in warehouses, kiln sites, compressor houses and sites, which can have quite an effect by leakage and spillage as it makes its way through water runoff inside and outside the factory. Steps such as daily inspection of oil seals and implementing a well-guided disposal policy for such oil may have avoided impacts such as the depletion of fauna and flora in lakes and drains within and outside the facility. The noise levels produced in cement plants range between 70 and 118db (decibels) (Aribigbola et al., 2012). The noise level standard prescribed for the industries in Nigeria is 90 to 115db. It is worth knowing that 90db is the maximum noise level that human beings can tolerate. Therefore, the use of different sizes and forms of ear muffles in cement plants are to be used to avoid injury to eardrums. Although this is largely complied with for the employees in the cement factory, the noise level for the village residents is always above the norm.

Forms of Pollution

The most important environmental problems arising from the industry's activity in the view of citizens of Ewekoro, Papalanto and its surroundings are the air pollution dust that sometimes affects not only visibility but also agriculture. Polluting water sources within the cities' aesthetic context pose a severe threat to residents' health and wellbeing. From the study, it is very clear that air pollution is the main environmental concern faced in the city of Ewekoro. This is not surprising, keeping in mind that the majority of respondents live within less than 2 km from the factory site. The cement factory has a noxious impact as shown in Fig. 7.2.

Impact of Industrial Waste on Health and Environment

Hazardous wastes contaminate soil, water and air (Akpan & Olukanni, 2020). The pollution of these three key components tied to the existence of mankind undoubtedly creates a precarious relationship detrimental to sustainable growth and development. Health impact includes exposure to toxic chemicals through air, water and soil media; exposure to infection

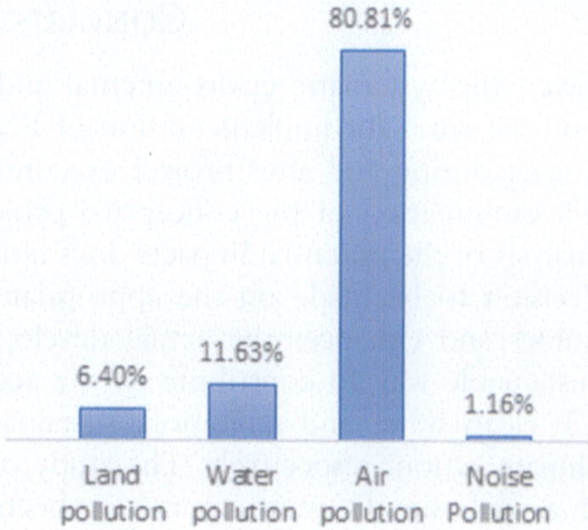

Fig. 7.2 Distribution of Environmental Pollution within the study area *Source* Aribigbola et al. (2012)

and biological contaminants, stress related to odour noise, vermin and visual amenity, risk of fires, explosions and subsidence, spills, accidents and transport emission (Olajumoke & Oluwagbemiga, 2017). An estimated 2 million working hours are lost to work-related illness while another two million people say they suffer from illness they believe was caused by their work. Industrial pollution directly affects health through serious chemicals they discharge. These chemicals, beyond a specified limit have adverse effects on human health. The effects are seen in the heart, blood, kidneys, reproductive organs, lungs, liver among others (Olajumoke & Oluwagbemiga, 2017). Waste from agriculture and industries can also cause serious health risks (Olukanni et al., 2020). Other than this, co-disposal of industrial hazardous waste with municipal waste can expose people to chemical and radioactive hazards. Uncollected solid waste can also obstruct storm water and runoff, resulting in the forming of stagnant water bodies that become the breeding ground of disease (Olukanni & Nwafor, 2019; Olukanni & Oresanya, 2018). Waste dumped near a water source also causes contamination of the water body or the groundwater source. Direct dumping of untreated waste in rivers, seas and lakes results in the accumulation of toxic substances in the food chain through the plants and animals that feed on it.

Conclusion

Given the systematic environmental and social impact analyses, mitigation measures for implementation of EIA is to ensure that any negative impact during and after project execution is averted. Consequently, the full examination of the conceptual project phases and a corresponding analysis of the potential impacts does not only enable for a well-informed decision to be made on the appropriateness of the project, but it also guides and enhances the actual development and implementation in a sustainable way to contribute to the accomplishment SDGs: 6, 11 and 13; clean water and sanitation, sustainable cities and communities and climate action, respectively. The study on Ewekoro cement plant shows that while significant attempts have been made by industry management to reduce noxious pollution effects, more needs to be done, especially in the area of environmental monitoring, so that the vibrations and other emissions mentioned earlier can be kept under control.

From an environmental management practitioner's point of view, the need to reduce the volume of carbon dioxide emissions from Portland cement cannot be overemphasized given the importance of carbon dioxide in the impact of greenhouse gases of global warming. Considering the quantity of carbon dioxide emitted per ton of cement, it is a must for the cement industry to use mineral admixtures. Efforts aimed at reclaiming the quarry site should be further expanded by converting the quarry site into parks and garden for recreational purposes. Measures such as forestation, scarification and final conversion into animal zoos and garden can be adopted. In this case people can visit and pay a token used to sustain such projects.

It is very important the cement factory authorities have fewer disturbing means for the workers to protect themselves from dust inhalation, and protect the atmosphere from the danger of dust by supplying super active dust control equipment. Cement factories' location should be strictly regulated in such a way that the danger of transportation of noise, dust from and heavy vehicles is kept under control and far from cities and towns. In addition, this expository review recommends the use of media (social networks and local mediums) to spread awareness to the public regarding the need for EIA in proposed projects and the availability of room for participation. This will further enhance the level of public recognition and participation in EIA processes in Nigeria.

References

Akpan, V. E., & Olukanni, D. O. (2020). Hazardous waste management: An African overview. *Recycling, 5*(3), 15–25.

Aribigbola, A., Fatusin A. F., & Fagbohunka A. (2012). Assessment of health and environmental challenges of cement factory on Ewekoro community residents, Ogun State, Nigeria. *American Journal of Human Ecology, 1*(2), 51–57.

Chang, A. P., & Lin, J. D. (2018). Defining green road project management scope by PDRI. *International Journal of Engineering Technologies and Management Research, 5*(10), 94–102. https://doi.org/10.5281/zenodo.1491892

Echefu, N., & Akpofure, E. (2002). Environmental impact assessment in Nigeria: Regulatory background and procedural framework. In *UNEP EIA Training Resource Manual*. https://doi.org/10.1115/GT2016-6914

Eromosele, I. C. (2015). *Environmental Impact Assessment (EIA) Analysis; Case Study: Final Report on Lagos Light Rail Transit (Blue Line) Project*. https://www.academia.edu/23483886/Environmental_Impact_AssessmentAnalysis_Case_Study_Final_Report_on_Lagos_Light_Rail_Transit_Blue_Line_Project

Glasson, J., Riki, T., & Andrew, C. (2012). Introduction to environmental impact assessment. In Professor John Glasson Oxford Brookes University (Ed.), *Recent trends and advances in environmental health* (4th ed.). Routledge. https://doi.org/10.1080/07293682.2012.747551

Ilalokhoin, P. O., Otaru, A. J., Odigure, J. O., Abdulkareem, A. S., & Okafor, J. O. (2013). Environmental impact assessment of a proposed cement plant in southwestern Nigeria. *IOSR Journal of Environmental Science, Toxicology and Food Technology, 3*(5), 83–98.

Inegbenebor, A. I., Mordi, R. C., Idowu, A. O., Siyanbola, T. O., Akanle, B., Evbuoma, I. K., & Inegbenebor, A. O. (2018). Consequences of the activities of a Nigerian cement industry on the environment. *International Journal of Applied and Natural Sciences, 7*(4), 67–74.

Lameed, G. A., & Ayodele, A. E. (2010). Effect of quarrying activity on biodiversity: Case study of Ogbere site, Ogun State Nigeria. *African Journal of Environmental Science and Technology, 4*(11), 740–750.

Lawrence, D. P. (2003). *Environmental impact assessment: Practical solutions to recurrent problems*. Wiley-Interscience. Cop.

Morris, P., & Therivel, R. (2001). *Methods of environmental impact assessment*. The Natural and Built Environment Series (2nd ed.). Spon Press.

Olajumoke, O. I., & Oluwagbemiga, O. (2017). Effect of industrial waste management on workers health in selected industries in Nigeria. *International Journal of Waster Resources Development, 7*, 278.

Olaleye, V. F. (2005). Ichthyofaunal survey of rivers within Ewekoro cement manufacturing operational areas. *Biodiversity & Conservation, 14*(9), 2171–2184.

Olukanni, D. O., & Oresanya, O. O. (2018). Progression in waste management processes in Lagos State, Nigeria. *Journal of Engineering Research in Africa (JERA), 35*, 11–23.

Olukanni, D. O., & Nwafor, C. O. (2019). Public-private sector involvement in providing efficient solid waste management services in Nigeria. *Recycling, 4*(19), 1–9.

Olukanni, D. O., Pius-Imue, F. B., & Joseph, S. O. (2020). Public perception of solid waste management practices in Nigeria: Ogun State experience. *Recycling, 5*(2), 8–14.

Oyinloye, M. A. (2015). Environmental pollution and health risks of residents living near Ewekoro Cement Factory, Ewekoro, Nigeria. *International Journal of Architectural and Environmental Engineering, 9*, 108–114.

Ogun State Government. (2001). *Ogun State World Bank Community-Based Urban Development Project; Final Environmental Impact Assessment* (Vol. 7).

Ogunba, O. A. (2004). EIA systems in Nigeria: Evolution, current practice and shortcomings. *Environmental Impact Assessment Review, 24*(6), 643–660. https://doi.org/10.1016/j.eiar.2003.10.019

REMA. (2008). *Sector guidelines for environmental impact assessment (EIA) for* (Issue December). https://www.eia.nl/docs/mer/diversen/rwanda-eia-guidelines-road-construction.

Transmission Company of Nigeria (TCN). (2018). *Esia of Lagos and Ogun States transmission lines and associated substations project (Lot 3).*

Wood, C. (2000), Screening and scoping. In N. Lee & C. George (Eds.), *Environmental assessment in developing and transitional countries.* Wiley.

Yusuf, K. A., & Duru, A. E. (2014). Trace metals characterization in environmental media: A Case study of cement production area Ewekoro, southwest, Nigeria. *American Journal of Environmental Protection, 3*(2), 83–89.

CHAPTER 8

Implications of COVID-19 Pandemic on Energy and Environment Research in Nigeria

Olatokunbo Ofuyatan, Joshua Ighalo, David Olukanni, Adewale Adeniyi, and John Oluwafemi

Introduction

In the last part of December 2019, a new strain of the Coronavirus known as COVID-19 began to spread from mainland China (Novel, 2020). Due to the high infection rate (Liu et al., 2020), it spread through most countries of the world within a few months (WHO, 2020). The emergence of this pandemic virus is unknown (El Zowalaty & Järhult, 2020). COVID-19 is a zoonotic virus. From phylogenetics analyses undertaken with available full genome sequences, bats appear to be the reservoir of COVID-19 virus, but the intermediate host(s) has not yet been

O. Ofuyatan (✉) · J. Ighalo · D. Olukanni · A. Adeniyi · J. Oluwafemi
Department of Civil Engineering, College of Engineering, Covenant University, Ota, Nigeria
e-mail: olatokunbo.ofuyatan@covenantuniversity.edu.ng

S. Folarin et al. (eds.), *The United Nations and Sustainable Development Goals*, https://doi.org/10.1007/978-3-030-95971-5_8

identified. The pandemic has a doubling widespread effect on the human-to-human transmission affecting the lower respiratory tract of patients with pneumonia (WMHC, 2020). The WHO announced that the official name of the 2019 novel coronavirus is coronavirus disease (COVID-19), early patterns have shown a trend similar to Severe Acute Respiratory Syndrome (SARS) and the Middle East respiratory syndrome (MERS) coronaviruses (Fehr et al., 2017). More specific statistics are not given in this paper as infection rates are so high that they quickly become outdated a few weeks after writing.

Nigeria is the most populated black nation on earth with a population of over 200 million people (NBS, 2018). Studies have shown that the aged have the highest fatality rate for COVID-19 (Dowd et al., 2020). Considering that Nigeria has a fairly young population (Stanislas & Iyah, 2016), there is a chance that the death rate might not be high in the country due to the poor existing healthcare system. The daily reported number of cases has been on the rise over the past week and this is likely going to continue for the short term. As of May 2020, there are over 3000 COVID-19 cases in Nigeria. This statistic is changing almost every day hence specific figures are not presented. The real number of infected persons is most likely far higher here than these reports. If this is true, it means there are numerous individuals unaware of their infection who currently are not in self-isolation. As in the case in Italy (Remuzzi & Remuzzi, 2020), there could be an explosion of reported cases, deaths and a total failure of the healthcare system to cope.

In a paper published on the 2nd of March by Mustapha et al. (2020) (and probably written a few weeks before that), strong optimism was expressed at the preparedness of the country for the COVID-19 pandemic. However by the 11th of March, Ebenso and Otu (2020) already raised questions on Nigeria's preparedness albeit not giving full discourse and the situation. A lot has changed in that time and now.

In this chapter, the implications of the COVID-19 pandemic on research in energy and environment are discussed. The extent of preparedness and the current scenario of Nigeria was gauged based on the synthesis of the efforts as a backdrop of Nigeria's population. The potential for positive environmental consequences of the lock-down due to the COVID-19 pandemic is highlighted.

The Current Scenario

As originated from the index case, the epicentre of COVID-19 outbreak in Nigeria was Lagos state (Durotoye et al., 2020). Most of the early cases were in Lagos state, Abuja and Ogun state. Lagos being the former headquarters of the government has the highest population density, Abuja being the headquarters of government and Ogun being an industrialised state. This has now rapidly spread to the northern part of the country. The healthcare system in Nigeria is quite poor for a population of over 200 million people. There has been a long history of poor funding, mismanagement and corruption in the health sector in Nigeria (Anaemene, 2016). The country neither has enough hospital beds nor ventilators for the COVID-19 pandemic and more ventilators were not purchased (Ibeh et al., 2020). There have been efforts to increase the available bed spaces, but these will not be enough at the peak of a crisis.

The indigenous educators and researchers are trying to seek all possible avenues to reawaken their sense of responsibility to avoid the Italian (Remuzzi & Remuzzi, 2020) and Iranian (Arab-Mazar et al., 2020) scenarios. Nigeria Centre for Disease Control (NCDC) has so far done an excellent job of updating Nigerians on the reported cases and sensitising the populace on appropriate measures and precautions for self-protection via her official Twitter feed (Reuben et al., 2020). However, the individuals with social media presence and those in the rural areas are not as enlightened about the pandemic. More awareness will need to be made at the grassroots level to avoid a high mortality rate from the pandemic (Olapegba et al., 2020). There would need to be more proactive testing as there are concerns that the current low numbers are due to few tests being done and numerous individuals are still moving about completely oblivious of their infection. Finally, there needs to be more government investment in the health sector (in the short term) so that personal protective equipment (PPE), ventilators and other needed infrastructure can be put in place (Adesegun et al., 2020). It must, however, be said that this is a little too late as there are production orders from numerous countries and manufacturers are currently struggling to meet up.

A Changing Paradigm in the Environment

Recent studies have shown that human activities have led to polycyclic aromatic hydrocarbons in sediments and marine organisms in the coastal environment (Sun et al., 2018), poor nutrient cycling and food web dynamics in lacustrine ecosystems (O'Beirne et al., 2017), reduced taxonomic and functional diversity of bacterio-plankton communities in lotic ecosystems (Meziti et al., 2016), dwindling ungulates (M'soka et al., 2017), sea-birds (Miller et al., 2019) and fish (Teichert et al., 2016) populations and a host of others (Mahmoud & Gan, 2018). Reduced human activities could lead to the amelioration of environmental pollution as most pollution sources are known to be anthropogenic (Adeniyi & Ighalo, 2019; Ighalo and Adeniyi, 2020a). It could also lead to ecological changes as animal, hunting and feeding routines, gestations, breeding and migration patterns could also change.

Several key questions are relevant in the domain of the research area. How has this period of self-isolation, quarantine and restricted public movement and reduced commercial activities affected the extent of environmental pollution in Nigeria? What air, water and soil quality parameters are most improved due to the lock-down and which are unchanged? If there are other significant environmental changes during this period, what are they? And what are the mechanisms and processes facilitating it? What significance does this bear in the long term for environmental pollution research, if any? What will be the long-term implications environmental implications of the COVID-19 pandemic on the environment especially in the domain of sustainability and climate change? These issues are all in the domain of research in environmental science and pollution.

It is highly likely that indigenous journals in environmental science and engineering would begin special issues on the subject and put up call-for-papers to encourage researchers to investigate these observations in scientific studies. The authors foresee a new generation of research papers focused on data inventorying on the recent developments in the environment. Investigations will abound on the mechanisms of environmental pollution and how the recent changes in the dynamics have affected these mechanisms. Furthermore, ecological research would not be left behind as the way organisms relate with the physical surrounding would change both the aquatic, terrestrial and arboreal domain.

Though this might not lead to drastic policy changes in Nigeria, there is a likelihood of policy adjustments (slackening) in environmental laws if long-term positive environmental influences are observed. Furthermore, there would be a pressing need by industries affected by the lock-down to make up for lost ground in productivity and profit. This would indirectly place more pressure on the environment in due course.

Based on this, the authors express scepticism on the true long-term positive environmental implications of the pandemic in Nigeria. All stakeholders might not be ready to take advantage of this opportunity except there are drastic post-pandemic changes in modus operandi down to the ones regarding the most basic lifestyle patterns. This is where the issue of sustainability needs to be revisited. Sustainability is a concept that boils around avoidance of the depletion of natural resources to maintain an ecological balance (Hueting & Reijnders, 2004). Sustainable processes try to minimise and mitigate the negative environmental impact. These sustainable processes are monitored by economic, social and environmental indicators (Amrina & Vilsi, 2015). A potential way of banking on the post-pandemic environmental advantage is to maintain focus on the tenets of sustainability in most of its applied domain.

Implications on Energy and Environmental Research

African countries are at high risk of being decimated by the pandemic due to lack of preparedness but there are already improvements in this regard in recent times (Gilbert et al., 2020). Most research labs are closed and researchers are now working and teaching from home. Global research output is likely to be on the decline in the coming months in most specialisations in science, engineering and technology if the lock-down due to the pandemic continues. In this section, the authors discuss the current and potential implications of COVID-19 pandemic on energy and environment research in Nigeria and the place of computer-based simulations as an alternative solution for research productivity. There are generic scenarios presented in this discussion, the peculiar challenges of the indigenous African researchers are carefully highlighted.

In most African countries, it is quite difficult to get funding for research activities (Teferra & Altbachl, 2004) even before these pandemic times. This has made it difficult for researchers to publish quality papers (in SCOPUS indexed journals). Research output in STEM from African countries has been relatively quite low in quality and quantity (North et al., 2020). Furthermore, most indigenous researchers fund their energy and environment research by themselves. The COVID-19 pandemic might not in itself affect funding in this scenario, as it was almost non-existent in the first place. However, there are other short and long-term implications for indigenous researchers.

In the short term, access to labs is one of the major issues. Tertiary institutions in most of these developing countries have been shut down and only virology labs (in a few cases) are allowed to run. This would mean that experimental studies would be difficult to perform at these times. With the COVID-19 likely to be around till the summer and maybe beyond (Yong, 2020), it means that the already meagre research productivity would be greatly hampered. Furthermore, already running research works have now been prematurely paused or terminated due to the pandemic (Jacob et al., 2020). Distractions from family members and the psychological hindrance from working from home are general factors that are affecting researchers in these times. However, peculiar to the Nigerian researcher is the lack of stable electricity and internet connections in their homes to sustain office levels of productivity. These are usually available on the university campuses where research works were always done.

In the long term, there are bound to be physical health issues on the researchers due to extended periods of self-isolation. Humans are social animals (Frith & Frith, 2007). Mental health could be a problem too for those who have self-isolated without the presence of family. There is likely to be a downturn in the growth of the already weak economy and economic depression in more severely hit countries (Ozili, 2020). Researchers might get laid-off and research students might have to discontinue studies. This is also a significant challenge in the long term. This would mean that the post-pandemic research contributions from Nigeria to energy and environment research are likely to be epileptic at best.

In the area of energy policy, Nigeria is usually quite reactive (and not proactive) to such challenges. There have been recent policy adjustments in Nigeria to mitigate the cost of electrical energy. What else can be done about these issues? This discussion would only make suggestions regarding the measures researchers can take to improve research productivity. Other wider issues would require more technical analysis and investigations to come up with a sustainable and workable road map.

The Way Forward

The indigenous researchers in energy and environment have always shown little interest in *silico* studies. This research team has tried to change that paradigm over the past year as we have utilised computer-based models (Ofuyatan & Edeki, 2018b) in investigating a variety of renewable energy systems ranging from pyrolysis (Adeniyi et al., 2019c; Ighalo & Adeniyi, 2019), steam reforming (Adeniyi et al., 2019a, 2019b) and air gasification (Adeniyi et al., 2019d; Ighalo and Adeniyi, 2020b). This is a call to researchers in energy and environment in Nigeria in particular and developing African countries in general to embrace the opportunities in process modelling and simulations to advance their research. It would be very important that we take up this gauntlet in times when we are have being affected by the pandemic. Though it was quite important in the pre-pandemic times, such studies are even more important now with restricted access to labs (Ofuyatan & Edeki, 2018a). If we do not accept such a challenge, then we could end up experiencing a near-zero research output and productivity in the coming months in light of the current global health challenges.

Conclusions

In this paper, the current and potential implications of COVID-19 on energy and environment research in Nigeria were discussed. Due to the high infection rate and lack of vaccine and cure, COVID-19 has now affected most countries of the world. The extent of preparedness and the current scenario of Nigeria was gauged based on the synthesis of the efforts as a backdrop of Nigeria's population. More isolation centres will need to be prepared across the 36 states on the federation as there is likely to be an upsurge in the reported cases in the coming months. There would need to be more proactive testing as there are concerns that the current low numbers are due to few tests being done and numerous individuals are still moving about completely oblivious of their infection. There needs to be more government investment in the health sector (in the short term) so that personal protective equipment (PPE), ventilators and other needed infrastructure can be put in place.

The potential for positive environmental consequences of the lockdown due to the COVID-19 pandemic is highlighted. Some important questions were raised on the subject in the domain of research in environmental science and pollution. How has this period of self-isolation, quarantine and restricted public movement and reduced commercial activities affected the extent of environmental pollution in Nigeria? What air, water and soil quality parameters are most improved due to the lock-down and which are unchanged? If there are other significant environmental changes during this period, what are they? And what are the mechanisms and processes facilitating it? What significance does this bear in the long term for environmental pollution research, if any? What will be the long-term environmental implications of the COVID-19 pandemic on the environment especially in the domain of sustainability and climate change?

For research in energy and environment, there is a lack of access to labs, psychological hindrance of working from homes and lack of stable electricity and internet connections at homes. In the long term, there are bound to be physical and mental health issues on the researchers due to extended periods of self-isolation (especially for those without the presence of family in their locations). This is a call to indigenous researchers in energy and environment area in developing Nigeria to embrace the opportunities in process modelling and simulations to advance their research.

References

Adeniyi, A. G., & Ighalo, J. O. (2019). Biosorption of pollutants by plant leaves: An empirical review. *Journal of Environmental Chemical Engineering, 7*, 103100 http://dx.doi.org/10.1016/j.jece.2019.103100

Adeniyi, A. G., Ighalo, J. O., & Abdulsalam, A. (2019a). Modelling of integrated processes for the recovery of the energetic content of sugarcane bagasse. *Biofuels, Bioproducts & Biorefining, 13*(4),1057–1067. http://dx.doi.org/10.1002/bbb.1998

Adeniyi, A. G., Ighalo, J. O., & Aderibigbe, F. A. (2019b). Modelling of integrated processes for the pyrolysis and steam reforming of rice husk (Oryza sativa). *SN Applied Sciences, 1*, 841. http://dx.doi.org/10.1007/s42452-019-0877-6

Adeniyi, A. G., Ighalo, J. O., & Amosa, K. M. (2019c). Modelling and simulation of banana (Musa spp.) waste pyrolysis for bio-oil production. *Biofuels*, 1–5. http://dx.doi.org/10.1080/17597269.2018.1554949

Adeniyi, A. G., Ighalo, J. O., Onifade, D. V., & Adeoye, A. S. (2019). Modelling the valorisation of poultry litter via thermochemical processing biofuels. *Bioproducts & Biorefining, 14*, 242–248. https://doi.org/10.1002/bbb.2056

Adesegun, O. A., Binuyo, T., Adeyemi, O., Ehioghae, O., Rabor, D. F., Amusan, O., Akinboboye, O., Duke, O. F., Olafimihan, A. G., & Ajose, O. (2020). The COVID-19 crisis in Sub-Saharan Africa: Knowledge, attitudes, and practices of the Nigerian Public. *The American Journal of Tropical Medicine and Hygiene*: tpmd200461.

Amrina, E., & Vilsi, A. L. (2015). Key performance indicators for sustainable manufacturing evaluation in cement industry. *Procedia CIRP, 26*, 19–23.

Anaemene, B. U. (2016). Health sector reforms and sustainable development in Nigeria: A historical perspective. *Journal of Sustainable Development in Africa, 8*, 50–66.

Arab-Mazar, Z., Sah, R., Rabaan, A. A., Dhama, K., & Rodriguez-Morales, A. J. (2020). Mapping the incidence of the COVID-19 hotspot in Iran–implications for travellers. *Travel Medicine and Infectious Disease, 34*, 101630

Dowd, J. B., Rotondi, V., Adriano, L., Brazel, D. M., Block, P., Ding, X., Liu, Y., & Mills, M. C. (2020). Demographic science aids in understanding the spread and fatality rates of COVID-19. medRxiv.

Durotoye, I., Odunola, R., Adeyemi, O., Akanmu, A., Bolarinwa, O., Adeboye, M., Abdullahi, A., Bolajoko, Z., Durosinmi, W., & Adebisi, G. (2020). Pertinent roles of African higher institutions in the COVID-19 pandemic response: the University of Ilorin, Ilorin, Nigeria; an African model. *The International Journal of Health Planning and Management*. https://doi.org/10.1002/hpm.2984

Ebenso, B., & Otu, A. (2020). Can Nigeria contain the COVID-19 outbreak using lessons from recent epidemics? *The Lancet Global Health*. https://doi.org/10.1016/S2214-109X(20)30101-7

El Zowalaty, M. E., & Järhult, J. D. (2020). From SARS to COVID-19: A previously unknown SARS-CoV-2 virus of pandemic potential infecting humans–call for a one health approach. *One Health, 9*, 100124

Fehr, A. R., Channappanavar, R., & Perlman, S. (2017). Middle East respiratory syndrome: Emergence of a pathogenic human coronavirus. *Annual review of medicine, 68*, 387–399.

Frith, C. D., & Frith, U. (2007). Social cognition in humans. *Current Biology, 17*, R724–R732.

Gilbert, M., Pullano, G., Pinotti, F., Valdano, E., Poletto, C., Boëlle, P.-Y., D'Ortenzio. E., Yazdanpanah, Y., Eholie, S. P., & Altmann, M. (2020). Preparedness and vulnerability of African countries against importations of COVID-19: A modelling study *The Lancet, 395*, 871–877.

Hueting, R., & Reijnders, L. (2004). Broad sustainability contra sustainability: The proper construction of sustainability indicators. *Ecological Economics, 50*, 249–260.

Ibeh, I. N., Enitan, S. S., Akele, R. Y., Isitua, C. C., & Omorodion, F. (2020). Global impacts and Nigeria responsiveness to the COVID-19 pandemic. *International Journal of Healthcare and Medical Sciences, 6*, 27–45.

Ighalo, J. O., & Adeniyi, A. G. (2019). Thermodynamic modelling and temperature sensitivity analysis of banana (Musa spp.) waste pyrolysis. *SN Applied Sciences, 1*, 1086. http://dx.doi.org/10.1007/s42452-019-1147-3

Ighalo, J. O., & Adeniyi, A. G. (2020a). Adsorption of pollutants by plant bark derived adsorbents: An empirical review. *Journal of Water Process Engineering, 35*, 101228. http://dx.doi.org/10.1016/j.jwpe.2020.101228

Ighalo, J. O., & Adeniyi, A. G. (2020b). Modelling of thermochemical energy recovery processes for switchgrass (Panicum virgatum). *Indian Chemical Engineer*. http://dx.doi.org/10.1080/00194506.2020.1711535

Jacob, O. N., Abigeal, I., & Lydia, A. (2020). Impact of COVID-19 on the higher institutions development in Nigeria. *Electronic Research Journal of Social Sciences and Humanities, 2*, 126–135.

Liu, Y., Gayle, A. A., Wilder-Smith, A., & Rocklöv, J. (2020). The reproductive number of COVID-19 is higher compared to SARS coronavirus. *Journal of Travel Medicine*.

M'soka, J., Creel, S., Becker, M. S., & Murdoch, J. D. (2017). Anthropogenic effects on the density of migratory and resident ungulates in a human-inhabited protected area. *Ecological and, 55*, 618–631.

Mahmoud, S. H., & Gan, T. Y. (2018). Impact of anthropogenic climate change and human activities on environment and ecosystem services in arid regions. *Science of the Total Environment, 633*, 1329–1344.

Meziti, A., Tsementzi, D., Ar. Kormas, K., Karayanni, H., & Konstantinidis, K. T. (2016). Anthropogenic effects on bacterial diversity and function along a river-to-estuary gradient in Northwest Greece revealed by metagenomics. *Environmental Microbiology, 18*, 4640–4652.

Miller, J. A., Furness, R. W., Trinder, M., & Matthiopoulos, J. (2019). The sensitivity of seabird populations to density-dependence, environmental stochasticity and anthropogenic mortality. *Journal of Applied Ecology, 56*, 2118–2130.

Mustapha, J. O., Adedokun, K. A., & Abdullahi, I. N. (2020). Public health preparedness towards COVID-19 outbreak in Nigeria. *Asian Pacific Journal of Tropical Medicine, 13*, 197.

NBS. (2018). *Demographic statistics bulletin 2017 Nigerian Bureau of Statistics*.

North, M. A., Hastie, W. W., & Hoyer, L. (2020). Out of Africa: The underrepresentation of African authors in high-impact geoscience literature. *Earth-Science Reviews*, 103262.

Novel CPERE. (2020). The epidemiological characteristics of an outbreak of 2019 novel coronavirus diseases (COVID-19) in China. *Zhonghua liu xing bing xue za zhi= Zhonghua liuxingbingxue zazhi, 41*, 145.

O'Beirne, M., Werne, J., Hecky, R., Johnson, T., Katsev, S., & Reavie, E. D. (2017). Anthropogenic climate change has altered primary productivity in Lake Superior. *Nature Communications, 8*, 1–8.

Ofuyatan, O. M., & Edeki, S. (2018). Dataset on the durability behavior of palm oil fuel ash self compacting concrete. *Data in Brief, 19*(2018), 853–858.

Ofuyatan, O. M., & Edeki, S. (2018). Dataset on predictive compressive strength model for self-compacting concrete. *Data in Brief, 17*(2018), 801–806.

Olapegba, P. O., Iorfa, S. K., Kolawole, S. O., Oguntayo, R., Gandi, J. C., Ottu, I. F., & Ayandele, O. (2020). Survey data of COVID-19-related Knowledge, risk perceptions and precautionary behavior among Nigerians. *Data in Brief, 30*, 105685.

Ozili, P. K. (2020). Covid-19 pandemic and economic crisis: The Nigerian experience and structural causes. *Journal of Economic and Administrative Sciences*. Available at SSRN 3567419. https://doi.org/10.2139/ssrn.3567419

Remuzzi, A., & Remuzzi, G. (2020). COVID-19 and Italy: What next? *The Lancet*.

Reuben, R. C., Danladi, M. M., Saleh, D. A., & Ejembi, P. E. (2020). Knowledge, attitudes and practices towards COVID-19: an epidemiological survey in North-Central Nigeria. *Journal of Community* health, 1–14.

Stanislas, P., & Iyah, I. (2016). Changing religious influences, young people, crime and extremism in Nigeria. In *Religion, faith and crime* (pp. 325–345). Springer.

Sun, R., Sun, Y., Li, Q. X., Zheng, X., Luo, X., & Mai, B. (2018). Polycyclic aromatic hydrocarbons in sediments and marine organisms: Implications of anthropogenic effects on the coastal environment. *Science of the Total Environment, 640*, 264–272.

Teferra, D., & Altbachl, P. G. (2004). African higher education: Challenges for the 21st century. *Higher Education, 47*, 21–50.

Teichert, N., Borja, A., Chust, G., Uriarte, A., & Lepage, M. (2016). Restoring fish ecological quality in estuaries: implication of interactive and cumulative effects among anthropogenic stressors. *Science of the Total Environment, 542*, 383–393.

WHO. (2020). *Coronavirus disease 2019 (COVID-19): Situation report, 51*. World Health Organization.

WMHC. (2020). *Wuhan municipal health and health commission's briefing on the current pneumonia epidemic situation in our city*.

Yong, E. (2020). *How the pandemic will end*.

CHAPTER 9

Evaluation of Drivers and Barriers to Vertical Architecture Construction for Public Housing Delivery in Lagos Megacity

Adedeji Afolabi and Rapheal Ojelabi

Introduction

In order to address the socio-economic needs of the Nigerian populace, there is a need to meet their housing provision needs. Ibem et al. (2011) asserted that urban housing provision in Nigeria is in deep crisis despite the successive government's haphazard approach to tackling the housing deficit across several states both at the federal and state levels. The state of Nigeria's housing deficit continues to be worsened by the continuous rural–urban migration (Akinmoladun & Oluwoye, 2007), uncontrolled population growth rate (Olotuah, 2010), inefficient policies toward housing (Ibem et al., 2011), high cost of land and insufficient

A. Afolabi (✉) · R. Ojelabi
Department of Building Technology, Covenant University, Ota, Ogun State, Nigeria
e-mail: adedeji.afolabi@covenantuniversity.edu.ng

S. Folarin et al. (eds.), *The United Nations and Sustainable Development Goals*, https://doi.org/10.1007/978-3-030-95971-5_9

landmass (United Nations-HABITAT, 2006), misappropriation and politics (Mustapha, 2002), human-induced and natural disasters (Afolabi et al., 2018). Statistics show that Nigeria needs approximately 17 to 20 million houses to address the housing deficit within the country (Centre for Affordable Housing Finance Africa, 2018). However, the annual capacity to provide housing units stands at a meager 100 thousand units compared to the housing demand and needs. Another pointer is uncontrolled Nigeria's population growth rate put at 3.2% annually, which means that the over 193 million people, according to the 2016 census (National Population Commission, 2016), would have grown to over 410 million people by 2050 (United Nation's World Population Prospects, 2017). Comparing the data of the housing capacity that is presently achievable by the Nigerian government and a population that would triple in the next 30 years, the housing situation would be a disaster. In Ibem et al. (2011), it was reported that since 1962, the Nigerian government had not met its national development plan on housing provision. Therefore, there is a need to rethink the housing solutions that have been used by previous governments. Sadly, the housing deficit affects the low-income earners direly (Olotuah & Aiyetan, 2006) mainly because of issues dealing with affordability.

Examining the proportion of rural–urban migration in Lagos megacity, Okupe (2002) and Enisan and Ogundiran (2013) found out that the people in urban centers had gone four times higher 2010 compared to data available in 1950. Lagos State suffers more from the effect of rural–urban migration due to the notion of rural dwellers seeking for a better life. Lagos State, as the commercial nerve center of Nigeria, has seen its population double in the last two decades and a projection of 32.6 million people by 2050. This would make Lagos State the sixth largest megacity in the world. Statistics from Nwannekanma and Gbonegun (2018) showed that 87 people migrate to Lagos State per hour daily. This value will continue to increase due to the lack of restriction in the rural–urban migration and increasing rate of poverty in the rural areas. So, Lagos State needs to plan for its citizens and its visitors in terms of housing supply to address the increasing rate of homelessness. In preparing for housing provision with Lagos State, the relatively constant land mass area of 3577 Km^2 needs to be considered. Apart from homelessness, Lagos State grapples with many slums springing up due to the housing deficit. The slum settlements have been put at over 100 within

Lagos State (Ilesanmi, 2010). Due to the limited land resource, the provision of housing units needs to move away from horizontal supply to the vertical supply of houses. Apart from these realities, one of the sustainable development goals of the United Nations is "Sustainable Cities and Communities". In this goal 11, the aim is to have cities and communities that are inclusive, safe, resilient, and also sustainable. This study evaluates the state of public housing while trying to proffer sustainable solutions to Lagos megacity in terms of vertical architecture construction. Therefore, this study was aimed at evaluating the drivers and barriers to vertical architecture construction for public housing delivery in Lagos megacity. The following research questions formed the basis for carrying out this study;

- Which parameters can drive investment and implementation of vertical architecture construction in public housing delivery in Lagos megacity?
- What are the barriers to large-scale vertical architecture construction in public housing delivery in Lagos megacity?
- How can vertical architecture construction in public housing delivery be achieved in Lagos megacity?

Research Method

The study is quantitatively utilized a survey research design to turn the research questions highlighted into a project that can be tested. This helped to monitor and observe the perception of the research participants concerning the subject matter of vertical architecture construction within the study area. The survey research design was cross-sectional to draw a sample from the population of the study. The population is comprised of research participants with a primary interest in the construction industry and the built environment. The primary subjects include Architects, Builders, Engineers, Estate Surveyors and Valuers, Quantity Surveyors, and Urban and Regional Planners. The study location is Lagos megacity in Nigeria. The study utilized a non-probability sampling technique, precisely a quota-purposive sampling technique in selecting the sample size for this project. This method was deemed adequate due to the lack of comprehensive data on the number of registered and unregistered construction professionals actively involved in the built environment in Lagos State. A quota of 150 construction professionals was decided for this study. The concept of data collection utilized the instrument of a well-structured questionnaire. This helped gather, collate, and aggregate the primary responses from the respondents. The design of the data collection instrument comprised of four (4) sections from A to D. In section A, the background information of the research participants were measured while section B to D helped obtain responses on the research objectives. A total of 77 fully completed questionnaires were returned, which were analyzed in this study. This represented a 51.3% questionnaire retrieval rate for the survey. The data collected was analyzed using the SPSS v.23 data analytical tool. Statistical tools for data analysis highlighted in this study include cross-tabulation of frequencies, percentages, mean score, principal component analysis (PCA), and categorical regression (CAT-REG) tests.

Result and Discussion

This section consists of the data analysis of the areas in the questionnaire instrument. From the 77 questionnaires retrieved, the data were coded and analyzed using the SPSS data analytical tool. In the result and discussion, the presentation comprised of the background information, drivers, barriers, and measures toward the implementation of vertical architecture construction in public housing. Table 9.1 showed the summarized background information on the professional background, the educational status of the research participants, the industry work experience, and the sector of the construction industry the research participants belonged to. In all, the design team comprising of Architects and Engineers had a significant representation in this study. The conceptualization of vertical architecture construction starts with the design and planning, in which the design team contributes a considerable stake.

Drivers of Vertical Architecture Construction in Public Housing Delivery

Extensive studies have been done in terms of public housing in the Nigerian environment. The drivers of vertical architecture construction in public housing delivery were gathered from previous studies in Mustapha (2002), Akinmoladun and Oluwoye (2007), Olotuah (2010), Ibem et al. (2011), and Afolabi et al. (2018). In Table 9.2, construction professionals such as Architects, Quantity Surveyors, Estate Surveyors, and

Table 9.1 Background information on research participants

Participants' characteristics	*Professional background*						*Total*
	Arch	*Bldr*	*QS*	*Engr*	*ESV*	*URP*	
Highest academic qualification							
OND/HND	0	3	0	0	0	0	3 (3.9%)
B.Sc/B.Tech	3	5	6	17	4	4	39 (50.6%)
M.Sc/MPM	15	3	0	6	1	2	27 (35.1%)
Ph.D	4	3	1	0	0	0	8 (10.4%)
Working experience							
1–10 years	6	6	6	15	4	5	42 (54.5%)
11–20 years	12	6	1	6	1	1	27 (35.1%)
21–30 years	4	2	0	2	0	0	8 (10.4%)
Sector							
Contracting	8	11	4	13	2	0	38 (49.3%)
Consulting	7	0	1	4	3	0	15 (19.5%)
Government	3	0	1	5	0	6	15 (19.5%)
Client sector	0	0	1	1	0	0	2 (2.6%)
Educational sector	4	3	0	0	0	0	7 (9.1%)
Total	22 (28.6%)	14 (18.2%)	7 (9.1%)	23 (29.8%)	5 (6.5%)	6 (7.8%)	77(100%)

Urban Planners perceive that the spate of housing deficit can be a significant driver for implementing vertical architecture construction. At the same time, Builders believe that vertical architecture construction would come at the forefront of public housing, mainly due to the housing deficit and the increasing population. The overall mean score showed that housing deficit, population, and low cost of building materials would be the primary drivers in the full implementation of vertical architecture construction in public housing delivery. In the studies by Akinmoladun and Oluwoye (2007) and Ademiluyi and Raji (2008), they affirmed the worsening housing situation attributed to the increasing population, rapid urbanization insufficient response of the Federal and State governments to the housing needs of the people. The link between housing deficit and population drivers of vertical architecture construction in Lagos megacity is very glaring. The reality, as portrayed in Olotuah (2000), is that the existing housing units are inadequate to meet the needs of the increasing population in Lagos megacity. The situation is worsened because Lagos megacity is the commercial nerve center for Nigeria, and many people

Table 9.2 Drivers of vertical architecture construction in public housing delivery

Drivers	*Arch*	*Bldr*	*QS*	*Engr*	*ESV*	*URP*	*Overall MS*	*Ranking Index*
Housing deficit	4.41	4.29	4.57	4.26	4.40	4.83	4.39	1st
Population	3.95	4.29	3.71	4.35	4.20	3.83	4.12	2nd
Low-cost building materials	3.95	4.21	3.86	3.74	4.20	4.00	3.95	3rd
State of the economy	3.73	3.79	3.57	3.96	3.60	3.50	3.77	4th
Availability of technology	3.73	3.71	3.71	3.78	3.20	3.67	3.70	5th
Congestion	3.73	3.57	3.57	3.26	3.80	3.33	3.52	6th
Urban planning	3.50	3.29	3.43	3.61	3.20	3.50	3.47	7th
Cost of land	3.41	3.64	3.71	3.22	3.60	3.50	3.44	8th
Rate of urbanization	3.50	3.36	3.43	3.48	3.40	3.33	3.44	8th
Access to land	3.32	3.21	3.57	3.52	3.20	3.00	3.35	10th
Size of land mass	3.55	2.79	3.86	3.43	3.00	3.33	3.35	10th
Political influence	3.14	3.43	3.29	3.09	3.20	3.67	3.22	12th
Efficient designs	2.86	3.00	3.14	3.39	3.40	2.67	3.09	13th
Sustainable practices	3.00	2.93	2.86	2.83	2.80	3.33	2.94	14th
Level of innovation	2.95	3.07	2.71	2.74	3.00	2.83	2.88	15th

in rural areas see it as the engine room for prosperity. This assertion is confirmed in Enisan and Ogundiran (2013) that rural–urban migration accounts for 65% of the urban population growth experienced in Lagos megacity. The data available shows that the urban population would reach about 5 billion people by 2030, most of which would come from Asia and Africa (UN-HABITAT, 2006). Presently, more than half of the world's total population dwells in urban areas such as the Lagos megacity, and by 2050 this is projected to have increased by another 20% (World Bank, 2008). Despite the fixed supply of land in Lagos megacity, the increasing population and housing deficit have metamorphosed into overcrowding, slums, substandard housing, and inability to deal with the large volumes of human-generated waste (Jiboye, 2011). Lagos, as a megacity, needs to prepare for the explosive population growth through vertical architecture construction as there would be massive pressure on the available housing stock and its supporting infrastructure.

To give a clearer understanding of the drivers identified in this study, the study utilized principal component analysis (PCA) to reduce the variables and characterize the variables based on similarities that exist between them. Table 9.3 showed the Principal Component Analysis (PCA) on drivers of vertical architecture construction in public housing delivery. In the PCA test, the variables were reduced from 15 to 10 variables and characterized into a 3-component solution. Component 1 was titled country-specific factors based on the variables that appeared under the component. These country-specific factors include Availability of Technology, Political Influence, Access to Land, State of the economy, Urban Planning, and Rate of Urbanization. These country-specific factors are associated with the internal workings of the country under study. This means that for vertical architecture construction to begin as a full-fledge housing policy or full implementation in public housing, there is a need to have adequate technology to power it.

Table 9.3 Principal component analysis (PCA) on drivers of vertical architecture construction

Component		*Dimension*		
		1	*2*	*3*
Country-specific factors	Availability of technology	0.751	−0.102	0.121
	Political influence	0.651	0.252	−0.119
	Access to land	0.592	0.020	−0.212
	State of the economy	0.552	−0.284	0.087
	Urban planning	0.521	−0.056	0.171
	Rate of urbanization	−0.508	−0.243	0.154
Land resources factors	Cost of land	−0.059	0.810	0.100
	Congestion	0.200	0.784	−0.163
	Low-cost building materials	0.163	0.520	0.290
Housing deficiency factor	Housing deficit	−0.155	0.307	0.596

Technology in terms of the crane technology, the capacity, the technical know-how, and the facilities to spearhead vertical construction. Al-Kodmany (2018) argued that the twenty-first Century is increasingly thinking of vertical construction, which is evident from tall buildings in many cities. However, does Nigeria or Lagos megacity possess adequate technology to build above 40 floors called skyscraper? Whereas, Igwe et al. (2017) asserted that Lagos megacity's building technology is still rudimentary compared to many developed cities worldwide. The analysis showed that political influence/power is another factor that should be considered as a driving force. The political influence comes from the leadership commitment to housing, the political will, policies, and political agenda toward public housing. The study by Jiboye (2011) argued that the delivery of dignified public housing units requires appropriate political will, which is based on the conviction from the government due to its responsibility to the citizen. In the past, there have been good housing policies instituted by previous governments, but the bane is the lack of continuity and consistency. Jiboye (2011) opined that selfish political reasons have to be shelved aside to attain sustainability in housing provision. Adequate provision of houses to its citizens by the government should be seen as an avenue to better the lives, improve the well-being and productivity of the citizenry. Jiboye (2011) suggested that the government at different tiers need to start making realistic targets in housing provision irrespective of the political leaning of each government to avert the impending crisis. One such policy should be facilitating procedures that empower the private sector in urban development and housing delivery issues. In component 2, it was titled land resources factors as it mainly had to deal with the cost of land, congestion, and low cost of building materials. In the study by Ezeigwe (2015), the high price of land was noted as a significant barrier to housing delivery. The high bureaucracy mostly influences the high cost of land in Lagos in obtaining land titles (Oshodi, 2010). This is compounded with the unfriendly provisions in the 1978 Land Use Act, which most private developers have decried. However, Enisan and Ogundiran (2013), Ibimilua and Ibitoye (2015) suggested the intervention of the government through policies that emphasize easy accessibility to land at low cost and policies that would enhance the reduction of building materials' prices. This study posits that with the high cost of land, private developers need to think upward, that is, vertical construction in buildings. Urban land is an asset that must be exploited to the fullest to bring adequate profit. The third component was titled housing deficiency factor, mainly due to the variable of the housing deficit as a driver for vertical architecture construction in public housing delivery. This is confirmatory to the result in the mean score in Table 9.2 that housing deficiency is one of the main drivers that would spur the government and other stakeholders to implement massive vertical architecture construction in public housing delivery. As stated earlier, the Nigerian housing supply deficit has been put at over 17 to 20 million while the housing production capacity is at a hundred thousand units annually (Centre for Affordable Housing Finance Africa, 2018). Only sustainable solutions can help tackle the housing deficit and meet the target in the housing supply.

Barriers to Vertical Architecture Construction in Public Housing Delivery

This study noted that massive investment into vertical architecture construction in public housing is not in place, and this can be attributed to several barriers, as identified in this research. In Table 9.4, the main barriers identified in this study are the high cost of building materials, inadequate investment funding, and ineffective and inconsistent housing policies. The study showed that overall, construction professionals are concerned about cost and policies as significant inhibitors to vertical architecture construction in public housing delivery. This corroborated in previous studies by Enisan and Ogundiran (2013); Ibimilua and Ibitoye (2015) and Okafor (2016). The findings from this study showed the interconnection between the drivers and the barriers influencing vertical architecture construction in public housing delivery.

Inferential statistics using categorical regression (CAT-REG) was performed on the 16 identified barriers to vertical architecture construction in public housing delivery. Using the availability of technology for venturing into vertical architecture construction as the dependent variable and the barriers as the predictor variables, the CAT-REG test was performed. From the model summary, the strength of the influence that exists between the model and the dependent variable is calculated at R^2 = 91.2% ($F = 22.478$; Asymp. Sig. = 0.000). From the CAT-REG solution in Table 9.5, the significant barriers facing vertical architecture construction in public housing delivery are mainly epileptic power supply (beta factor = 19.4%; $F = 4.542$; Asymp. Sig. = 0.015) and poor land policies

Table 9.4 Barriers influencing non-implementation of vertical architecture construction

Barriers	*Mean score*	*Std. Deviation*	*Ranking Index*
The high cost of building materials	3.99	0.803	1st
Inadequate investment funding	3.92	0.914	2nd
Ineffective and inconsistent housing policies	3.61	0.746	3rd
Poor land policies	3.45	0.717	4th
High risk investment	3.45	0.699	4th
Politics and partisanship	3.31	0.544	6th
Bureaucracy in permits and approvals	3.27	0.599	7th
Lack of technical know-how	3.25	0.610	8th
Lack of high-rise construction technology	3.22	0.641	9th
Poor maintenance culture	3.21	0.635	10th
Lack of capacity from construction firms	3.17	0.657	11th
Poor town and urban planning	3.09	0.672	12th
Epileptic power supply	2.97	0.584	13th
Inadequate steel production locally	2.87	0.570	14th
Single-ownership culture	2.86	0.601	15th
Poor fire service delivery	2.84	0.586	16th

(beta factor = 83.3%; F = 79.271; Asymp. Sig. = 0.000). The statistical significance in the independent variables of epileptic power supply and poor land policies showed that there is a likelihood that it can influence vertical architecture construction in public housing delivery, and it is caused by something other than chance. This means that these variables require further discussion because they can predict the influence on vertical architecture construction. The epileptic power supply is one of the bane reducing the productivity of Nigeria. Without an adequate power supply, vertical architecture construction may become impossible. Tall buildings consume high energy from operations of the HVAC to the lift systems and other ancillary installations. Nigeria presently generates 4000 megawatts (MW) of electricity for a population of over 200 million, whereas South Africa, on the same continent, generates over 51,000 megawatts (MW) for a population of 56 million.

Table 9.5 CAT-REG of barriers facing vertical architecture construction in public housing delivery

Barriers	*Standardized coefficients*		*df*	F	*Sig*
	Beta	*Bootstrap (1000) Estimate of Std. Error*			
Lack of high-rise construction technology	0.076	0.194	2	0.153	0.858
Ineffective and inconsistent housing policies	0.018	0.100	1	0.033	0.856
Inadequate investment funding	0.007	0.108	1	0.004	0.950
Single-ownership culture	−0.069	0.083	2	0.696	0.503
Epileptic power supply	0.194	0.091	2	4.542	0.015
Poor maintenance culture	0.045	0.178	2	0.062	0.940
Poor fire service delivery	0.071	0.128	1	0.310	0.580
Inadequate steel production locally	−0.163	0.103	1	2.490	0.121
Lack of technical know-how	−0.168	0.157	3	1.157	0.335
Poor land policies	0.833	0.094	2	79.271	0.000
Poor town and urban planning	0.230	0.149	1	2.372	0.130
Bureaucracy in permits and approvals	0.193	0.167	1	1.336	0.253
High risk investment	−0.010	0.103	1	0.009	0.926
Politics and partisanship	0.088	0.106	1	0.687	0.411
High cost of building materials	−0.108	0.071	1	2.281	0.137
Lack of capacity from construction firms	0.068	0.103	2	0.433	0.651

Dependent Variable: Availability of Technology

Conclusion

This study was aimed at evaluating the drivers and barriers to vertical architecture construction for public housing delivery in Lagos megacity. The state of housing deficit, increasing population, and low cost of building materials would mainly drive the urgency to invest and implement vertical architecture construction in public housing delivery in Lagos megacity. These vertical architecture construction drivers have further categorized as country-specific factors, land resources factors, and housing deficiency factors. The significant barriers to large-scale vertical architecture construction in public housing delivery in Lagos megacity were the high cost of building materials, inadequate investment funding, and inefficient & inconsistent housing policies. Further inferential tests showed the stakeholders need to be concerned about the epileptic power supply and the poor land policies for the actualization of vertical architecture construction in Lagos megacity. Therefore, the study noted that the first steps in the realization of vertical architecture construction in Lagos megacity are through the involvement of the private sector in the form of a Public–Private Partnership (PPP) program in vertical architecture construction, Increase in housing investment from all stakeholders in the housing sector and the Increase in the training of construction professionals to handle the technicalities involved in vertical architecture construction.

References

Ademiluyi, I. A., & Raji, B. A. (2008). Public and private developers as agents in urban housing delivery in Sub-Saharan Africa: The situation in Lagos State. *Humanity and Social Sciences Journal, 3*(2), 143–150.

Afolabi, A. O., Ojelabi, R. A., Bukola, A., Akinola, A., & Afolabi, A. (2018). Statistical exploration of dataset examining key indicators influencing housing and urban infrastructure investments in megacities. *Data in Brief, 18*, 1725–1733.

Afolabi, A., Oluwatayo, A., Oyeyipo, O., Ojelabi, R., & Fagbenle, O. (2018). Assessment of designers' perception of post conflict housing schemes for internally displaced persons. *Construction Economics and Building, 18*(1), 27–47.

Akinmoladun, O. I., & Oluwoye, J. (2007). An assessment of why the problems of housing shortages persist in developing xountries: A case of Study of Lagos Metropolis, Nigeria. *Pakistan Journal of Social Science, 4*(4), 589–598.

Al-Kodmany, K. (2018). Sustainability and the 21st century vertical city: A review of design approaches of tall buildings. *Buildings, 8*(102), 1–40.

Centre for Affordable Housing Finance Africa. (2018). Housing finance in Nigeria. Accessed on 25th January 2019 from http://housingfinanceafrica.org/countries/nigeria/

Enisan, O., & Ogundiran, A. (2013). Challenges of housing delivery in metropolitan Lagos. *Research on Humanities and Social Sciences, 3*(20), 1–9.

Ezeigwe, P. (2015). Evaluation of the causes of housing problems in Nigeria: A case study of Awka the capital city of Anambra State. *Journal of Economics and Sustainable Development, 6*(20), 1–7.

Ibem, E. O., Anosike, M. N., & Azuh, D. E. (2011). Challenges in public housing provision in the post-independence era in Nigeria. *International Journal of Human Sciences, 8*(2), 421–443.

Ibimilua, A. F., & Ibitoye, O. A. (2015). Housing policy in Nigeria: An overview. *American International Journal of Contemporary Research, 5*(2), 1–7.

Igwe, P. U., Okeke, C. A., Onwurah, K. O., Nwafor, D. C., & Umeh, C. N. (2017). A review of housing problems. *International Journal of Environment, Agriculture and Biotechnology (IJEAB), 2*(6), 3092–3099.

Ilesanmi, V. O. (2010). Urban sustainability in the context of Lagos megacity. *Journal of Geography and Regional Planning, 3*(10), 240–252.

Jiboye, A. D. (2011). Ensuring sustainable development through effective housing delivery process in Nigeria. *African Journal of Social Sciences, 1*(2), 36–45.

Mustapha, I. (2002). Overview of housing and urban development programme since independence. *Housing Today-Journal of the Association of Housing Corporations of Nigeria, 1*(6), 28–30.

National Population Commission. (2016). National Population Estimates. Accessed on 25th January 2019 from https://nigerianstat.gov.ng/download/474

Nwannekanma, B., & Gbonegun, V. (2018). Divergent views trail calls for adoption of vertical city development. Accessed on 25th January 2019 from https://guardian.ng/politics/divergent-views-trail-calls-for-adoption-of-vertical-city-development/

Okafor, B. N. (2016). The residential housing problem in Anambra State (A case study of Onitsha Metropolis). *International Journal of Civil Engineering, Construction and Estate Management, 4*(2), 1–18.

Okupe, O. (2002). Problem of real estate developers in Nigeria. *A paper presented at a workshop organized by the Nigerian Institute of Quantity Surveyors*, Abuja.

Olotuah, A. O. (2000). The challenge of housing in Nigeria. In *Effective housing in 21st century in Nigeria, Environmental Forum Federal University of Technology, Akure, Nigeria* (pp. 16–21).

Olotuah, A. O. (2010). Housing development and environmental degeneration in Nigeria. *The Built & Human Environment Review, 3*, 42–48.

Olotuah, A. O., & Aiyetan, A. O. (2006). Sustainable low-cost housing provision in Nigeria: A bottom-up, participatory approach. In D. Boyd (Ed.), *Proceedings of 22nd Annual ARCOM Conference, 4–6 September, Birmingham, UK, Association of Researchers in Construction Management* (Vol. 2, pp. 633–639).

Oshodi, L. (2010). *Housing, population and development in Lagos, Nigeria*. International Development and Urban Governance. www.worldpress.com.

UN-HABITAT. (2006). *National trends in housing—Production practices volume 4: Nigeria*. United Nations Centre for Human Settlements.

United Nation's World Population Prospects. (2017). World Population Prospects 2017. Accessed on 25th January 2019 from https://population.un.org/wpp/

World Bank. (2008). *Urban poverty: A global view*. Prepared by Judy L. Baker for the World Bank Group. http://www.worldbank.org/urban/

PART II

African, Global Development and Sustainability

CHAPTER 10

ECOWAS and the Challenges to Regional Integration in West Africa

Samuel Ibok and Adetomiwa Atayero

Introduction

Preceding the creation of ECOWAS, West Africa was comprised of states that developed from dissimilar and unique colonial experiences and administrations which demarcated the boundaries of the fifteen states in the sub-region. These states were carved out by colonial masters during the scramble and partition of Africa. The termination of the Second World War saw the birth of nationalism and political transformation in Africa. The call for independence by African elites through diverse nationalist movements was a means to end the devastating dependence on colonial masters and a means of instituting self-rule in Africa. This resulted in the attainment of independence by many African countries. During the post-independence era, traces of dependence persisted, and it was against this backdrop that African leaders saw the need to unite and promote interdependence among African states, end dependence on the colonial masters,

S. Ibok · A. Atayero (✉)
Department of Political Science and International Relations, Covenant University, Ota, Ogun State, Nigeria

S. Folarin et al. (eds.), *The United Nations and Sustainable Development Goals*, https://doi.org/10.1007/978-3-030-95971-5_10

and foster development in the West African sub-region (Baran, 1973; Dos Santos, 1970; Rodney, 1972).

The initial attempt at integration can be traced to 1975 when the CFA franc was created as the sole currency for francophone countries in the region. It was Liberian President, William Tubman in 1964 that proposed the establishment of an economic union for West Africa. A treaty was contracted in 1965 by just four states (Guinea, Cote d' Ivoire, Sierra Leone, and Liberia). In 1972, a proposal was made to establish a unification of states in West Africa. General Yakubu Gowon the then head of state of Nigeria and the head of state of Togo, Gnassingbe Eyadema were instrumental in the spread of the idea of integration (Rasheed, 2020). Their efforts resulted in the Treaty of Lagos in 1975. The treaty was initially signed by sixteen West African states. These states were Burkina Faso, Sierra Leone, Benin, Mali, Cape Verde, Senegal, Nigeria, Liberia, Ghana, Guinea Bissau, Mauritania Niger, The Gambia, Guinea, Togo, and Cote d' Ivoire (Akinyemi & Aluko, 1984). Mauritania extracted its affiliation from ECOWAS in 2000. ECOWAS still faces different forms of obstacles that frustrate its efforts at regional integration. This ranges from corruption, political instability, domineering tendencies of some states, terrorism, among others. This paper is organized into five sections. After the introduction, relevant literature is examined. In the third segment, succinct information on the structure and fundamental principles of ECOWAS is provided. The fourth section puts into context the efforts of ECOWAS towards regional integration and the prevailing challenges to this targeted integration. The final segment concludes the work and offers adequate recommendations.

Review of Related Literature

It is important to note that scholarly literature on ECOWAS achievements and efforts in fostering regional integration is rich (Adetula, 2009; Adetula, Bereketeab, & Jaiyebo, 2016; Ajiye, 2019; Best, 2006; Fayomi & Adeola, 2015). However, minimal attention has been given to the prevailing challenges of regional integration in West Africa. This study aims at filling this gap in the literature. According to Ibietan and Ekhosuehi (2013), ECOWAS has been afflicted by divisions based on political history. They also assert that the economies of ECOWAS states are not complimentary, ensuing in low intra-regional trade (Onah & Ibietan, 2009).

More so, the disunion based on lingual lines (Francophone and Anglophone) induced by colonial heritage, demographic, and monetary fiscal alignment has had a disrupting influence on ECOWAS (Equere, 1984). According to the African Development Report (2001), the re-occurrence of border conflicts and political instability is having remarkable effects on economic activities and integration efforts in the West African sub-region. Bundo (1997) argues that a development culture is absent within governments and people in the West African sub-region. Similarly, the activities of terrorists have adversely affected integration efforts in the sub-region. Adekunle (2010) maintains that the cost of doing business in the ECOWAS sub-region is unreasonably expensive. This is caused by the frequent collection of bribes by customs and immigration officers and touts along the West African corridors (Adekunle, 2010; Odularu, 2006).

Poor road networks and shortage of adequate alternative means of transportation adversely affect trade, development and discourage integration (Bala, 2017; Dean-Swarray et al., 2014). From the foregoing, it can be asserted that there are serious challenges facing ECOWAS in its mission of regional integration in the West African sub-region.

The crucial concepts in the paper are elucidated in the following segment to avoid misconceptions and ambiguities.

Development

It is apposite to note that there is no agreement among scholars as to the definition of development (Gertzl, 1995). The concept of development is not strictly an economic affair, it is, however, a multidimensional process that involves modification or transformation from a less to a more desirable state (Aniekan & Otoabasi, 2013). It implies a situation where an economically unstable country can create and sustain a yearly growth in its Gross National Product. The Rio Conference in 1992 introduced Sustainable Development as a new form of development. This denotes development that addresses the need of the current generation and does not in any way jeopardize the resources available to the future generations (Aniekan & Otoabasi, 2013).

Dependency

It should be noted that the terms dependence and dependency are recurrent themes in contemporary international relations. They reveal the mutual yet detrimental nature of the relations between the core and peripheral countries or what many scholars term as the North/South dialogue (Okereke & Ekpe, 2002). Dependence refers to the pattern of outward reliance of well-integrated nation-states on each another (Caporaso, 1978). Dos Santos (1970) defines dependency as a situation that shapes the configuration of the world economy in a way that some countries are favoured at the loss of others and this further confines the possibility of development in poor underdeveloped countries. The context of dependency in this work is a departure from the traditional perception which portrays a core and periphery relationship. Accordingly, dependency in this work suggests interdependence between peripheral nations targeted at expediting some form of development.

Globalization

There is no consensus among scholars as to the definition of the term globalization. It has been defined as an all-encompassing network of political, cultural, socioeconomic, and interconnections and processes which transcend state boundaries (Yeates, 2001). It has to do with the procedure by which diverse societies and economies become more narrowly incorporated (Nilson, 2010). Similarly, it is seen as the spread of information, technology, products, and jobs across national borders and cultures (Klopp, 2020). Regional integration is inherently a facilitator of globalization because it creates room for the transfer of ideas, cultural exchange, monetary transfers, and so forth. This is depicted in the level of similarities among ECOWAS member states.

Theoretical Framework

The need to apply theories to issues in the international system cannot be overemphasized. Theories are used to make predictions based on observed behavioural patterns (Hollis & Smith, 1990). The exclusion of blockades to commerce and free trade is a core part of the modern interdependency theory which is also called the theory of liberal institutionalism. The growth of regional economic integration in Europe was stimulated by the notion that interstate struggle can dwindle by establishing a common interest in trade and economic partnerships between states in the same region (Hollis & Smith, 1990). States can expand the conceptions of self-interest to broaden the scope of collaboration by belonging to international institutions (Keohane & Nye, 1977). Liberal institutionalist seeks to demonstrate that states can cooperate in the absence of a powerful player to implement obedience to treaties. The progress of economic interdependency corresponds with the decay in the value of territorial conquest for countries (Rosecrance, 1986).

There is abounding literature on the concept of regionalism. It has to do with the voluntary association of countries with their neighbours to resolve conflicts among themselves (Ernst, 1971). Similarly, it establishes peace between neighbouring countries and narrows the gap between countries (Egbo, 2012). Regional integration can lead to peace and security in that region (Daniel, 1999). ECOWAS reflects an intrinsic desire by the peoples of West Africa for cooperation. It is essentially the structural embodiment of their belief in a collective attack against the persisting problems of underdevelopment in tropical Africa (Akinyemi & Aluko, 1984). In another vein, regional integration is regarded as a valuable means of loosening the various forms of the dependence of the developing world in the developed world (Inotai, 1991).

Structure and Fundamental Principles of ECOWAS

ECOWAS like most regional organizations has a distinct structure that engenders the smooth operation of the community and prevents anarchy. It has three arms of governance which are the legislature, executive, and judiciary. The organization has the authority of heads of states and government. It is also the highest policymaking body. It comprises the heads of states and the government of member states. The next body is the Council of Ministers. Other organs include Community Parliament, the Community Court of Justice, ECOWAS Bank for Investment and Development Specialized Technical Committees. Some specialized agencies of the community include ECOWAS Gender and Development Centre, Intergovernmental Action Group Agents money laundering and Terrorist Financing in West Africa (GIGABA), West African Health Organization, West African Monetary Agency (WAMA), and many others.

The community is directed by some fundamental principles that guide the nature of the relationship between its member states and they reflect the values of ECOWAS.

Equality and independence of member states. This principle is given the greatest attention because the territorial integrity of its members must on no account be infringed upon. There is also the principle of non-aggression between member states. Another principle is the preservation of regional peace, security, and stability through the promotion of good neighbourliness. The peaceful resolution of disagreements among member states, vigorous collaboration between bordering countries, and the advancement of a peaceable atmosphere as a precondition for economic development is another principle of the community.

Recognition, protection, and promotion of human rights in harmony with the requirements of the African Charter on Human Rights is another principle of the community. The elevation and consolidation of a democratic system of governance in each member state as envisaged by the declaration of political principles adopted in Abuja on 6th July 1991 is also a fundamental principle. Accountability, social justice, economic and popular participation is another fundamental principle. All member states are expected to recognize and abide by all these fundamental principles.

Efforts Towards Regional Integration

ECOWAS in its attempt to realize its aim of integration in West Africa developed and implemented some unique strategies. These strategies go beyond just promoting cooperation but also attempt to accelerate development in the region.

Trade and Market Integration

It should be noted that ECOWAS places market integration and trade at the centre of its aims. Article (3) of the ECOWAS Revised Treaty proposes the elimination of all forms of blockades to trade and coordination of trade guidelines for the formation of a Free Trade Area (FTA), Common Market, Customs Union, and an ensuing conclusion into a Monetary and Economic Union. Each member state will, however, retain its fixed barriers to trade with non-member states. In other words, the barriers to trade are to be applicable only in trade relations with states that are not part of ECOWAS. ECOWAS member states have agreed to a mutual process to which various groups of goods will profit from the decrease and elimination of tariffs. The ECOWAS Trade Liberalization Scheme (ETLS) implemented in 1979 with a contract on artisanal handicrafts, agricultural, and unprocessed products, and protracted to industrial products in 1990, serves as the core agenda for market and trade integration in ECOWAS as it addresses protocols regarding the unrestricted movement of persons, goods, and transportation. Additionally, ECOWAS has executed a Connectivity and Customs programme to make it easier for goods to be moved in the sub-region. ECOWAS is also working in three vital areas to foster competition and investment policies. These include the formation of the ECOWAS Common Investment Market, investment climate promotion as well as financial market integration. ECOWAS has been firm in its relations with other sub-regional organizations in West Africa.

Harmonization of Immigration Programmes

This involves the adoption of strategies that are directed at increasing the level of cooperation and interaction among the countries within a particular region. This will increase the level of collaboration among the member states of ECOWAS. Following this philosophy, ECOWAS has developed the necessary legal mechanism to promote the free movement of its citizens in the sub-region. Article 59 of the ECOWAS Treaty entreats its member to ensure citizens of ECOWAS states will be given the right of entry, residence, and the right of establishment. By this provision, ECOWAS states are to recognize these as rights of citizens of West African states in their respective territories thereby honouring the stipulations of the Protocols relating thereto.

Collaboration in Transport

ECOWAS made it clear in the 1975 Treaty that member states need to develop progressively mutual communication and transport policies through the enhancement and extension of their prevailing and communication links as well as the creation of innovative ones. This was to foster the physical connection of member states and the advancement of better movement of goods, persons, and services within the community. ECOWAS reiterated in the 1993 revised Treaty and subsequent decisions, protocols, and resolutions of the need to pursue these goals. The creation of roads to link capital cities of member states is part of the general objectives of ECOWAS (Egbo, 2012).

Conflict Resolution and Peacekeeping Initiatives

The subject of development cannot be discussed in isolation from that of security in West Africa since both are interdependent. The political history of West African countries since independence in the early 1960s has been unstable (Best, 2006). This accounts for the attention that ECOWAS gives to security and peace in West Africa. This led ECOWAS members to form a sub-regional military alliance (ECOMOG) in 1990.

ECOMOG forces were subsequently deployed in the various conflict areas and their presence helped to bring some level of sanity and order within these places. This development reflects the multidimensional nature of new regionalism where various elements in regional cooperation are to complement each other in other to promote the development of the regionalization process.

Cultural and Social Integration

In a bid to attain social and cultural integration in West Africa, ECOWAS is encouraging its citizens to take an interest in its affairs, and it has set up several measures to achieve this target. Article 61 of the ECOWAS treaty beckons on its members to work together with a mindset to mobilize and utilize the different segments of their populations, adequately ensure their effective integration and their inclusion in the social development of West Africa.

To realize this aim, member states are to ensure the harmonization of their Social Security laws and labour laws; coordinate their policies to promote the creation of youth and women's platforms and professional associations as a medium of guaranteeing mass participation in the integration activities of ECOWAS; support the exchange of experiences and information on literacy, professional training and employment; and cooperate in the promotion of sporting activities with a view of uniting the region's youth and also ensure their balanced development.

Challenges with Regional Integration in West Africa

There are numerous challenges facing the regional integration of states in West Africa. Some of these challenges have been itemized below:

Colonial Legacy

The legacy of colonialism in the newly independent states of Africa has left the people and especially the leadership shackled to their colonial masters, economically, socially, and politically. For example, France still has a strong influence on the policies in Francophone countries of West Africa (Egbo, 2012). Continuous ties with colonial masters have been discouraged in literature particularly by many African scholars. (Ake, 1978; Bala, 2017; Nkrumah, 1965; Rodney, 1972). However, the governments of West African states have refused to reconsider. According to Equere (1984), the matrimony between ECOWAS states and their colonial masters reduces intra-regional trade. This is because ECOWAS member states prefer to trade with their colonial masters than trading with fellow member states.

Anglophone/Francophone Divide

The ongoing relations between Anglophone and Francophone West African countries have been clothed with suspicion in the sense that they are always trying to outsmart one another to protect the interests of their bloc (Chidozie & Abiudun-Eniayekan, 2017). This divide has constrained the development of much greater coordination; better intelligence gathering and sharing; and more efficient border controls, which will require tackling the corruption that is prevalent in several customs services and police forces (Ibrahim, 2020). Correspondingly, the member states of the community may have to go against the principles of the community in a bid to please their colonial masters. The Anglophone and Francophone states use English and French, respectively, as their official languages and this language difference reduces the freedom of communication and consequently on trade (Equere, 1984).

Terrorism

West Africa is witnessing a difficult stage in its evolution. The inability of the member states of ECOWAS to manage terrorism and insecurity generally has resulted in the loss of lives and property across the region (Ibrahim, 2020). The action of ECOWAS to this has been very inconsequential and some of these terrorist groups have merged with other bigger terrorist organizations (Ibrahim, 2020). To this end, they have gained international recognition and patronage and have become key players in the International system. If the issue of terrorism is not tackled swiftly, it may just happen that the region may be given the nomenclature "axis of terror".

Clashing Interests of Member States

It is common knowledge that in the international system there are no permanent friends and no permanent enemies, but only permanent interest. From the forgone statement, it can be deduced that the member states of ECOWAS may tend towards taking actions that would best suit their interests as a state rather than the collective interest of the community.

A contemporary example is the closure of the Nigerian border by the Nigerian government (Rasheed, 2020). This action is against the ECOWAS agreement on trade liberalization and the attempt to create a borderless West African sub-region. On the other hand, sovereign states have the right to shut their borders for diverse reasons including based on an outbreak of diseases as well as for economic reasons. In as much as ECOWAS appealed for the re-opening of the borders, no official sanction is yet to be placed on Nigeria. This has created some form of speculation as to whether the inaction of ECOWAS is because Nigeria is its major stakeholder.

Fear of Domination

This has always been a major concern of the member states and to a considerable extent, it is a great impediment. An example is the fact that some states consider Nigeria to be a threat and hegemon in West Africa (Iheme, 2006). Also, Nigeria is indisputably the most populated black country in the world and it also has the largest market in Africa. In a bid to balance Nigeria's power, some states deliberately refrain from direct relations with the Nigerian government and sometimes these states try to project themselves as also been powerful. The fear of Nigeria exerting hegemonic influence over smaller nations of ECOWAS is not easy to dismiss and it has led the former to grant concessions to validate that such fears are unsubstantiated (Ebiefie, 1984).

Political Instability

One unique feature of the West African sub-region is the prevalent political instability (Egbo, 2012). It is often said that democracy has been relegated in these countries and this is expressed in the abuse of the fundamental human rights of citizens by the governments represented in ECOWAS and their failure to abide by the rule of law. Governments of member states are commonly accused of rigging elections, inflating election results, and committing other forms of electoral malpractice.

Excessive Mobility of Community Citizens

There are several concerns by governments of member states, particularly the more prosperous ones over the provision of ECOWAS that articulates the free mobility of citizens of the community. This is because it may inspire movement away from low-wages areas to high-wages areas. The influx of Community citizens from less prosperous sister nations will in time strain the patently inadequate public utilities and security apparatus of high-wage ECOWAS countries. Some states feel the available jobs may be taken by community citizens who may provide cheap labour which would be at the expense of their citizens (Akinyemi & Aluko, 1984).

Conclusion and Recommendation

The kernel of this paper is to examine the role of ECOWAS in fostering regional integration in the West African sub-region. In doing so, it stated that ECOWAS plays a vital role in integrating the sub-region and it produced several measures to realize its goals. However, the integration processes have been slowed down by certain impediments which include terrorism, colonial legacy, political instability, among others.

The paper recommends that all ECOWAS member states should abide by the fundamental principles of the community. Also, the Anglophone/Francophone divide in ECOWAS should be reduced through friendly relations. Additionally, the government of member states should find a lasting solution to the security challenges that have plagued West Africa.

More so, social media should be used as a tool to project the achievements of ECOWAS and the government of member states should manage the media in their respective countries properly. Social media platforms should be utilized to de-escalate xenophobic tendencies by Community citizens. Lastly, the respective governments of member states should also uphold the key principles obtainable in democracy and respect the rule of law.

References

Adekunle, B. (2010). Joint trade post at ECOWAS borders. Nigerian Tribune. Retrieved August 25, 2020, from http://www.tribune.com.ng/index.php/opinion/2370-joint-border-at-ecowas-borders.html

Adetula, V. (2009). ECOWAS and the challenges of integration in Africa. In U. Ogwu, & W. Ali, *Milestones in regional integration* (pp. 15–58). NIIA.

Adetula, V., Bereketeab, R., & Jaiyebo, O. (2016). *Regional economic communities and peace building in Africa: The Experiences of ECOWAS and IGAD.* Nordic Africa Institute.

African Development Report. (2001). *Fostering good governance in Africa.* African Development Bank.

Ajiye, S. (2019). Integration and the potency of ECOWAS protocols in the drift towards statehood. *International Journal of Economics, Commerce and Management, 7*(2), 578–599.

Ake, C. (1978). *Revolutionary pressures in Africa.* Zed Press.

Akinyemi, A., & Aluko, I. (1984). Introduction. In I. Aluko, A. Akinyemi, & S. Falegan, *Readings and documents in Ecowas* (pp. 3–28). Nigerian Institute of International Affairs.

Aniekan, E., & Otoabasi, A. (2013). *Readings in International Political Economy.* Book House.

Bala, M. (2017). The challenges and prospects for regional and economic integration in West Africa. *Asian Social Science, 13*(5), 24–33.

Baran, P. (1973). *The political economy of growth.* Peguin.

Best, G. (2006). *Introduction to peace and conflict studies in West Africa.* Spectrum Books Ltd.

Bundo, A. (1997). ECOWAS and the future of regional integration in West Africa. In R. Lavergne (Ed.), *Regional integration and cooperation in West Africa* (pp. 29–47). Africa World Press, IDRC.

Caporaso, J. (1978). Dependence, dependency and power in the global system: A structural behavioral analysis. *International Organization, 32*(1), 13–43.

Chidozie, F., & Abiudun-Eniayekan, E. (2017). ECOWAS and the 'New scramble' for Africa: Interrogating the francophone/anglophone dynamics. *Journal of International Politics and Development (JIPAD), 15*(1), 81–104.

Daniel, B. (1999). *The revival of regional integration in Africa.*

Dean-Swarray, M., Adekunle, B., & Odularu, G. (2014). Policy recipe for fostering regional integration through infrastructure development and coordination in West Africa. In D. Seck (Ed.), *Regional economic integration in West Africa* (pp. 29–36). Springer.
Dos Santos, T. (1970, May). The structure of dependence. *American Economic Review*, *9*, 231–236.
Ebiefie, E. (1984). Central provisions of the Treaty of ECOWAS. In A. Akinyemi, S. Falegan, & I. Aluko, *Readings and documents on ECOWAS* (pp. 109–117). Nigerian Institute of International Affairs.
Egbo, S. (2012). *International organizations and regional integration.* John Jacob's Classic Publishers Ltd.
Equere, U. (1984). Problems and prospects of the Economic Community of West African States. In A. Akinyemi, S. Falegan, & I. Aluko, *Readings and documents on ECOWAS* (pp. 553–572). Nigerian Institute of International Affairs.
Ernst, B. (1971). The study of regional integration: Reflections on the joy and anguish of pretheorizing. In N. Leon & A. Staurt (Eds.), *Regional Integration: Theory and Research* (pp. 3–4). Havard University Press.
Fayomi, O., & Adeola, L. (2015). ECOWAS and sub-regional integration in West Africa. *Covenant University Journal of Politics and International Affairs (CUJPIA), 3*(1), 29–40.
Gertzl, C. (1995). *The new world order.* Development Bulletin.
Hollis, M., & Smith, S. (1990). *Explaining and understanding international relations*. Oxford University Press.
Ibietan, J., & Ekhosuehi, O. (2013). Trends in development planning in Nigeria: 1962 to 2012. *Journal of Sustainable Development in Africa, 15*(4), 297–311.
Ibrahim, J. (2020, January 3). 2020, Nigeria and the West Africa challenge. Premium Times Newspaper. Retrieved January 4, 2020, from https://opinion.premiumtimesng.com/2020/01/03/2020-nigeria-and-the-west-africa-challenge-by-jibrin-ibrahim/
Iheme, F. (2006). The role of ECOWAS in conflict management. In G. Best (Ed.), *Introduction to Peace and Conflict Studies in West Africa* (pp. 253–269). Spectrum books Ltd.
Inotai, A. (1991). *Regional integration among developing countries revisited, trade policy division, country economics department*. World Bank.
Keohane, R., & Nye, J. (1977). *Power and interdependence.* Harper Collins Publishers.
Klopp, C. (2020). *What is globalization*? INVESTOPIA. Retrieved July 2, 2020, from https://www.investopedia.com/termsg/globalization.asp
Nilson, T. (2010). Good for Living? On the relationship between globalization and life expectancy. *World Development, 30*(9), 1191–1203.

Nkrumah, K. (1965). *Neo-colonialism the last stage of imperialism*. Thomas Nelson and Sons Ltd.

Odularu, G. (2006). Trade facilitation as a tool for promoting regional development in Africa. *NIIA Nigeria Forum, 27*(3–4), 126–136.

Okereke, O., & Ekpe, A. (2002). *Development and underdevelopment: The politics of North-South divide*. John Jacob Classic Publishers.

Onah, R., & Ibietan, O. (2009). Democratic stability and regional economic integration: The economic community of West African States (ECOWAS) experience. *Nigerian Journal of Public Administration and Local Government, 15*(1), 17–32.

Rasheed, A. (2020, January 2). Nigeria's border closure: Pros, cons and consequences. PUNCH NEWSPAPER. Retrieved January 4, 2020, from https://punchng.com/nigerias-border-closure-pros-cons-and-consequences/

Rodney, W. (1972). *How Europe underdeveloped Africa*. Bolge-Loveuture Publication.

Rosecrance, R. (1986). *The rise of trading state*. Basic Books INC.

Yeates, N. (2001). *Globalization and social policy*. Sage.

CHAPTER 11

Academic Performance and Secondary School Students' Disposition: Imperatives for Sustainable Development Solutions for the Africa We Want

Olawale Olonade, Ibukun Balogun, Tayo George, Christiana Adetunde, Mercy Ozoya, and Mercy Adebayo

Introduction

Education is one of the vital foundation and functional aspects of human development. That is, education is one of the social institutions that make up society. It is an essential tool for promoting economic expansion and national development (Franklins & Nelson, 2015). Education has been legally recognized as a human right since the Universal Declaration of Human Rights enactment in 1948 (UNICEF, 2007). During the formative years of a child, formal education is already considered right from

O. Olonade (✉) · I. Balogun · T. George · C. Adetunde · M. Ozoya · M. Adebayo
Department of Sociology, Covenant University, Ota, Nigeria
e-mail: olawale.olonade@covenantuniversity.edu.ng

S. Folarin et al. (eds.), *The United Nations and Sustainable Development Goals*, https://doi.org/10.1007/978-3-030-95971-5_11

kindergarten to the tertiary level. This formal education aims to promote personal development and encourage individuals to participate effectively in a free society.

In Nigeria, formal education is divided mainly into three parts. They include a primary school, secondary school, and the university. The Nigerian structure of education is a 6–3–3–4 system, and in this structure, a child is required to spend six years in primary school, three years in junior secondary school, three years in senior secondary school, and the last four years in a university or other tertiary institution (Adekunle et al., 2021). For this study, the focus is on the secondary level of education, with first of its kind established in 1859.

A student's attitude toward his or her academics is the overall and most important factor that determines the academic performance of such a student. In many situations, all the materials needed for quality education are provided, but the right attitude to work is not reciprocated. However, there are situations where the materials needed for quality education are not available, but students have a positive attitude (Davies, 2010). According to Freeman & Davies, (2010), in the early stages of education, girls are more encouraged to do better in school than boys, and they tend to have higher grades. In secondary school, academic performance is of absolute importance to people who have vested interest in school, such people may include parents, principals or proprietors, teachers, and the public at large. A student's strengths and weaknesses are identified in secondary school because secondary school helps in setting a foundation for lifelong learning and development, and this can also have effects on students' academic performance (Goni et al., 2015). This is why various departments serve as a platform to help students in their areas of strength. They include the science class, commercial class, and art or humanities. Research has shown that boys do better than girls in sciences, and girls do better in creativity (art). Studies have shown that boys do better than girls in sciences, and girls do better in creativity (art) (George et al., 2020; Adekunle et al., 2021).

Secondary schools today have different operational activities, which can significantly contribute to boys' and girls' attitudes toward their academics. Some of these activities are dependent on some factors. These factors include the quality and quantity of education given, the surrounding environment, and teachers' involvement in academic matters. Secondary schools also form their student's careers as boys and girls decide their area of focus for their respective careers (Wangu, 2014).

Therefore, this study examines the various attitudes of students and how it has affected academic performance and suggests the way forward for the attainment of sustainable development for the Africa we want.

Research Questions

I. What are the attitudes of secondary school students toward their academic performance?
II. What are the effects of the attitudes of students toward their academic performance in secondary schools?

The Concept of Education

Education is as old as man. Education does not have a clear definition, as it has been defined in several ways. Education is a process through which society transmits from one generation to another its accumulated skills, knowledge, and values. Education is the basis for each nation's development and empowerment. It plays a vital role in understanding and engaging in today's world's day–to–day activities. It builds one's character and plays a significant role in communicating one's culture, beliefs, and values to others in society (Sommerfeldt, 2013). Educations' fundamental purpose is to transfigure the human personality into a perfect pattern through a synthetic process of body development, emotion sublimation, mind enrichment, and spiritual enlightenment. It is a lifestyle preparation here and hereafter. A society cannot grow without education. Whether a society is formed by contact or communication, education plays a role in preserving and transmitting social values (Adie & Ushie, 2018).

Education is described as a process of development in which the human being passes from infancy to maturity, the process through which he gradually adapts himself to his physical and spiritual environment in various ways. Education is, therefore, nothing but a purposeful practice designed to maximize the capacity of a person (Bhardwaj, 2012). Education is also a learning process that fosters the ability to attain knowledge, abilities, values, beliefs, and behaviors. Methods of learning include storytelling, debate, teaching, practice, and guided study. Education can occur in a formal or informal environment, and any interaction that has a formative impact on how one thinks, acts, or feels can be called educational (Wikipedia).

Education has become very relevant in recent times, as most people participate in this matter. Moreover, it cannot be separated from the life of man. Education plays a crucial role in a country's development. If a country does not have adequate education, other countries that support education can leave it behind (Rita & Johan, 2014). Many people consent that in their lives to be educated is very important. Most of them choose a reputable school that is perceived to be the best educational institution for them. The higher quality of the school they select, the lower the price they have to pay for their education (Rita & Johan, 2014).

Education is classified, therefore, into two: formal and informal education. Formal education is an organized learning model, structured and governed by laws and standards, subject to strict objectives, methods, and curriculum content (George et al., 2020). Formal education is institutionalized, deliberate, organized, and funded by public organizations and approved private bodies. This consists primarily of initial training designed for children and youth before their first entrance into the labor market (Adekunle et al., 2021). Formal education started in Nigeria at the first primary school in Badary, Lagos, 1843. Methodist missionaries owned the school. Later on, the first secondary school was established by Christian missionaries. It is called the CMS grammar school and was created in Lagos in 1859 (National Bureau of Statistics, 2015).

The education system in Nigeria is a 6–3–3–4 system. This system was developed to promote functionality in society by bringing forth graduates that can make use of their intelligence, heart, and hands (Abdulwali, 2019). This system provides a child with six years in primary school, three years in junior secondary school, and if the child excels in academic performance, moves and spends three years in senior secondary and then proceeds to a higher institution where he or she spends four years.

Secondary school education, which is the focus of this study is divided into two sections: junior and senior secondary school. The junior school is the continuation of primary education and introduces more academic subjects to students for three years. In the third class, JSS3, the student writes the Basic Education Certificate Examination to proceed to the senior secondary school, for another three years. The senior secondary school is a more advanced class since it gives room for students to choose what class they want to be for career purposes. The classes include: science class, commercial class, and art or humanities. At the end of the last class in the senior school, students take part in writing the Senior Secondary Certificate Examination (SSCE), in which they must attain a minimum of

5 credits, including English and Mathematics. Also, students sit for the Joint Admission and Matriculation Board (JAMB) to gain admission into a higher institution. So, this level of education is very crucial to the career path of every student, hence, the need to be more focused.

Non-formal or informal education is a form of learning that can take place outside a standardized curriculum. It involves a student's interests in a regular classroom program but is not confined to that environment. Informal education can take place by engaging in a conversation, exploring, and even through experience. Informal education can occur at any place and time. It is not an arranged form of learning. This kind of learning is a natural process that helps people learn new things. It helps to develop groups, connections, and partnerships that create a positive environment for learning. However, our concern in this paper is on formal education at the secondary level.

Attitudes and Their Formation

Attitudes are the cognitive orientations people have due to past or present experiences that affect how they see situations, people, objects, events, and how they react to them positively or negatively (Peteros et al., 2019). Attitudes are the positive or negative perceptions or feelings regarding a person, an object, or the media. There are three interconnected elements or qualities which change in direction or strength. The emotional element or component describes our feelings, the cognitive element or component that explains our beliefs, what thoughts we have, and the behavioral element or component that portrays our experiences and actions (Bakanauskas et al., 2020).

Attitudes are the organizations of certain beliefs, behavioral tendencies, and feelings toward a subject or an object (Tsagem, 2020). As individuals grow in society through training and social interaction, attitudes are learned, acquired, and formed. Through direct contact or firsthand experience either from parents, teachers, peers, or relations, attitudes are cultivated, learned, and developed, and from this early stage, they grow and become part of the individual. Attitudes are also formed and developed from indirect sources; this includes: social media through the persuasion of others.

It is essential to know that attitudes are not permanent because they are learned and not innate; attitudes are subject to change. Though learned, it could also be unlearned through new contact, practice, and experiment. Attitudes can be changed from positive to negative, acceptable to unacceptable, unfavorable to favorable, and vice versa. Emotions greatly influence attitudes; this can be either through sensory reactions, that is, attitudes portrayed through the five senses, which include touching, seeing, tasting, hearing, and smell. Also, the values of individuals contribute to attitudes. Many people are guided by various systems that can determine how they perceive certain things.

Attitudes of Students Toward Academics

Lewy introduced the concept of attitudes toward academics (1986). It was then defined as the individual behavior, feelings expressed toward school, and school experience. Attitudes toward school are correlated with academic attainment and achievement. Students who excel in their academic works have positive attitudes toward learning. On the other hand, students who have poor academic performance project a negative attitude toward learning, and they feel that school will not allow them to excel in the future (Candeias et al., 2010). A student's academic performance is when a student can engage in personal or group study on the things taught by the teacher and can put down his or her knowledge into written or oral form in a test or an examination.

Attitudes and academic achievement are interrelated because they are essential factors ensuring student success. Thus, students' attitudes toward academics affect their performance (Hussaini et al., 2015). Just as gender differences apply to other concepts, so also does it apply to attitudes? Girls tend to be more optimistic, and they display positive attitudes toward academics, whereas boys are less inspired and display negative attitudes toward academics and school (George et al., 2020).

A student's attitude is an essential factor that contributes to having a good result (Sejcova, 2006). When a student shows a positive attitude toward their academics, the academic performance gets better (Kubiatko, 2013). Academic accomplishment is referred to as the advancement, improvement in terms of gained knowledge and abilities by an individual. According to a study conducted by Fisher, Hell and Schult in (2013), teenage girls show a more positive attitude toward learning than boys, and boys' attitudes reflect their results. In addition to this, Magalhães et al. (2010) contributed and said that boys have little or no motivation toward school and display negative attitudes toward learning, and girls, on the other hand, are highly motivated and show positive attitudes toward academics.

Some of the factors that significantly influence students' attitudes toward their academics are the subject taught and learned, the rules and demands of the learning institution, and other academic activities. The secondary education of an individual also contributes mostly to the life of a student. This is because secondary education sets the foundation for future education and choices, and so when there is a good foundation, it makes it easier for students when faced with future challenges of their schools, careers, and life as a whole (Kpolovie et al., 2014). Educational attainment is described as a student's positive approach toward the school that may not fully reflect in outstanding achievement, though it will be shown to achieve the best individual outcome regarding the student (Herd et al., 2019).

The attitudes put toward learning and school activities determine the kind of academic performance yielded. Most people believe that poor academic performance results from just low intelligence and neglect their personal efforts and attitudes that substantially affect their performance. Students' academic performance or achievement is considerably connected with the attitudes they put and show toward school. Such attitudes could be displayed in their behaviors, beliefs, or feelings.

A student's academic performance solely lies on his or her ability to recall information and convey knowledge through written or spoken forms. When a student directs a positive attitude toward learning, the academic performance is better because the attitudes have affected how they think, behave and act toward learning (Kpolovie et al., 2014).

Attitudes are said to either be positive or negative. They comprise values, emotions, beliefs, and so on; hence, they affect one's reaction and thinking to particular situations regarding teaching and learning. Attitudes play a significant role in affecting a person's behavior and can help predict other people's behaviors. Though not precisely measurable, attitudes are derived from observable responses and attitudes representing a pattern of conviction and emotion.

Functionalist Theory

This study's theoretical framework will be based on a functionalist theory of attitudes that was propounded by Daniel Katz. He believes attitudes are determined by the roles and functions they perform for us. People have individual attitudes because it helps them to achieve their set objectives. Katz explained this theory based on four different perspectives. Firstly, he describes attitudes as a function for the instrumental purpose. This instrumental purpose posits that specific attitudes are formulated to aid rewards. Because people want to avoid punishment or sanction they portray attitudes that tend to favor them (Happer et al., 2019).

When students know there is a reward for good academic performance, a positive attitude will be directed toward learning because they do not want the stigma directed toward poor academic performance. Katz also explained this theory of attitudes as a function of knowledge. He posits that knowledge is gained through attitudes and attitudes provide criteria for evaluation, through stereotype levels of understanding come in place, and clarity and order can be given to specific situations in life. Students develop a sense of understanding and knowledge by putting the right attitudes to the right things. When they direct positive attitudes and energy toward academics, they are open to new knowledge, and because of the understanding they have, they know how to react to certain situations and circumstances (Happer et al., 2019).

Furthermore, Katz describes attitudes as a form of value expression. The attitudes we have to portray our values and beliefs, for example, if I am a Christian, my values and beliefs are guided by Christianity, reflecting on my attitudes. Therefore, my reaction and attitude to a situation may differ from the attitudes and reactions of a non-believer or a non-Christian. A student's attitude toward academics can show how much value he or she has toward academics. Students who are never interested in extra co-curricular activities that show negative attitudes toward learning and have poor academic performance show that they do not value school. Lastly, Katz describes attitudes as a function or acts posited due to our ego defense mechanism. Some attitudes are used as a cover-up to hide certain things or truth we are scared of letting loose, which may be hurtful if they went out in the open, so there is a showcase of another attitude to avoid unwanted attention (Katz, 1960).

Methods

This study adopts a descriptive survey design method. Google form questionnaire was circulated on the social media platform with 224 responses retrieved and analyzed. The study population is secondary school students in Lagos State, Nigeria. This method was adopted because it allows reaching a broader population and because the data was collected during the coronavirus pandemic lockdown.

Results and Findings

Research Question 1: Attitudes of Secondary School Students Toward Their Academic Performance

Table 11.1 shows that 43.6% of respondents agree to study harder when they have low grades, and 34.5% strongly agree with the same assertion. On the other end of the scale, 4.5% and 2.7% of respondents disagreed and strongly disagreed with the same, respectively. 14.5% of respondents were neutral, not sure of their study habits after getting low grades. This shows a strong determination of students to get better, having performed poorly in previous attempts. Figure 11.1 shows respondents' general acceptance of their need to seek academic assistance when struggling with their studies. 44.5% agree to ask for academic assistance, 33.6% strongly agree, 15% were neutral, 3.6% disagree, while 2.3% strongly disagreed with the variable.

Table 11.1 Attitudes of secondary school students

	Agree	*Disagree*	*Neutral*	*Strongly agree*	*Strongly disagree*
Study harder with low grades	96	10	32	76	6
Willing to ask for academic assistance	98	8	33	74	5
Spend free time studying	46	55	100	9	10
Start studying at term beginning	20	31.4	30.9	8.2	9.5
Study when test is near	39.5	13.2	20	22.3	5
Actively participate in class discussions	41.4	12.7	28.6	15	2.3
Have daily study time	30.5	24.1	32.3	8.6	4.5
Spend less time with friends	14.1	28.2	35.9	3.6	15
Finish assignment on time	31.8	15.9	37.3	6.8	5

Source Field Survey June (2020)

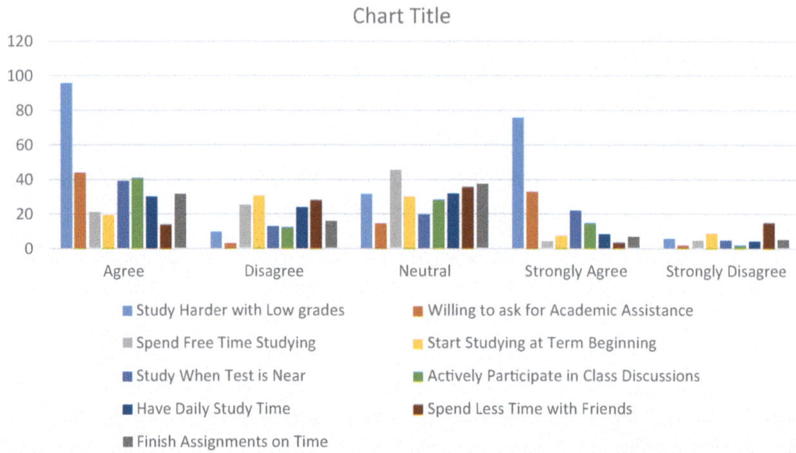

Fig. 11.1 Bar Chart depicting attitudes of secondary school students

The table also gives an insight into how secondary school students in Lagos state utilize their free time. 20.9% and 4.1% agree and strongly agree, respectively, to spending their free time for studies. This statistic is just a little lower than the 25% and 4.5% who disagree and strongly disagree with the same. However, a considerable number of students, 45.5%, are neutral and cannot decide how they use their free time.

Secondary school students in Lagos state do not fancy starting personal studies so early in the term. 20% start studying at the beginning of the term; a further 8.2% strongly agree. 31.4% disagree, and 9.5% strongly disagreed with starting their studies at term beginning, while 30.9% were neutral. Students, therefore, prefer to study close to their test or exam period. A total of 61.8% agree to study when a test is near, while only 18.2% disagree to same, 20% are also neutral. This is also well reflected in students' preference for having daily study time. In Table 11.1 30.5% agree to have a daily study time, 8.6% strongly agree, 24.1% disagree, 8.6% 32.3% are neutral. This is well reflected in how students only study close to their test or exam periods.

From the table, it can be deduced that only 15% do not actively participate in class discussions. Although 28.6% of respondents are neutral, 56.4% of students seemingly enjoy partaking in class discussions.

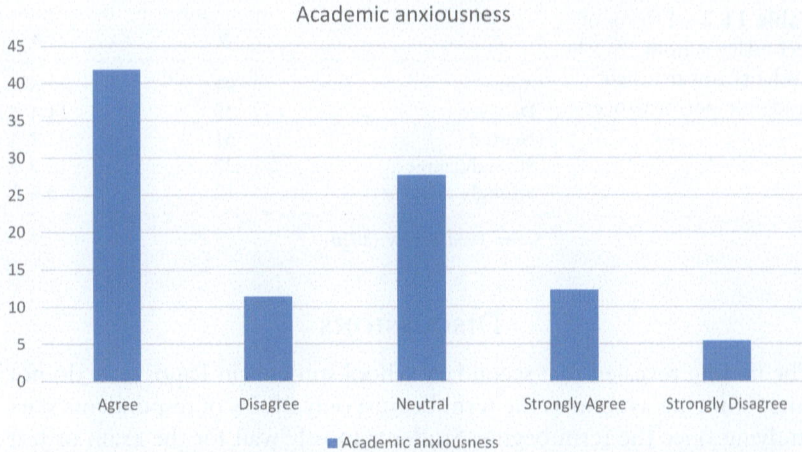

Fig. 11.2 Bar Chart depicting respondents anxiousness about academics

The field results show that secondary students do not give up their social life concerning studying more. 14.1% agree, 3.6% strongly agree, 28.2% disagree, 15% strongly disagree, and 35.9% are neutral about spending less time with friends because of their academics. The total of 43.2% that disagrees is somehow off 17.7% that choose to focus more on their academics than social life.

In Table 11.1, 31.8% agree, 6.8% strongly agree, 15.9% disagree, 5% strongly disagree, and 37.3% are neutral about finishing their assignments on time. From Fig. 11.2, it can be deduced that though most respondents are neutral, the second-highest group of respondents are those who are eager to finish their assignments on time. Unlike theirs, study habits which are delayed much later in the term, secondary school students in Lagos state seem to take their assignment completion seriously. Perhaps, this might be due to the short-timed nature of such assignments.

Research Question 2: Effects of Boys' and Girls' Attitudes Toward Their Academic Performance in Secondary Schools?

Table 11.2, 41.8% agree, 12.3% strongly agree, 11.4% disagree, 5.5% strongly disagree, and 37.3% are neutral in their anxiety about academics.

Table 11.2 Effects of secondary school students toward their academic performance

	N	%
Agree	92	41.8 %
Disagree	25	11.4 %
Neutral	61	27.7 %
Strongly agree	27	12.3 %
Strongly disagree	12	5.5 %

Source Field Survey (2020)

Discussions

The finding revealed that secondary school students in Lagos state do not fancy studying as soon as the term begins; only 28.2% of respondents start studying once the term begins. Students mostly wait for the exam or test periods to study seriously; 61.8% of respondents say they study when a test is near. This corroborates Adeniyi's (2011) submission, which shows such study habits eventually result in poor performance by students, especially in exams.

This submission also resonates with how students spend their free time. This study has revealed that only 25% of students spend their free time on additional studies. The statistics further reveal where their priorities lie. Instead of using such time for additional studies, secondary students prefer to spend more time with their social circle, friends. When posed with that option, only 17.7% of students pass up the opportunity to spend more time with their friends. Bakanauskas et al. (2020) highlighted this by stating the impact of such extra studies on subjects such as mathematics.

Secondary school students in Lagos state also show little toward having daily study time. A handful, 32.3%, are undecided about the use of study time, and with a further 32.7% not having a daily study time, it is pretty clear that students are only generally interested in studying to pass rather than studying to know. This has reflected on society as the "study to pass" nature of the educational system has affected the job market. This is also subscribed to by Herd et al., (2019), who focused on employability in Nigeria regarding the education system on offer.

In Table11.2, only 30.9% prefer academic activities over recreational activities. The statistic is not alarming due to the previously discussed attitudes of secondary students. However, this is not to say a preference for recreation is entirely inadequate. Many scholars have revealed recreation to be responsible for better academic performance in students if well utilized. Candeias et al. (2010) recorded the following to be benefits accrued by students to participate in recreational activities: time management skills, respect for others, academic performance, sense of belonging/association, ability to multi-task, ability to develop friendships, group cooperation skills, communication skills, multicultural awareness, and problem-solving skills.

Studies carried out by Chang et al. (2014) reveal that physical activity before cognitive test-taking has positive effects. A meta-analysis by Lambourne and Tomporowski (2010) found that following exercise, mental processes continue to accelerate, and memory storage is enhanced. These studies are valuable to university administrators in the quest to increase student academic performance and student persistence. Moreover, this may well key into secondary school students' preference in Lagos state if well utilized.

In Table 11.2, a total of 54.1% of students admit to being anxious about their academics. This again can be traced as a by-product of their erstwhile discussed attitude toward their academics, studying only close to exam or test period. The "study to pass" syndrome is sometimes a cause of anxiety as students only cram notes for exam purposes, a view also shared by Agba (2013).

Conclusion

These papers examine attitudes and academic performance among secondary school students in Lagos State. The study found that poor study habits and attitudes are mostly responsible for poor academic performance among secondary school students. Lack of interest in academic study, lackadaisical attitudes exam-centered approach to study has a more significant influence on academic performance. Therefore, it is imperative to revive the culture of reading among secondary school students and ensure that there is proper and conducive learning environment for students, especially in public schools, to stimulate their interest in their studies.

References

Abdu Raheem, B. (2012). The influence of gender on secondary school students' academic performance in South-West. *Nigeria, Journal of Social Sciences, 31*(1), 93–98.

Abdulwali, C. (2019). *Academic performance in Embu west district*. Kenyatta University.
Adekunle, E. O., Olonade, O. Y., Ayodele, O. T., & George, T. O. (2021, January). Technological advancement and child–friendly education in Nigeria: A post-COVID review proceedings of INTCESS 2021. *8th International Conference on Education and Education of Social Sciences*, 18–19.
Adeniyi, V. (2011). *Studying to pass: Implication for students*. Macmillan.
Adie, E. U., & Ushie, A. D. (2018). Integrating African folklore into drama-in-education pedagogy for cultural development in Nigerian primary schools curriculum. *Humanitatis Theoreticus Journal, 1*(1).
Agba, R. (2013). *Why students must develop study habits*. Rixmas Publishing Company.
Bakanauskas, A. U., Kondrotiene, E., & Puksas, A. (2020). *The theoretical aspects of attitude formation factors and their impact on health behaviour* (p. 83). https://doi.org/10.1515/mosr-2020-0002
Bhardwaj, M. J. (2012). Implementing experiential learning: It' snotrocket science. In M. Reynolds & R. Vince (Eds.), *Experiential learning & management education* (pp. 137–152). Oxford University Press.
Candeias, A. A., Rebelo, N., Oliveira, M., & Mendes, P. (2010). Pupils' attitudes and motivation toward learning and school–study of exploratory models on the effects of socio-demographics, personal attributes and school characteristics. *Research Gate, 1*(1), 1–18.
Chang, Y. K., Chi, L., Etnier, J. L., Wang, C. C., Chu, C. H., & Zhou, C. (2014). Effect of acute aerobic exercise on cognitive performance: Role of cardiovascular fitness. *Psychology of Sport and Exercise, 15*(5), 464–470.
Eagann, Figueroa, Shaarknes, Hurtado & Chang, (2011). *Student' atitudes toward learning and school – Study of exploratory models about the effects of socio-demographics and personal attributes*. Retrieved May 10, 2020 from http://www.projectored.uevora.pt/documentos/LICE.pdf
Fischer, F., Schult, J., & Hell, B. (2013). Sex differences in secondary school success: Why female students perform better. *European Journal of Psychology of Education, 28*(2), 529–543.
Franklins, A. S., & Nelson, E. A. (2015). *The Nigeria education system and vision 20: 2020*.
Freeman, D. (2010). *Trends in educational equity of girls and women*. United States Department of Education, National Centre for Educational Statistics.
George, T. O., Orbih, M. U., Olonade, O., Onwumah, A., & Olaonipekun, T. (2020, June). Personal learning obstacles and the adoption of ICT among female students in selected public secondary schools in Ogun state, Nigeria. *SOCIOINT 2020—7th International Conference on Education and Education.*

Goni, B. O., Wali, K. K., Kaltum, A. D., Ali, M. K., & Mohammed, M. K. (2015). *Kinship systems, gender norms, and household bargaining: Evidence from the matrilineal belt*. Harvard Mimeo.

Happer, C., McGuinness, P., McNeill, F., & Tiripelli, G. (2019). Punishment, legitimacy and taste: The role and limits of mainstream and social media in constructing attitudes towards community sanctions. *Crime, Media, Culture, 15*(2), 301–321.

Herd, P., Freese, J., Sicinski, K., Domingue, B. W., Mullan Harris, K., Wei, C., & Hauser, R. M. (2019). Genes, gender inequality, and educational attainment. *American Sociological Review, 84*(6), 1069–1098.

Hussaini, I., Foong, L. M., & Kamar, Y. (2015). Attitudes of secondary school students towards biology as a school subject in Birninkebbi Metropolis, Nigeria. *International Journal of Research & Review, 2*(10), 596–600.

Katz, D. (1960). The functional approach to the study of attitudes. *Public Opinion Quarterly, 24*(2), 163–204.

Kpolovie, P. J., Joe, A. I., & Okoto, T. (2014). Academic achievement prediction: Role of interest in learning and attitude towards school. International *Journal of Humanities Social Sciences and Education (IJHSSE), 1*(11), 73–100.

Kubiatko, M. (2013). The comparison of different age groups on the attitudes toward and the use of ICT. *Educational Sciences: Theory and Practice, 13*(2), 1263–1272.

Lambourne, K., & Tomporowski, P. (2010). The effect of exercise-induced arousal on cognitive task performance: A meta-regression analysis. *Brain Research, 1341*, 12–24.

Magalhães, J., Rebelo, A., Oliveira, E., Silva, J. R., Marques, F., & Ascensão, A. (2010). Impact of loughborough intermittent shuttle test versus soccer match on physiological, biochemical and neuromuscular parameters. *European Journal of Applied Physiology, 108*(1), 39–48.

Peteros, E., Columna, D., Etcuban, J. O., Almerino, Jr. P., & Almerino, J. G. (2019). Attitude and academic achievement of high school students in mathematics under the conditional cash transfer program. *International Electronic Journal of Mathematics Education, 14*(3), 583–597. https://doi.org/10.29333/iejme/5770

Rita, J & Johan H. (2014). Education nowadays. *International Journal of Educational Science and Research*. Vol. 4

Sejčová, Ľ. (2006). *Pohľad na kvalitu života dospievajúcich* Album.

Sommerfeldt, E. J. (2013). The civility of social capital: Public relations in the public sphere, civil society, and democracy. *Public Relations Review, 39*, 280–289.

Stanford University Press Small group classroom discussion. *Discourse and Society 14*(2), 115–132. Social support, school attitudes, and behavior-adjustment problems. *Educational Sciences: Theory & Practice 6* 234–240.

Tsagem, S. Y. (2020). Self-concept, attitude to course of study and academic achievement among students of tertiary institutions in Katsina state, Nigeria.

UNICEF. (2007). The state of world's children 2007. Investing in women's rights to advance the rights of both women and children. *Flagship Report*. https://www.unicef.org/reports/state-worlds-children-2007

Wang M. J. (2014). The impact of gender differences on students' academic performance in secondary school in Ndumberi division, Kiambu county, Kenya in science subjects and languages.

CHAPTER 12

Global Production, Consumerism, Supply Chain, and Rural Economy in Africa

Olawale Olonade, Janet Adeleke, Olaniyi Ayodele, and Tayo George

Introduction

Globalization of production has flourished worldwide due to the systematic removal of barriers in trade and economic activities (Islam, 2015). Producing goods in a particular location is no longer a necessity. Although products can label a particular nation, their various parts can be from different locations. The interconnectedness in production implies that the world has turned into a global village, making the manufacturers receive benefits across different cultures and inexpensive labour across the globe

O. Olonade (✉)
Departement of Sociology, Covenant University, Ota, Nigeria
e-mail: olawale.olonade@covenantuniversity.edu.ng

J. Adeleke · T. George
Lagos, Nigeria

O. Ayodele
Departement of International Relations, Coveant University, Ota, Nigeria

S. Folarin et al. (eds.), *The United Nations and Sustainable Development Goals*, https://doi.org/10.1007/978-3-030-95971-5_12

(Ravenhill, 1999; Islam, 2015). In recent times, companies have moved to other parts of the globe to get products at a low price. Also, because of resources embedded in different countries, these multinational companies explore and discover them and then invest. For instance, China is the place where parts of Honda are being made, and it is then assembled in Pakistan and has the engine design in Japan. This is a precise instance of the global supply chain. Therefore, production is distributed into three different places and is distributed and sold globally. Also, consumers demand to contribute to the gains, sustainability, and growth in manufacturing that is being made in the international market (Issahaku et al., 2020). Therefore, there is a need to increase consumer awareness and understand the necessity of making better, socially conscious products that match their taste and the practical means and vehicle through which these products get to the final consumers (Bulus & Ango, 2012).

Many of the global trade is between corporations and within their global supply chain, thereby suggesting that most economic activity in the international realm is overseen, owned, and controlled by corporations (Dau et al. 2019). Hence, the management of its supply chain system, aimed at getting to the consumers leading to a high consumption rate, is worked towards, while components and raw materials may arrive from various other countries for assemblage in yet another state. Finally, products may be sold to customers worldwide (Kolade et al. 2020).

Africa is undoubtedly blessed and endowed with Natural resources such as Tin, Iron Ore and Cocoa, and many more but under-utilized instead of exploited and harnessed by the Western countries. Multinational corporations' source for products and services from places worldwide makes the most public benefits in the quality and cost of production factors (Islam, 2015). These include land, labour, and capital Agriculture, forestry, and mining remain crucial sectors in Africa, specifically in rural places, and are significant contributors to global productions. It is disheartening to see that these rural dwellers still live in abject poverty and are highly underdeveloped. These areas' conditions are overlooked, not forgetting that the farms and ranches are the backbones of rural economies and farmers, the foremost stewards of the lands. These multinational companies increase every day and require the use of these raw materials. What are their contributions to these rural areas' economy and what are their effects on the lives and environment of the rural people are the questions that this paper seeks to answer?

Conceptualization of Terms

Global production is one whose related links and nodes (branch) extend spatially across national boundaries. As Fahreen and Subhabrata (2019) observed, global productions refer to the rise in neoliberal economics, which has occasioned a substantial change in how the market, state, and society relate and in the worldwide division of labour. World Bank Structural Adjustment Programs (SAP) in developing countries make it compulsory for states to create an enabling or friendly business environment (Fahreen & Subhabrata, 2019). So, global production can be referred to as interconnectedness and interrelatedness of businesses, making it easy for multinational corporations to penetrate developing economies to extract raw materials and the attendant consequences.

Multinational Corporations (MNCs): This can be defined as a company or group of companies with subsidiaries in more than one country. It is an enterprise that maintains and directs value-adding activities in many countries across the globe. As argued by Beuselinck et al. (2018), MNCs are of greater importance in an increasingly interconnected global economy. This position is corroborated by the United Nations Conference on Trade and Development report in 2014. According to the report, almost 50% of the world's gross domestic product is obtained from subsidiaries of multinational corporations, which are located outside their countries, and 70% of the total assets of the world's largest 100 multinationals are invested overseas (Beuselinck et al., 2018). With the enormity of the multinational corporations' economic implications, it is therefore vital to examine its vis-à-vis Africa rural economy.

Consumerism: The concept of consumerism depicts a socio-economic imperative and philosophy that promotes an ever-increasing amount in consumers' acquisition of goods and services. As put by Lister (2016), consumerism generally has to do with consumption. It is an uncontrollable consumption pattern and one key feature of the global economy (Olonade, Busari, Egherevba et al., 2021).

Supply Chain: the concept of supply chain refers to individuals, companies/industries, resources, technology, and activities in the global market. It also involved the establishment and product transaction, from the transfer of raw materials from the merchant to the industrialist and then to its ultimate distribution to the final consumer (ElMessiry & ElMessiry, 2018).

Theorizing

World System Theory

The World System Theory will be useful in explaining the issue discussed in this paper. Immanuel Wallerstein (1974) developed this theory. This theory is a macro-sociological standpoint and takes cognizance of the world economy as the unit of analysis that sees the world's composition as unequally skewed in favour of one party against the other. The economy of nations is referred to as the core/metropole or the world's peripheral/satellite system (Wallerstein, 1974). The world-system theory grouped the world economies into three main categories or levels: the core, periphery, and semi-periphery.

The core comprises a highly advanced and developed economy, which absorbs the more significant part of the global export and raw materials. It implies the existence of a world economic system that benefitted some countries. In contrast, there is a high level of exploitation among other countries; that is, the most advanced nation's control and exploit the less developed nations for labour and raw materials, for example, Canada, Japan, France, the United Kingdom, Italy, Germany, and the United States of America. On the other hand, the periphery comprises weak economies that are reliant on shipping a few commodities, such as rice or coffee, or mineral resources such as copper or zinc, to the core countries. Most African countries belong to these periphery countries and often face many exploitations by the core countries. The semi-peripheral—are countries positioned and are dominated by the core, while they take advantage of the periphery, such countries are China, India, and Brazil.

For a peripheral continent like Africa, where a western government or company (Multinational Corporation) purchases thousands of hectares of land in Africa intending to plant it with food or biofuel crops for export back to the western countries to be used for the production are faced with deprivation and exploitation (Uduji et al. 2019). The Western states and multinational companies take advantage of the cheap labour and resources and gain even much more than the African nations selling the lands in the long term, which provides the raw materials such as cash crops. The foreign investment resulted in foreign-owned plantations and not expanded industry and development of those areas.

The World System theorists posit that the international economic system is fundamentally imbalanced. Also, the economic power of core nations and multinational corporations is so high that the periphery will always grapple with exploitation. Put succinctly, Africa, being a peripheral continent, is hugely exploited. Rural areas where these materials are grown are used without being developed, exposing them to so many hazards. This paper will state a lot of multinational companies that exploit the land and resources in Nigeria (For example) and the state of those areas.

Global Production

Production at a global level is buying products and facilities in places across the world to enjoy immensely public benefits in the quality and price of production factors such as labour, land, and capital. Only a small part is done in the industry, while the larger part of the production is done from various locations, some national and other international (Henderson & Nadvi, 2011).

Global production connotes the fact that the world has turned into a global village. It implies manufacturers (multinational companies) getting profits across various countries with low-priced labour across the globe and natural resources for the production needed. It involves the multinational companies fragmenting their activities at the international level, establishing every production phase in countries where it can be completed at a cheaper cost, around the globe (Dicken, 2003). Global production is one whose corresponding links and nodes extend spatially across national boundaries (Fahreen & Subhabrata, 2019). This concept combines sequenced and interrelated activities in the process of value creation. According to Arfi et al. (2018) global production entails an established network of inter-organizations connected and collected by a single product or service that linked together states, households, and enterprises. Global production is best explained by the activities of Multinational Corporation, which is hereby discussed below.

Multinational Corporations

There are several definitions of MNCs; worthy of note are its various attributes. MNCs invest directly in other countries for profits. They comprise a body industry and a collection of outlets in different nations. Also, an MNC can also be referred to as a commercial enterprise that upholds its foreign direct investment and maintains value-added holdings in several countries (Duangjun, 2021). Operating in foreign nations alone does not make an enterprise multinational. Instead, a multinational corporation must invest resources such as financial, managerial talent, marketing skills, and technology to engage in production in a foreign land (Beuselinck et al., 2018).

According to Aguilera and Grøgaard (2019), a multinational corporation or international corporation is a business with many countries' establishments. Similarly, multinational corporations were identified by the International Labour Organization (ILO) as an organization with headquarters in their home countries and have many of their operations in host countries. As opined by Islam (2015), an international corporation is a business establishment that controls or owns products or offers services in several countries across the globe.

It is usually prominent in home countries and manufactures or sells products or offers services in different countries. They can make use of their international presence to manipulate cheap labour services.

Africa

Africa's continent is the second world's largest and second most-populous continent, which covers 20.4% of the earth's total area. Africa is a continent rich and abundant in mineral resources, such as gold, petroleum, iron, tropical fruits, diamonds, wood, salt, and cobalt. However, Africa as a continent is bedeviled with myriads of challenges when it comes to international business. They are always at the receiving end of international laws and usually the dumping ground for global production. As it stands, 1% of global production occurs in Africa (Osabuohien et al., 2019). Factors responsible for this include lack of skills, inadequate power supplies, global competition infrastructural deficit, transportation challenges, commercial feasibility, cross-border delays, and lack of government support for small and medium scale businesses.

African local markets in each country are usually tiny in size to appeal to multinationals' investment. Furthermore, many local production projects' viability is affected by the hindered regional integration and the trade barriers removal.

About 70% of people in Africa reside in rural areas, and nearly 60% of the globally accessible new farmlands are in Africa (Sulle, 2017). Hence, the economic growth and development of Africa are primarily dependent on improved agriculture and rural productivity.

Africa has many natural resources, including diamonds, salt, tin, petroleum, cocoa, and many others. Much of its natural resources are discovered, used, and overexploited by more dynamic groups, thereby exploiting African resources. Scholars have attributed several factors attracting investors to the region, including the availability of cheap labour, low cost of arable land, and Africa's weak institutional framework (Sulle, 2017; Osabuohien et al., 2019). However, despite the abundance of these natural resources, many Western Nations often exploit Africa's natural resources today and further cause poverty in Africa.

Consumerism

Consumerism is the consumption of goods and services. It is referred to as economic and social processes and thoughts that promote the purchase of products and services at an unprecedented level (Lister, 2016). Consumption is the culture or ideology of excessive use of material goods or services sprouting from the desire to buy what we want, apart from what we need to survive (Olonade, Busari, Imhonopi et al., 2021). Consumerism places value upon the excessive consumption of material goods and services. For example, as children, we only got what we wanted during our birthdays, as birthday presents, but we were not limited to birthdays again as we grew old. It is an obsession with buying material goods or items.

It is a theory that a continual increase in the consumption of goods is sound economically. It is the constant increase in an individual's needs and desires for services and products. It is people's behaviour that spends money heavily on products and services. It takes different forms, and this depends on the individual or family income. It is a high level of excessive consumption, far beyond any reasonable wants or needs. Consumption is what people do; consumerism, on the other hand, is understood by sociologists as societal characteristics and a powerful philosophy that conditions people's world view, identities, relationships, behaviour, and values (Cole, 2018). Consumerism as an ideology is a driver that drives people to consume and find fulfilment and excitement via consumption, which increases massive production of goods and a continual increase in sales (Olonade, Busari, Imhonopi et al., 2021).

Consumerism defines people—they desire and pursue goods not just for their usefulness but, more importantly, because of what those things represent to them. They answer the identity question. Individuals want to use the latest and most trending product to outshine other customers to prove their worth and social class (Olonade, Busari, Imhonopi et al., 2021). In consumerism, the understanding of humans, affiliation with others, and mostly, their ability to fit in and be respected by the larger society.

Consumption habits define how humans understand one another, how they affiliate with others, and overall, the extent to which they fit in with and are valued by society. Consumer practices broadly define social and economic value.

Supply Chain

The supply chain comprises merchants that supply raw materials, manufacturers that transform the raw materials into finished goods, storerooms where goods are stored, delivery points delivered to the consumers, and ultimate users (Osabuohien et al., 2019). In short, the supply chain is all the processes involved in the production processes. Without the supply chain, no manufacturer will give customers their desired goods when they needed them, in a particular location, and at a reasonable cost. Therefore, multinational companies should maintain several critical attributes of their global supply chain, including safe transportation to the customers, the minimum social standard for suppliers, product types and sources essential, and sustainability in the supply chain.

Methods

This paper examines global production from a macro perspective using secondary data sources, including previous research articles, official reports, and archival materials. This method is adopted due to the study's broad nature and the need to work within the available resources.

Global Production, Supply Chain, Consumerism and the Nigeria Rural Economy.

Many of the global trade is between companies and within their global supply chain, thereby suggesting that most economic activity in the international realm is overseen, owned, and controlled by corporations. Hence, the management of its supply chain system, aimed at getting to the consumers leading to a high consumption rate, is worked towards, while components and raw materials may arrive from various other countries for assemblage in yet another country (Issahaku et al., 2020). Finally, products may be sold to customers across the globe.

According to Yeung and Coe (2015), the main goal of Global Production and international corporations is to attain the lowest production of goods for the global markets. The objective is achievable by acquiring the most effective localities for the creation, and they try in every way possible to maximize productivity, which is achieving maximum results and minimum cost. The nature aims and objectives of the Multinational Corporation are maximizations of profits at the least possible price. Therefore, the multinationals' foreign direct investment is not to improve the economy of the foreign countries but for exploitation (Beuselinck et al., 2018).

The problem is producing imported consumption in areas where hunger is prevalent, mainly when local subsistence farmers are displaced. Although most third-world nations are endowed with land and other natural resources, they are bereft of both the financial and technical capacity to improve them (Stolle & Huissoud, 2019). These activities create an opening for the MNCs to exploit these resources.

These MNCs exploit the rural areas, export those raw materials, use them for production, and return them to resell (Uduji et al., 2019). Multinational companies decide the prices to sell those products, and they become unaffordable by the rural dwellers, where the raw materials are grown. Nigerian society is mostly a rural community. As observed by Kolade et al. (2020), the most important production factors in Nigeria's rural economy and livelihoods are natural resources and land. As argued by Fahreen and Subhabrata (2019), The World Bank, the International Monetary Group (IMG), and the World Trade Organization (WTO) execution of globalization policies have generally restructured the economy of the rural areas and had significant effects.

Firstly, the policy encouraged the commercialization and privatization of land and resources, followed by deregulation. The second effect is that these policies bring about the land use Acts of 1978, which the government used to obtain a vast expanse of land resulting in momentous land grabs, and the private sector drives this land grab, national government, and multinational corporations (Otive, 2012). The intensification of large-scale land acquisition reinforced by the globalization policies is much evidence in the rural areas. Hence, the liberalization and opening up of private foreign investment have resulted in the acceleration of large-scale land acquisition in rural areas by multinational companies. Below is the table consisting of multinational companies and the land acquired by them for their production activities (Table 12.1).

Table 12.1 Showing multinational companies and the land acquired by them for production

Company	*Country*	*Land Acquired*	*Crop Type*	*Source*
Viscount Energy China	Nigeria		Sugarcane plantation	Fris and Reenberg (2010)
International Trans oil corporation of USA	Odogwu, Ibaji L.G.A. Kogi State	31,000 hectares	Ultra-modern factory for the production of ethanol fuel	Odogwu (2012) cited in Attah (2013)
Union De Initiative S. A de CV Mexican Company		2,000 hectares		Attah (2013)
TRANS4mation Agroted Limited	Arochukwu, Abia State	10,000 hectares	Agricultural Production	Otive (2012)
NNPC	Benue, Jigawa, Gombe, and Kebbi	20,000 hectares	Sugarcane	Nigeria Tribune (July 15, 2008)
Niji farms	Ilero, Ibadan	5,00 hectares	Cassava	www.nijigroup.com
Shell Petroleum Development Company			Petroleum	http://Shell.com.ng
ESPRO asphalt production company	Ife, Osun State		Building and construction materials	

Source Author's computation

Negative Impact of Global Production Activities in Rural Areas

Rural Poverty: This becomes endemic. According to Townsend (1999), poverty can be referred to as the lack of necessary resources to allow involvement in the activities, customs, and diets commonly approved by society.

Environmental Degradation: This is more obvious among the oil-producing companies/firms in Nigeria. These companies degrade the environment, farmlands, wildlife, rivers through gas flaring, oil spillages, and others (Ibaba, 2009).

Cost of Products: Farm production is for export rather than local consumption and the prices set by global producers and multinational corporations rather than domestic markets.

Restructuring: This has to do with changes in the local economy's structure (Such as decrease in wages, reduction of full-time work) that leads to impoverishing small ranchers and farmers and farms sales.

Structural Distortion: The principle of industrialization in Africa has given multinational corporations the freedom to choose their line of operations, the locations of their industries, and other production processes.

Slave Labour: Multinational corporations take advantage of the rural workers by paying them small wages and using them.

Environmental Threats: For the sake of profit, these global campaigns contribute to pollution and also make use of non-profit renewable resources, which poses severe risks to the environment.

Pushing Local Firms out of Business: In rural economies, these multinational companies use economies of scale for driving the local firms out of their businesses.

Market Dominance: The market dominance of multinational companies makes it hard for local small firms to succeed and thrive.

Others include land degradation, deforestation, soil erosion, soil fertility loss, waterlogging, salinity and toxification of soils, damage, and destruction of coral reefs, mangroves, and fisheries. There is also a loss of biodiversity and ecosystem and pollution of air and water bodies.

Conclusion

Through their various activities in foreign countries, MNCs have wreaked much havoc on the African economy in environmental problems, violation of human rights, and non-technology transfer, among others. There is an urgent need to improve agriculture in Africa, and her economy needs to develop in other to ensure food is available for her increasing population, thereby achieving food security. Therefore, to attain sustainable food security and development, a fair deal needs to be struck between agricultural exports, increasing every day and serving local needs. Also, there should be binding rules and regulations set up by the government and strictly agreed/adhered to by international bodies and multinational corporations, which will ensure the protection of local farmers and keep the integrity of Africa's environment, soil, and water.

Recommendation

The following should become necessary to improve the rural economy by the Multinational Corporation:

1. The MNCs should partner with farmers and not just take advantage of the rural areas.
2. The government should actively participate in the activities of this Multinational Corporation in rural areas.
3. There should be a standard agreement between multinational corporations and the rulers/heads and government as to their contribution to the rural areas' economy.
4. There should be a standard rule for payment of workers' salaries; suppose possible pay per hour to avoid labour and slave trade and workers' exploitation.

References

Adesina, A. (2012). (April 3, 2017): *Agricultural transformation agenda nigerian economy, and labor conditions of developing countries: The Nigerian experience. Acquiescence*. www.futureagriculture.org/global-land-grab

Aguilera, R. V., & Grøgaard, B. (2019). The dubious role of institutions in international business: A road forward. *Journal of International Business Studies, 50*(1), 20–35.

Arfi, W. B., Hikkerova, L., & Sahut, J. M. (2018). External knowledge sources, green innovation and performance. *Technological Forecasting and Social Change, 129*, 210–220.

Arshinder, Kanda & Deshmukh, S., G., (2008): Supply Chain Coordination

Attach, N. E. (2013). Land grabbing in Nigeria and response: Protest or challenges (World bank Techical Paper. no. 444). Washington D.C. Corporations on the Nigerial Economy. *European Journal of Social Sciences, 19*(3), Critical Issues in Asian Development, Oxford University Press.

Beuselinck, C., Cascino, S., Deloof, M., & Vanstraelen, A. (2018). Earnings Management within Multinational Corporations. *The Accounting Review American Accounting Association, 94*(4), 45–76. https://doi.org/10.2308/accr-52274July2019

Cole, N. L. (2018). *Consolidating the social, environmental and economic risks, challenges and opportunities in gold mining: An overview*

Dau, G., Scavarda, A., Scavarda, L. F., & Portugal, U. J. (2019). The Healthcare sustainable supply chain 4.0: The circular economy transition conceptual

Framework with the Corporate Social Responsibility mirror. *Sustainability,* 11, 3259. https://doi.org/10.3390/su11123259

De Schutter, O. (2011). *Forum on global land grabbing: How not to think land debates*. www.landgrabs.org/21079. Domestic Prices in Commodity Markets during the Past 25 Years. *World Bank Economic Review. 12*(3), 503–28.

Dicken, P. (2003). *Global shift: Reshaping the global economic map in the 21st century*. Sage.

Duangjun, A. (2021). *Developing a strategic model to enhance foreign direct investment by evaluating thailand's potential market opportunities* (Doctoral Dissertation, Central Queensland University).

ElMessiry, M., & ElMessiry, A. (2018, June). Blockchain framework for textile supply chain management. *International Conference on Blockchain* (pp. 213–227). Springer.

Esekland, G. & Harrison, A. (2003) (June 6, 2017): Moving to Greener Pastures? *European Journal of Business and Social Sciences, 1*(6), 67–76. Farmland Threatens Food Security for the Poor. Oakland: The Oakland Institute. Federal Ministry of Agriculture and Rural Department.

Fahreen, A., & Subhabrata, B. B. (2019). Contested compliance regimes in global production networks: Insights from the Bangladesh garment industry. *Human Relations, 72*(2), 272–297.

Gisselquist, D., & Grether, J-M. (2000).: An Argument for Deregulating the Grabbing Three: Critique of Large Scale Investment in Farmland. *Journal of Peasant Studies, 38*(2), 249–279. Land Grabbing for Agrofuels. Retrieved on the 12/06/17 from www.foeeafrica-up-for-grabs. Latin American Challenge to East Conventional Wisdom. World Bank Economic Review, 11 (1): 33–57.

Henderson, J., & Nadvi, K. (2011). Greater China, the challenges of global production networks and the dynamics of transformation. *Global Networks, 11*(3), 285–297.

Ibaba, I. S. (2009). Horizontal inequalities and peacebuilding in the Niger delta. *Study of Peace and Conflict, 2008*, 103–115.

Islam, R. (2015). Globalization of Production, Work, and Human Development: Is a Race to the Bottom Inevitable? 2015 UNDP Human Development Report Office THINK PIECE

Issahaku, H., Mahama, I., & Addy-Morton, R. (2020). *African Journal of Economic and Management Studies,11*(2), 331–351 © Emerald Publishing Limited. 2040–0705 DOI https://doi.org/10.1108/AJEMS-03-2019-0124

Kolade, O., Mafimisebi, O., & Aluko, O. (2020). Beyond the Farm Gate: Can Social Capital Help Smallholders to Overcome Constraints in Africa's Agricultural Value Chain? In E. S. Osabuohien (Ed.), *The Palgrave Handbook of Agricultural and Rural Development in Africa*, (insert page number, place of pub and publisher) https://doi.org/10.1007/978-3-030-41513-6_6

Lister, J. (2016). Consumerism. Accessed on researchgate. 14/09/2020

Morisset, J. (1998). Unfair Trade? The Increasing Gap between World and Morocco. World Bank Policy Research Working Paper no. 3368, Washington DC. Multinationals and the Pollution Haven Hypothesis., *Journal of Development Economics,70*(1), 1–24.

Olonade, O. Y., Busari, D. A., Imhonopi, D., George, T. O., Iruonagbe, T. C., & Adetunde, C. O. (2021). Shopaholic Phenomenon, Choice of Shopping Place, and the Development of Megamalls in Ibadan, Nigeria. *IBIMA Business Review*. https://ibimapublishing.com/articles/IBIMABR/2021/280834/ DOI: https://doi.org/10.5171/2021.280834

Olonade, O. Y., Busari, D. A., Egherevba, M., Imhonopi, D., Alo, O. A., George, T. O., Asamu, F. F., & Adetunde, C. O. (2021). Megamalls and lifestyles of urban dwellers in selected cities in southwest Nigeria. *African Journal of Reproductive Health, 25*(5s) (Special Edition), 54.

Onodugo Vincent. A. (2012): Multinational Corporations (MNCs) and employment

Osabuohien, E. S., Efobi, U. R., Herrmann, R. T., & Gitau, C. M. (2019). Female labor outcomes and large-scale agricultural land investments: Macro-micro evidence from Tanzania. *Land Use Policy, 82*, 716–728.

Otive, I. (2012): Large Scale Land Acquisition in Africa: Current and Recent Ozoigbo, B. I,

Ozoigbo, B. I. & Chukuezi, C. O. (2011).: The Impact of Multinational Perspectives, Empirical Studies and Research Directions. *International Journal of Production Economics,115*(2), 316–335

Stolle, D., and Huissoud, L. (2019). Undemocratic Political Consumerism. In Magnus oström, Michele Micheletti, and Peter Oosterveer (eds). *The Oxford Handbook of Political Consumerism.*

Sulle, E. (2017). Social differentiation and the politics of land: Sugar cane outgrowing in Kilombero, Tanzania. *Journal of Southern African Studies, 43*(3), 517–533.

Townsend, R. F. (1999). Agricultural Incentives in Sub-Saharan Africa: Policy Transfer of Agricultural Technologies to Developing Countries. *World Bank Economic Review, 14*(1), 111–127.

World Bank. (1995). *Rural Development. Sector Policy Paper.* Washington D. C: World Bank.

Uduji, J. I., Okolo-Obasi, E., & Asongu, S. A. (2019*). Corporate social responsibility and rural women's role in sustainable agricultural development in sub-Saharan Africa: Evidence from the Niger Delta in Nigeria.*

Wallerstein, I. (1974). The rise and future demise of the world capitalist system: Concepts for comparative analysis. *Comparative Studies in Society and history, 16*(4), 387–415.

Yeung, H. W. C., & Coe, N. (2015). Toward a dynamic theory of global production networks. *Economic Geography, 91*(1), 29–58.

CHAPTER 13

Internal Displacement and the Feminisation of Vulnerability in Africa: Implications for the Actualisation of the UNSDGs

Faith Olanrewaju, Olujide Adekeye, and Oluseyi Ogunnowo

Introduction

Internal displacement is a relatable phenomenon because of its prevalence in the world today. Global displacement crisis poses enormous challenges to the international humanitarian community mostly because of the vulnerability displaced persons face as well as other social crises emanating from displacement (Joshua et al. 2021; Olanrewaju et al. 2020; Olanrewaju et al., 2019). As such, vulnerability is an intricate part of displacement. To concisely explicate displacement vulnerabilities, the Impoverishment Risk and Reconstruction (IRR) model developed by

F. Olanrewaju (✉) · O. Ogunnowo
Department of Poltical Science and International Relations, Covenant University, Ota, Nigeria
e-mail: faith.olanrewaju@covenantuniversity.edu.ng

O. Adekeye
Department of Psychology, Covenant University, Ota, Nigeria

S. Folarin et al. (eds.), *The United Nations and Sustainable Development Goals*, https://doi.org/10.1007/978-3-030-95971-5_13

Michael Cernea argues there are nine risks that cause displaced persons to be vulnerable and expose them to traumatic experiences: homelessness, landlessness, joblessness, food insecurity, marginalisation, increased mortality and morbidity, loss of access to common services and property, the loss of educational opportunities and social disarticulation (Cardoso et al., 2016).

The apparent purposes of humanitarian action compel an inclusive response in keeping up with the principles of neutrality, universality and humanity which are informed by needs-based and rights-based approaches. The accomplishment of this entails a comprehensive examination of the gendered norms, power roles and dynamics which shape why and how all people irrespective of their genders experience exclusion and violence in crises. Since the last half of the twentieth century, gender matters in development, security and peace, governance and humanitarian action have received increased attention, leading to the adoption of the Convention on the Elimination of All Forms of Discrimination against Women in 1979, Beijing Platform for Action in 1995 and Women, Peace and Security agenda at the United Nations (UN) Security Council Resolutions 1325, 1820, 1888 and 1960 among others. One of the fallouts of the world's commitments and calls to action on gender matters is the feminisation of displacement (United Nations, 2020).

Displacement has been supposedly framed a feminine and gender issue. Humanitarian practices and policies have taken gender to synonymously mean women, who are labelled as homogeneously vulnerable. The feminine face of displacement has been hinged on women's exposure to gendered based violence such as rape, lower levels of socio-economic development, insecurity, engagement in survival sex, transactional sexual relationships and formal sex work in exchange for protection, goods, money and other forms of compensation as well as the general deterioration of their wellbeing (Cazabat et al, 2020). Also, yearly analysis of the displacement figures shows that women and children are the majority of the displacement victims which makes them the focus of the displacement and gender narrative. Arising from the above, men constitute "the forgotten minority" (Barbelet & Wake, 2017). This lop-sided approach to displacement discourse and humanitarian intervention makes internal displacement under-represented in all forms of narrative—from advocacy, international discourse and research as relating men and displacement (UN OCHA, 2018). The study takes a different tow as it discusses the male face of displacement in other to provide a more gendered approach to the African displacement narrative. It fills the gap in literature by evaluating how the feminisation of displacement affects men and the impacts it could have on the actualisation of the UN SDG goals of gender equality (Goal 5), eradication of gender-based and domestic violence (Goal 5), as well as the actualisation of peace and security on the continent.

Methods

Data collection is anchored on the systematic review of existing studies, to identify articles that are related to the displacement of persons in Africa. To guarantee the maximum standardised methods of the review process, the PRISMA guidelines for systematic review guided the research. The authors undertook a sequential search of articles from search engines such as Google Scholar, AJOL, SCOPUS, Science Direct and PubMed. Only studies published between January 1, 2000, and August 30, 2020, were included in the study. These periods underscore the era of incessant conflicts and attendant displacement of persons in Africa. Titles with related text-based search terms were used with a combination of the following concepts and terms: "Gender and Internal Displacement in Africa" and "Internal Displacement in Africa." We included studies on internal displacement that used both quantitative and qualitative studies to analyse displacement and issues that affect displaced women and men. The authors also thought that the inclusion of these diverse methods could enhance the quality and value of the review. The status of internal displacement within Africa and sex of displaced persons were the major inclusion criterion. Articles not explicitly discussing the nexus between displacement and gender of displaced persons were excluded. Articles centred on other categories of forcefully displaced persons such as asylum seekers and refugees as well as those not differentiating between internally displaced people and categories of populations such as voluntary migrants were excluded from the study.

The article searching and selection process was piloted by the lead author. Four stages of screening were carried out as regards the selection of literature for the study. At the first stage, the key search terms were searched in websites and databases. Secondly, with the use of the inclusion and exclusion criteria, the titles and abstracts were reviewed to categorise the relevant articles. At the third stage, the full text of the remaining studies was reviewed to check if the studies met the pre-determined inclusion criteria. Lastly, at the last stage, there was an in-depth review of the remaining studies. The titles and contents of the articles were screened to evaluate their suitability for addition to the analysis. All the used data was in the public domain so the authors did not require any ethical approval.

Our search returned 12,767 studies. After the screening of titles for relevance (studies analysing the effects of internal displacement on men and women), 12,559 had unrelated themes. 208 titles and abstracts were reviewed. 89 studies were excluded for reasons such as duplications. Studies that did not specify either or both sex were excluded. We, therefore, assessed a total of 71 full-text papers for the final review. After the application of the screening criteria, 61 studies were excluded because they could not provide relevant information on the issues the study seeks to address. Only 10 studies that met the inclusion criteria were included in the study. Fig. 13.1 shows the result of the screening process for the systematic review of literature.

Results

The following study characteristics were extracted: type and year of study and region, country and methodology. The locations of the studies were Sudan ($n = 2$), Uganda ($n = 2$), Nigeria ($n = 2$), Kenya ($n = 1$), Africa ($n = 2$), Sierra Leone ($n = 1$). The methodology of the studies was diverse but many included quantitative survey. They are as follows: cross-sectional survey ($n = 5$), systematic review ($n = 1$), mixed methods ($n = 2$) and focus group ($n = 2$), North ($n = 2$), Central Africa ($n = 4$), East Africa ($n = 1$), West Africa ($n = 2$), combination of African countries ($n = 1$). All 10 studies focused on women. The results of the study are categorised according to several sub-topics that are linked to features of the displacement of internally displaced people such as physical and mental health ($n = 10$) conflict ($n = 10$), Coping strategies ($n = 6$) and life quality ($n = 7$).

Conflicts and the Displacement Nexus

The reviews show that conflict is a major cause of displacement in Africa. In countries like Nigeria, Sierra Leone and Uganda, decades of conflicts have reinforced protracted displacement. Out of 10, 8 studies both explored and referred to the effects of conflicts on displacement (Amodu et al., 2020; Reis et al., 2002; Singh et al., 2015; Olanrewaju 2018a; Olanrewaju 2018b; Getanda et al., 2015; Obol et al., 2011; Amowitz

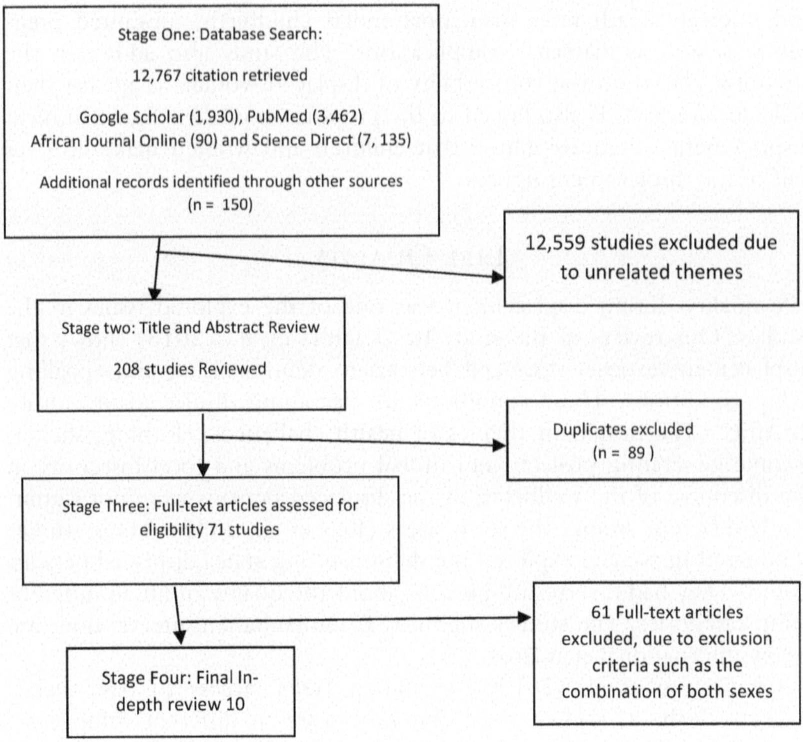

Fig. 13.1 Flowchart of study selection

et al., 2002). The study by Robert et al., (2009) argued that IDPs are largely based in conflict-affected areas.

Genderisation of Displacement

Four of the studies referred to the level of the vulnerability of men, women and children. Olanrewaju et al., (2018b) qualitative study acknowledged that children and women are more susceptible to men during displacement because they are more at risk of gender-based violence, sex trafficking, sexual coercion and forced labour. For Amodu et al. (2020), women's vulnerability could be the result of their inability to access women-specific care which brings about the risk of mortality and intensify death rates from unattended childbirth, unwanted pregnancy as well as maternal complications. The study also adds that the attention placed on the vulnerability of displaced women as against their male counterparts is also linked to the proportion of their figure in most displacement situations stating that children and women make up over half of the displacement figures.

Life Quality

Life quality during displacement was one of the explored issues in the studies. Our review of the study by Getanda et al., (2015) shows that displacement exposes displaced persons to dehumanising and appalling living conditions. These conditions are becoming displacement culture in Africa. The dominant themes of health challenges, clothing, shelter, income-generating projects, nutritional problems and food insecurity in the discourse of the wellbeing of the displaced persons were not significantly different among the study areas (Reis et al., 2002). Three studies conducted in Nigeria explored the dehumanising states displaced persons live in. They had diverse submissions about the quality of life in different camp categories. The studies submit that humanitarian interventions are below international standards.

Olanrewaju et al. (2018a), examined IDPs' access to basic needs such as clothing, shelter, food and healthcare in different camp categories—faith-based camp, formal camp and informal IDP settlements located in Abuja, the Federal Capital Territory and Adamawa state, north-east Nigeria. Their study was conducted with four different groups of displaced women specifically single girls, elderly women, nursing mothers and widows. A total of 12 focus group discussions with one hundred and sixteen (116) focus group participants were conducted. The study found that the displaced women did not have adequate supports relating to the protection of their rights to basic necessities such as cloth, shelter and food. They found that though there were gaps in coverage of basic needs, most of the IDPs in mostly faith-based and government-managed camps had more access to rations of food, shelter and potable water than their counterparts in informal IDP settlements. Olanrewaju et al., (2018a) attributed these gaps to corruption and lack of accountability of public office holders, the absence of inclusive and effective institutions of the government and limited proportion of government spending towards the management of IDPs.

General Physical and Mental Health

All the 10 studies reviewed for this study discussed the health challenges affecting displaced persons. The discourses dwelt on issues of mental health, sexual health and malaria. The studies argue that lack of access to basic essentials of human life like blankets, covered shelter and clothing have mental and physical health implications on IDPs; for instance, this increased risks of ailments such as diarrheal disease, malaria and acute respiratory illnesses. The study by Kim et al., (2007) and that of Getanda et al., (2015) study conducted in Kenya shows that IDPs had psycho-traumatic experiences (anxiety, depression, fear, suicidal thoughts) induced by the poor quality of life lived during displacement.

Roberts et al., (2009) cross-sectional survey in northern Uganda and Amowitz et al., (2002) study in Sierra Leone analysed the influence of marital and gender status on mental health outcomes and war-related sexual violence against women, respectively. Amowitz et al., (2002) argue that mental health outcome results were instigated by sexual violence perpetrated against displaced women by combatants, civilians and their partners. The sexual violence sometimes resulted in physical injuries such as vaginal bleeding, swelling, pain, uterine pain, sexually transmitted disease and vaginal discharge. In addition to the above, Amodu et al., (2020) associated the mental health of displaced women in Africa to lack of family and financial aid to assist them with coping, overwhelming caregiving responsibilities, continuous experiences of violence, family dysfunction, loss of family members and other psychological distresses. Badri et al., (2012) study in Omdurman city Sudan showed that PTSD was more related to loss of physical assets like goods, livestock, property and the loss of close acquaintances such as families and friends that were kidnapped or got disconnected from them. Amowitz et al., (2002) argue that displaced women face post-traumatic stress disorders (PTSD) mostly due to the anxiety of being attacked by armed groups, concerns about the future of their children and family as well as the fear of the unknown.

Coping Strategies

Three studies addressed the coping strategies of displaced persons. Olanrewaju, Omotoso and Alabi (2018b), Reis et al., (2002) and Roberts et al., (2009) reported some sources of emotional and physical/material supports adopted by respondents. The qualitative study by Olanrewaju et al., (2018b) showed that economic empowerment schemes is stressed as one of the most applauded ways to cope with displacement trauma. Before being empowered, the women lacked access to finance to meet essential needs such as food, proper clothing and good shelter. As such, their ability to get earnings from the learned skills paved the way for them to fund some of their basic needs and finance their reintegration back into the society. The study found that only a small portion of displaced women got trained with economic skills due to the limited resources available for the interventions. Men were not included in the economic empowerment schemes.

Two studies by Olanrewaju et al., (2018b) and Roberts et al., (2009) also agreed that family ties were effectively adopted by displaced persons to cope with the pains and distresses of displacement. Persons who lost family members to deaths and other mishaps lacked family ties as a coping mechanism. According to respondents in the study conducted by Getanda et al., (2015), social support from the government also played pungent roles in protecting displaced persons from poor well-being and mental health. Various governments in collaborations with NGOs and individuals provided the IDPs with food, clothing and shelters. However, most of the IDPs were dissatisfied with the quality of interventions they got from their governments.

Discussion

This study deals with the feminisation of displacement paying particular attention to how the near exclusion of men in the African displacement narratives aggravates men's vulnerability and impedes the realisation of some of the UN SDGs. Among the most significant findings of the paper are that humanitarian actors and policymakers due to the quest for gender equality have engendered discrimination against men in humanitarian interventions. More explicitly, though the experience of displacement is fundamentally disenfranchising for both males and females, there is widespread acknowledgement of the vulnerability of displaced women by policymakers, governments, humanitarian actors and academic literature (Holloway et al., 2019), while the plights of men are widely unacknowledged. This invariably makes displaced men constitute a group of the "forgotten minority". This paper argues that the feminisation of displacement in Africa is a discriminatory approach to humanitarianism and contradicts the landmark Universal Declaration of Human Rights (1948) which reaffirms that "All human beings are born free and equal in dignity and rights...irrespective of sex..."; and can impede the actualisation of the UN goals such as gender equality, gender discrimination and the human rights of all among others.

Sexual violence in a conflict situation is a weapon of war (UN Security Council Resolutions 1325, 1820, 1888 and 1960). During displacement, everyone can be affected by it be they men, women, girls and boys, however, the narratives have been concentrated on the female plights stating that it is more prevalent among them (Call to Action, 2015: 6). According to Kirby (2015), in the past two decades, men and boys have been both potential and actual victims of gender stereotypes and sexual and gender-based violence, rather than simply perpetrators, though the evidence is nascent. In the face of hunger, food insecurity, men could also be at risk of sexual exploitation and abuse in return for food, shelter or other practises of survival sex. Similarly, during detention, men could be at the risk of demands for sexual favours or rape in return for release (UNHCR, 2012). However, the cases of men have been under-reported. In the African context, patriarchy, masculinity, religious orientations as well as cultural and social norms are reinforcing gender inequality by framing men as intrinsically strong and labelling those having such experiences as taboos (Sivakumaran, 2010). Although not prevalent in literature, the engagement in transactional sex is not restricted to only girls and women. Hardship and conflicts also lead to serial marriages where men marry influential women from the diaspora or within their clans, who could enhance their social status and provide them with financial security (Gardner & El-Bushra, 2016).

Humanitarian actors including international organisations have preferred to focus their economic empowerment interventions on women acknowledging that gender discrimination and socially constructed roles denied women alternate sources of livelihood and disenfranchisement from economic opportunities (IASC, 2017). The programmes seek to educate young girls or transfer economic decision-making power to women through targeted cash transfers (Pearce, 2019). This seems not to acknowledge that displacement also separates men from their means of livelihood and disempowers them from providing for their families (Tower, 2020). This study argues that focusing economic empowerment interventions only on women impedes the global quest for the reduction of hunger and the actualisation of food security, poverty reduction and development. It agrees with the view of Cazabat et al., (2020) that assert that despite the milestones and progress, there is still a need for greater efforts in the incorporation of men in the empowerment adventure. This paper also argues that side-lining or excluding men will stand in the way of the actualisation of the empowerment of displaced women and ending domestic violence, especially in the post-displacement African society as their partners and spouses may resent their access to resources and desire to manage them (Pearce, 2019). Also, due to lack of economic opportunities, the vulnerability of men and boys, as well as the neglects of their essential needs, could degenerate over time and affect the wellbeing and welfare of their entire families—including women. This is in tandem with the study by Kaya and Luchtenberg (2018).

Also in the light of the above, when men's sources of income become inaccessible, they are likely to engage in very dangerous coping strategies to enable them to survive and fend for their families. Aside wilful conscription, they are at the risk of being recruited by armed groups in situations of violence/conflicts sometimes for pay since there are no other options for livelihood opportunities, or in exchange for protection. This could breed the grounds for more "Abubakar Shekaus" (Boko Haram insurgency leader in Nigeria) to be groomed, making the quest of an Insurgency-Free-Africa slim and dim. Similarly, school-age boys could be lured into engaging in child labour to assist their families to survive. This will interrupt their education as well as jeopardise their future. What this connotes is that the forceful or even willing recruitment of boys and girls into armed groups will increase the insecurity for the community and the nation at large, which will in turn foster more displacement in the future.

Conclusion and Recommendations

Africa lags in the implementation of the Guiding Principles on Internal Displacement. The management of the displacement crisis in Africa is a far cry from internationally expected standards. The International Organization for Migration mandate of leaving "to leave no one behind," for the creation of a more inclusive and equitable society has not been realised in the African displacement context. Although internal displacement affects men and women uniquely, there is the widespread acknowledgement of the vulnerabilities of women and girls, and contrarily, a widespread reluctance to acknowledge the experiences of men, because it concedes with the weakness of the male agency which negates popular societal structures in Africa. As such, the feminisation of displacement is a narrow, discriminatory and right denying approach to discussing and managing displacement and its ensuing vulnerability. This study recommends that the UN should pay attention to promoting a more equitable and effective response to internal displacement through a more holistic gender-sensitive implementation of the UN Guiding Principles on Internal Displacement and other humanitarian frameworks. The approach of exclusion of displaced men could be detrimental for national, continental and global peace and security as displaced men could be lured into social vices such as terrorism which will inevitably fuel the cycle of conflict and displacement in the future. Thus, there is the need for the revision of the UN Guiding Principles on Internal Displacement to encapsulate the specific needs of men and boys as it did for displaced women and girls in its Principle 4b.

References

Amodu, O., Richter, M., & Salami, B. (2020). A scoping review of the health of conflict-induced internally displaced women in Africa. *International Journal of Environmental Research and Public Health, 17*(4), 1280. https://doi.org/10.3390/ijerph17041280

Amowitz, L., Reis, C., Lyons, K., Vann, B., Mansaray, B., Akinsulure-Smith, A., Taylor, L., & Iacopino, V. (2002). Prevalence of war-related sexual violence and other human rights abuses among internally displaced persons in Sierra Leone. *The Journal of the American Medical Association, 287*(4), 513–521.

Badri, A., Crutzen, R., & Borne, V. (2012). Exposures to war-related traumatic events and post-traumatic stress disorder symptoms among displaced Darfuri female university students: An exploratory study. *BMC Public Health, 12*(603), 1–9.

Barbelet, V., & Wake, C. (2017). *Livelihoods in displacement: From refugee perspectives to aid agency response.* ODI.

Call to Action. (2015). *On Protection from GBV in Emergencies the Action Plan, 2016–2020*, P6.

Cardoso, L., Gupta, J. F., Shuman, S., Cole, H., Kpebo, D., & Falb, K. L. (2016). What factors contribute to intimate partner violence against women in urban, conflict-a_ected settings? Qualitative findings from Abidjan, Cote d'Ivoire. *Journal of Urban Health, 93*, 364–378.

Cazabat, C., Andre, C., Fung, V., Montandon, R., Patten, H., Ponserre, S. & Yasukawa, L. (2020). *Woman and girls in internal displacement.* Internal Displacement Monitoring Centre.

Gardner, J., & El-Bushra, J. (2016). The impact of war on Somali men, and its effects on the family, women and children. Rift Valley Institute Briefing Paper. Nairobi : Rift Valley Institute and UNICEF.

Getanda, E., Papadopoulos, C., & Evans, H. (2015). The mental health, quality of life and life satisfaction of internally displaced persons living in Nakuru County. *Kenya. BMC Public Health, 15*(755), 1–9.

Holloway, K., Stavropoulou, M., & Daigle, M. (2019). *Gender in displacement: The state of play*. HPG Working Paper.

Standing Committee [IASC]. (2017). *Policy on gender equality and the empowerment of women and girls in humanitarian action*. IASC.

Joshua, S., Samuel, S. I., & Olanrewaju, F. O. (2021). Between the Devil and the Deep Blue Sea: Insurgency and Humanitarian Conditions in IDP Camps in Nigeria. *International Journal of Cyber Warfare and Terrorism, 11*(1), 1–19.

Kaya, Z. N., & Luchtenberg, K. N. (2018). *Displacement and women's economic empowerment: Voices of displaced women in the Kurdistan region of Iraq*. Centre for Women, Peace and Security.

Kim, G., Torbay, R., & Lawry, L. (2007). Basic Health, Women's Health, and Mental Health Among Internally Displaced Persons in Nyala Province, South Darfur. *Sudan. American Journal of Public Health, 97*(2), 353–361.

Kirby, P. (2015). Ending sexual violence in conflict: The Preventing Sexual Violence Initiative and its critics. *International Affairs, 91*(3), 457–472.

Obol, J David Lagoro, K Christopher Garimoi, O. *Knowledge and misconceptions about malaria among pregnant women in a post-conflict internally displaced persons' camps in Gulu District*, Malar Res Treat. 2011; 107987. https://doi.org/10.4061/2011/107987. Epub 2011 Sep 14. PMID: 22312565; PMCID: PMC3265282.

Olanrewaju, F. Joshua, S. & Olanrewaju, A. (2020). *Natural resources, conflict and security challenges in Africa* (Article in Press). https://doi.org/10.1177/0974928420961742

Olanrewaju, F. Olanrewaju, A., Omotoso, F., Alabi, J.O., Amoo, E., Loromeke, E. & Ajayi, L.A. (2019). Insurgency and the invisible displaced population in Nigeria: A situational analysis. *Sage Open* 9(2): https://doi.org/10.1177/2158244019846207

Olanrewaju, F., Omotoso, F., & Alabi, J. O. (2018). Boko Haram insurgency and the management of internally displaced women in Nigeria: A situational analysis. *African Population Studies, 32*(1), 3622–3633.

Olanrewaju, F., Omotoso, F., & Alabi, J. O. (2018). Datasets on the challenges of forced displacement and coping strategies among displaced women in selected Internally Displaced persons' (IDP) Camps in Nigeria. *Data in Brief, 20*, 152–158.

Pearce, E. (2019). *We need to write our own names': Gender equality and women's empowerment in the Rohingya humanitarian response in Cox's Bazar*. Women's Refugee Commission.

Reis, C., Amowitz L. L., Hare-Lyons, K. et al. (2002). The prevalence of sexual violence and other human rights abuses among internally displaced persons in Sierra Leone: A population-based assessment. *Physicians for Human Rights.*

Roberts, B., Ocaka, K. F., Browne, J., Oyok, T., & Sondorp, E. (2009). Factors associated with the health status of internally displaced persons in northern Uganda. *Journal of Epidemiology and Community Health, 63*(3), 227–232.

Singh, P., Bhoopathy, S., Worth, H., Seale, H., & Richmond, R. (2015). Nutrition among men and household food security in an internally displaced persons' camp in Kenya. *Public Health Nutrition, 19*(4), 723–731.

Sivakumaran, S. (2010). Lost in translation: UN responses to sexual violence against men and boys in situations of armed conflict. *International Review of the Red Cross, 92*(877), 259–277.

Tower, A. (2020). The Gendered Impacts of Climate Displacement. Climate Refugees. Retrieved from https://www.climate-refugees.org/perspectives/genderedimpactsofclimatechange

UN. (2020). Twelve small actions with big impact for Generation Equality. Retrieved from https://www.unwomen.org/en/news/stories/2020/2/compilation-small-actions-big-impact-for-generation-equality

UN OCHA. (2018). Staying the course: delivering on the ambition of the World Humanitarian Summit, Agenda for Humanity Annual Synthesis Report 2018. In B. Ridsdel, L. Barajas, C. Benedek, R. Gupta, M. Easton and D. McDevitt (Eds).

UNHCR. (2012). Working with men and boy survivors of sexual and gender-based violence in forced displacement. Retrieved from https://www.refworld.org/pdfid/5006aa262.pdf

CHAPTER 14

Xenophobia and Africa's Prospects in the United Nations

Moses Saa-Aondo Andza and Isaac Iorhen Akuva

Introduction

The United Nations was established as a multilateral organization with the purposes of maintaining worldwide peace and security; developing relations among nations, fostering cooperation among nations in other to solve economic, social, cultural, or humanitarian international problems and providing a forum for bringing countries together to meet the UN's purposes and goals (Chapter I, Article I of the United Nations Charter). The founding fathers of the UN envisioned the aforementioned purposes as panacea for the attainment of comfortable living. It is in the light of this that the United Nations (2009) acknowledged the Department of Economic and Social Affairs of the UN Secretariat as a vital interface between global policies in the economic, social and environmental spheres and national action.

M. S.-A. Andza (✉) · I. I. Akuva
Department of Political Science, Federal University Dutsin-Ma, Dutsin-Ma, Katsina State, Nigeria

S. Folarin et al. (eds.), *The United Nations and Sustainable Development Goals*, https://doi.org/10.1007/978-3-030-95971-5_14

African countries at independence were inspired to join the multilateral organization not just because it promises to ensure world peace and security but as the United Nations (n.d.) noted, the multilateral organization holds unique capacities as the world's premier vehicle for international cooperation. And to actualize this, the organization's purposes were fashioned to include but not limited to supporting economic and social development as well as the promotion and protection of human rights which are prerequisites for the achievement of comfortable, healthy and secure living. Conscious of this therefore, African countries wasted no time in fulfilling the requirements for admitting new members into the United Nations and as such, they were so admitted following their application.

Since their admittance into UN, African countries have contributed towards the achievement of the UN as well as enjoyed tremendous support of the organization through the United Nations Office of the Special Adviser on Africa established in 2003. But Africa has been inundated with challenges that are capable of impeding the continent's unity and unanimous voice in the UN. One of such challenges that have assumed a worrying dimension is the issue of xenophobia among African countries. Xenophobia according to Mogekwu (2005) is the fear or hatred of foreigners or strangers embodied in discriminatory attitudes and behaviour, and often culminates in violence, abuses of all types and exhibition of all hatreds. The spate of the menace is widespread especially in South Africa, Libya, Algeria, Ghana and Kenya which to some extent have become the most hostile destinations in the world for African migrants (Claassen, 2017).

Xenophobic attacks in South Africa alone has claimed 148 lives of different African nationals between 2000 and 2019, 1,649,789 deportees between 2001 and 2011 (Department of Home Affairs in Dixon, 2015; Jeynes, 2017; Nyamnjoh, 2014; Sim, 2015). In 2012 and 2016, the Department of Home Affairs (2017, p. 30) indicated that South Africa deported 367,031 people from the top 10 African countries in the rainbow nation and in the wake of the 2019 xenophobic attacks, over 600 Nigerians were evacuated from the rainbow nation (Adebayo, 2019). According to Okeke (2019), Libya is also found to have deported thousands of fellow African nationals to their respective countries as Nigeria alone received 13,884 of its citizens as at December 6, 2019 in the wake of xenophobic attacks in Libya.

In Ghana, Tijani (2019) indicated that in 2018 and 2019, 723 Nigerians were deported on alleged illegal stay, cybercrime and prostitution. Buildings owned by Somalis in Kenya were pelted with stones, looted and in some instances, Somali nationals have been forced out of public service vehicles and beaten up aside the police frequently carrying out massive swoops, arresting anyone who looks like a Somali (Wambua-Soi, 2012). It is against this rising trend of xenophobic attacks among African countries that this paper explores the phenomenon to ascertain what it portends for the future of Africa in the United Nations.

This chapter is divided into seven sections beginning with an introduction as the first section, followed by theoretical framework, which is the second section. Section three identifies the causes of xenophobia on the African continent. Section four is an overview of xenophobic attacks on the African continent while section five dwells on the implication of xenophobia in Africa on the future of the continent in the UN. Section six is the conclusion and the chapter is wrapped up with recommendations in section seven.

Theoretical Framework

This paper adopts the conflict theory in explaining the cause(s) of xenophobic attacks among African countries and its implication on the future of Africa in the United Nations. As Crossman (2019) noted, the conflict theory originated in Karl Marx's work in early 1800 to mid-1800. However, many social theorists have built on Marx's conflict theory to strengthen it, grow it, and refine it over the years. The conflict theory seeks to scientifically clarify the general contour of conflict in the society: how conflict starts and varies, and the effects it brings. The central concerns of the conflict theory according to Coser (2006) are the unequal distribution of scarce resources and power, which breeds conflicts resulting to crisis and violence. And as it relates to our topic, if resources were evenly distributed, the dislike, fear or hatred that is embodied in discriminatory attitudes and behaviour that often culminates in abuses of all types, exhibition of hatred and violence which are the indices of xenophobia would have not been attributed to relative deprivation. The attacks on other African nationals and their businesses especially in Angola, Algeria, South Africa, Libya, Niger, Ghana and Kenya thus explains how distribution of scarce resources which is the fundamental premise of the conflict theory are central in explaining the spate of xenophobic attacks among African countries.

There is job scrunch in Africa and so getting a means of sustainable livelihood is arduous tasks which have made many skilled African migrants within the continent engage in unskilled labour. These unskilled labours through a segment of the workforce associated with minimal economic value for the work performed have interestingly ensured a comfortable, healthy and secure living for them. This thus has pitched the host communities of African migrants against them for utilizing the opportunities in their host countries to make ends meet therefore explaining the spate of xenophobic attacks among African countries. The consequence of this conflict (xenophobia among African countries) is the likely impediment of the continent's unity and lack of unanimous decisions in the UN which may result in the loss of relevance in the foremost multilateral organization. This thus may pose a serious challenge in galvanizing international support for Africa's initiatives and programmes. This theory like any other theory may have its flaws but its analytical prowess in explaining the adduced reasons for xenophobia and the consequences thereof on the future of Africa in the UN is not in doubt.

The Causes of Xenophobia on the African Continent

Claassen (2017) and a report published by Human Sciences Research Council in 2008 as cited in Onditi (2020) identified relative deprivation, specifically intense competition for jobs, commodities and housing, group processes including psychological categorization processes that are nationalistic rather super-ordinate, exceptionalism, or a feeling of superiority in relation to other Africans and exclusive citizenship that excludes others as the major causes of xenophobia among African nations. According to Harris (2001) xenophobia is caused by the fear of loss of social status and identity; a threat, perceived or real, to citizens' economic success; a way of reassuring the national self and its boundaries in times of national crisis.

The tendency for some people to make gains out of a bad situation or create a bad situation in order to make gains out of it cannot be ruled out as a cause of xenophobia among African countries. Politicians and conflict entrepreneurs participate through violent means in many of the active conflicts in Africa which they seek to increase their own power and wealth. It is interesting to note that in many countries on the African continent, conflicts can be a (or virtually the only) opportunity for some people to make a career in terms of power and finance hence the spate of xenophobia among African countries. Chutel (2019, p. 1) alluded to this when he held that "xenophobic violence has erupted in South Africa again, in a cycle that is now being fueled by politicians ramping up anti-immigrant rhetoric in a country where foreigners are easy targets. ... The 2015 attacks were fueled by comments made by Zulu King, Godwill Zwelithini as he flexed his political muscles".

Nevertheless, all the reasons alluded to in this paper as the causes of xenophobia in Africa are more or less symptomatic but that does not in any way invalidate their efficacy in explaining the menace of xenophobia on the continent. However, the main cause of xenophobia in Africa is the contradictions inherent in the political economy of the continent which Ake (1981) painstakingly explained. According to Ake (1981), the incorporation of the black continent into the global capitalist structure by western colonialism and imperialism is the incident which more than anything has influenced whatever has happened or will ever happen in modern-day Africa. The essential contradictions of capitalism which people increasingly cooperate to produce but the product is appropriated by an increasingly small number of people and the concentration of the working class which breeds frustration and aggression thus offers a more convincing explanation of the spate of xenophobic attacks among African countries. So, all the adduced causes of xenophobia in Africa have their roots in the political economy of the continent.

An Overview of Xenophobic Attacks among African Countries

In central Africa's Burundi, the IRIN (2009) avers that in security operations in which "foreigners" were rounded up ironically amid the country's evolving legislation to conform with requirements of the region's commitment to encourage the free flow of people and goods, about 4000 foreign nationals were deported as at February 1, 2009. While in East Africa's Kenya, Wambua-Soi (2012) noted that, there has been growing xenophobia against Somalis as buildings owned by them in Kenya are pelted with stones and looted among other degrading acts.

According to the BBC News October 26, 2006, Niger announced that it would deport to Chad the "Diffa Arabs" living in the Diffa region of eastern Niger numbering about 150,000. Though the decision was later shelved after two girls died and three women suffered miscarriages reportedly after fleeing government forces, the imprints of deep dislike, hatreds, and hostility against the "Diffa Arabs" had already been established. In Ghana, Nigerians have faced inhuman treatment and torture. The Guardian Newspaper August 2, 2019 reported that between January 2018 and January 2019, 723 Nigerians were deported on alleged illegal stay, cybercrime and prostitution which were based on suspicion without any proper investigation. As if that was not enough, the President of Ghana Union of Traders Association (GUTA) Dr. Joseph Obeng threatened that, "these foreign retailers have found a loophole in our retail laws and are capitalizing on that…we will not sit down and watch them take over our market" (The Guardian Newspaper August 2, 2019). And as it were, the Ghanaians made good their threat as over 600 shops belonging to Nigerians were recently locked up by Ghanian traders at the popular Opera Square Electronic market in the central business district of Accra.

In the North African country of Libya, Sub-Saharan African migrants have harrowing experiences of beatings, arson, and robbery that culminated into the summary deportation of thousands of Sub-African nationals. According to Okeke (2019), in the wake of renewed xenophobic attacks on Sub-Saharan African nationals in Libya in 2019, the oil richest North African country deported 168 Nigerians, raising to 13,884 Nigerians returned from Libya since April, 2017 as at December 6, 2019. Algeria like Libya has also repatriated 27,000 Sub-Saharan African migrants since 2015 (European Council on Refugees & Exiles, 2018). This led to the recall of the Guinean ambassador to Algeria by President Alpha Conde of Guinea in 2017 in response to the deep dislike, hatred and hostility by Algerians towards Guineans.

According to Eisenhammer and Paravicini (2018) about 300,000 Congolese fled Angola in 2018 in the wake of xenophobic violence in the southern African country. The account of pillage and death of over 10 Congolese contradicted assertions by the Angolan government that Congolese migrants were voluntarily returning home and that only one person died in a traffic accident. In South Africa, the spate of xenophobic attacks is a regular occurrence that often displaces tens of thousands of African migrants and their businesses and homes are also widely looted (Bearak & Dugger, 2008; McGreal, 2008). According to Nyamnjoh (2014), Sim (2015), Dixon (2015), BBC News September 17, 2019 and the Department of Home Affairs as cited in Jeynes (2017), xenophobic attacks in South Africa alone has claimed 148 lives of different African nationals between 2000 and 2019, 1,649,789 deportees between 2001 and 2011. While between 2012 and 2016, the Department of Home Affairs (2017, p. 30) indicated that South Africa deported 367,031 from the top 10 African countries in the rainbow nation.

The Implication of Xenophobia Among African Countries for Africa's Future in the UN

Xenophobic attacks among African countries may affect Africa's effective representation in the UN Security Council which undoubtedly, is the most powerful and influential organ of the UN. A non-permanent membership of the UN Security Council, which the African continent is entitled to produce at least two members is not primarily about the individual representative country(s) but it is first and foremost about the continent they represent and the UN-membership at large that they are supposed to represent and as such, UN members are bound by the decisions of the Security Council. This is predicated on Article 24(1) and 25 of the UN Charter which states respectively that, "In order to ensure prompt and effective action by the United Nations, its Members confer on the Security Council primary responsibility for the maintenance of international peace and security, and agree that in carrying out its duties under this responsibility the Security Council acts on their behalf" and "The Members of the United Nations agree to accept and carry out the decisions of the Security Council in accordance with the present Charter".

However, the spate of xenophobic attacks among African countries has the potential of furthering individual African nations' agenda in the UN Security Council instead of projecting the image and interest of the African continent as a whole. But it was Verbeke (2018, p. 2) that articulated in a security policy brief about the workings of the Security Council when he held that "It's not about glory and prestige, but about hard work and quality". So furthering their individual nations' agenda is therefore not tantamount to hard work and quality and as such, it will rather demean their status as non-permanent members of the most powerful organ of the UN. The consequences of this on the effective representation of Africa in the UN are manifold. First of all, countries of the African continent may be sidelined and outflanked especially by those who project the general interest of their continent and UN-membership at large. As Verbeke (2018, p. 2) held, "The UN Security Council is a no-nonsense decision making body. Its members are interested only in solving the problem at hand". The damage of African countries reputations in the UN Security Council may also make it difficult for its members on the Council to find their proper place in the setting of the UN Security Council. The permanent members with their dominance and other non-permanent members with their weight, power and authority will make it difficult for African countries with damaged reputation to find the right natural balance among other members of the Council. This thus will make them pathetic. Damaged reputation may also impede African countries on the Council to gain authority. This is because; members of the Council with damaged reputation cannot be entrusted with special missions and chair of the different Sanction Committees. As Verbeke (2018) noted, the Security Council is essentially a deliberative body and as such, it is the distribution of authority rather than power that counts, which paradoxically can result in small countries having a larger say in the Security Council than bigger countries.

As stipulated in rule 83 of the Rules of Procedure of the General Assembly of the UN, the non-permanent members of the Security Council are elected by two-thirds majority of the General Assembly present and voting. This means that, as there are 193 members of the General Assembly, and supposing that all of them are present and voting, a candidate must garner 129 votes to get elected. So all things being equal, there is no country that can get elected in the UN Security Council without the support of the African continent. This is because the African continent alone has 54 members representing 27.97 per-cent of the UN General Assembly and so if they are unanimous in their decisions in the multilateral organization, they would and always have had the tides in their favour in the UN General Assembly. This would have enhanced the continent's influence and relevance. But the question that arises from this is, will the spate of xenophobic attacks among African countries allow for such a united voice of the continent in the UN General Assembly? Recent events occasioned by the spate of xenophobic attacks among African countries indicate that xenophobia is capable of splitting the continent's voice in the UN General Assembly. The recalling of the Guinean Ambassador to Algeria by President Alpha Conde of Guinea in response to the xenophobic attacks on other Africans by Algerians in 2017 as recollected by Agbenonwossi (2018) and also the recalling of the Nigerian High Commissioner to South Africa by President Muhammadu Buhari in response to the spate of xenophobic attacks on other Africans by South

Africans in 2019 (Ameh, 2019) are pointers to a possible split of a united African voice in the UN General Assembly.

The European Council on Refugees and Exiles (2018) also noted that, the Algerian embassy in Bamako, Mali was vandalized by repatriated Malians from Algeria in anger of the xenophobic attacks they faced in Algeria. The same scenario played out in Nigeria as Nigerians went after South African business interest in the country. It might be the view of some people as even expressed by the Office of the Special Adviser on Africa (n.d.) at the UN that, Africa is increasingly speaking with one voice on global issues. This, the OSSA (n.d.) cited the Common African position on the UN Review of Peace Operations 2015, African Group perspective on Financing for Development Conference 2015 among others as examples of Africa's unanimous voice in the UN. This thus indicates that African countries may not necessarily bring their internal differences to bear on their representation in the UN and as such, they will work as one indivisible whole for a secured future of the continent in the organization. This thought is however countered by the phrase closely associated with the former Speaker of the United States House of Representatives Tip O'Neill as cited in Sote (2019) that, all politics is local and as such, the spate of xenophobic attacks among African countries will definitely exert on their thinking and decisions at the UN hence a split in the continent's voice in the multilateral organization may be inevitable.

Xenophobia among African countries will also expose to the UN and the international community that Pan-Africanism, the African Union, NEPAD, African Renaissance, Silencing the Guns Agenda 2063 and other African ideas and programmes are just but elite's projects that are not backed by current trends among African populations. This thus is an affirmation of Ajulor (2018) assertion that, many policies and programmes in African countries fail because of policy implementation challenges such as unrealistic goal settings, political patronage, and neglect of target beneficiaries and lack of consideration for the policy environment. This may therefore make it difficult for the continent to galvanize the UN's support for such initiatives and or programmes. Xenophobia among African countries will also expose the hypocritical nature of the continent to the commitment to achieving the purposes of the UN and adhering to international conventions and treaties. African countries are signatories to various international conventions and treaties that aim to protect strangers and foreigners in their countries. Article 4(a) of the International Convention on the Elimination of All Forms of Racial discrimination to which all African nations are signatory, requires state parties to declare, among others, an offence punishable by law, all dissemination of ideas based on racial superiority or hatred, incitement to racial discrimination, as well as acts of violence or incitement to such acts against any race or group of persons of another colour or ethnic organization. This provision is supposed to address the issue of xenophobia among African countries if they are not being hypocritical to international conventions and treaties. To confirm this hypocrisy, it is African government officials who are very conversant with the provisions of this convention that sometimes incite their fellow citizens to carry out xenophobic attacks on foreigners or strangers in their countries.

Conclusion

This chapter draws the attention of African political leaders to the implications of xenophobic attacks in African future in the United Nations. The analysis shows that xenophobia in Africa is on the rise and it has threatened relations among some countries in Africa. It is obvious there are no strategic measures to curb the phenomenon.

If xenophobia among African countries is not properly addressed, the phenomenon will have severe implications on the continued relevance of Africa in the UN. Therefore, the most important factors for a secured future of Africa in the UN are stability, security, peace and love for one another on the continent.

Recommendations

1. There should be a comprehensive reorientation of Africans to see themselves as equal human beings in Africa.
2. African governments should put in place mechanisms for skills acquisition for their citizens to bridge the gap between citizens and immigrants to address relative deprivations.
3. Primitive accumulation of wealth in Africa which drives people to engage in conflict in Africa should be de-emphasized.
4. Group processes that are super-ordinate should be encouraged over and above nationalistic ones by conscientizing the people on universal norms, treaties and conventions.

References

Adebayo, B. (2019, September 9). Nigeria to evacuate 640 citizens from South Africa after Xenophobic attacks. *CNN News*. https://edition.cnn.com/2019/09/09/africa/nigeria-to-evacuate-citizens-from-south-africa-intl/index.html

Agbenonwossi, E. (2018, January 17). Guinea's Alpha Code recalls ambassador to Algiers. *Medafrica*. https://medafricatimes.com/14898-guineas-alpha-conde-recalls-ambassador-to-algiers.html

Ajulor, O. V. (2018). The challenges of policy implementation in Africa and sustainable development goals. *International Journal of Social Sciences, 3*(3), 1497–1518.

Ake, C. (1981). *A political economy of Africa*. Longman Nigeria Plc.

Ameh, J. (2019, September 4). Xenophobia: Nigeria recalls high commissioner to South Africa, shuns WES. *Punch Newspaper*. https://punchng.com/breaking-xenophobia-nigeria-recalls-ambassador-to-south-africa-shuns-wes/

BBC News October 26, 2006. http://news.bbc.co.uk/2/hi/africa/6087048.stm

Bearak, B., & Dugger, C. W. (2008, May 20). South Africans take out rage on immigrants. https://www.nytimes.com/2008/05/20/world/africa/20safrica.html

Charter of the United Nations and Statute of the International Court of Justice San Francisco 1945. https://treaties.un.org/doc/publication/ctc/uncharter.pdf

Chutel, L. (2019, April 2). South Africa's election season rhetoric has sparked fresh xenophobic attacks on African migrants. https://www.google.com/amp/s/qz.com/africa/1585736/xenophobic-attacks-on-africans-in-south-africa-ahead-of-elections/amp/

Claassen, C. (2017). *Explaining South African xenophobia*. Working Paper No. 173. https://afrobarometer.org/sites/default/files/publications/Documents%20de%20travail/afropaperno173_xenophobia_in_south_africa.pdf

Coser, L. (2006). Conflict and critical theories. http://us.corwin.com/sites/default/files/upm-binaries/13636_Chapter7.pdf

Crossman, A. (2019, July 3). Understanding conflict theory. https://www.thoughtco.com/conflict-theory-3026622

Department of Home Affairs. (2017). White paper on international migration for South Africa. http://www.dha.gov.za/WhitePaperonInternationalMigration-20170602.pdf

Dixon, R. (2015, April 17). Attacks on foreigners spread in South Africa; Weekend feared. https://www.latimes.com/world/africa/la-fg-south-africa-foreigners-20150417-story.html

Eisenhammer, S., & Paravicini, G. (2018, October 25). Three days of violence that emptied an Angolan town of Congolese. *Reuters*. https://www.reuters.

com/article/us-angola-drc-violence-insight/three-days-of-violence-that-emptied-an-angolan-town-of-congolese-idUSKCN1MZ1UI

European Council on Refugees and Exiles. (2018, March 30). Algeria: Mass deportations of African migrants. https://www.ecre.org/algeria-mass-deportations-of-african-migrants/

Guardian News Paper August 2, 2019. https://m.guardian.ng/opinion/xenophobic-attacks-in-ghana/

Harris, B. (2001). A foreign experience: Violence, crime and Xenophobia during South Africa's transition. Centre for the Study of Violence and Reconciliation (CSVR).

International Convention on the Elimination of All Forms of Racial Discrimination Adopted and opened for signature and ratification by General Assembly resolution 2106 (XX) of 21 December 1965 entry into force 4 January 1969, in accordance with Article 19. https://www.ohchr.org/EN/ProfessionalInterest/Pages/CERD.aspx

IRIN, Burundi: Deportations not a sign of xenophobia—Minister, 4 February 2009. https://www.refworld.org/docid/498ab63fc.html

Jeynes, K. (2017, July 26). FACTSHEET: Detention and deportation of undocumented migrants in South Africa at the Lindela Repatriation Centre. https://africacheck.org/factsheets/lindela-repatriation-centre-migrants/

McGreal, C. (2008, May 20). Thousands seek sanctuary as South Africans turn on refugees. https://www.theguardian.com/world/2008/may/20/zimbabwe.southafrica

Mokegwu, M. (2005). African Union: Xenophobia as a poor intercultural communication. *Ecquid Novi-African Journalism Studies, 26*(1), 5–20.

Nyamnjoh, F. B. (2014). Exorcising the demons within: Xenophobia, violence and statecraft in contemporary South Africa. *Journal of Contemporary Studies, 32*(3), 397–401.

Okeke, I. (2019, December 6). Libya deports 168 Nigerians, raising to 15,731 members deported since 2017. https://businessday.ng/top-stories/article/libya-deports-168-nigerians-raising-to-15-731-number-deported-since-2017/

Onditi, F. (2020). *Conflictology: Systems, institutions, and mechanisms in Africa.* Lexington Books.

OSSA (n.d.). Speaking as one. https://www.un.org/en/africa/osaa/advocacy/onevoice.shtml

Rules of Procedure of the General Assembly of the United Nations (embodying amendments and additions adopted by the General Assembly up to September 2007), New York, 2008. https://www.un.org/depts/DGACM/Uploaded%20docs/rules%20of%20procedure%20of%20ga.pdf

Sim, D. (2015, December 30). South Africa Xenophobia: Anti-immigrant violence in Durban and Johannesburg (photo report). https://www.ibtimes.

co.uk/south-africa-xenophobia-anti-immigrant-violence-durban-johannesburg-photo-report-1496588

Sote, L. (2019, March 6). All politics is local. *Punch Newspapers*. https://punchng.com/all-politics-is-local/

Tijani, A. (2019, March 6). Ghana's deportation of Nigerians is a new chapter in a very ugly history that must end. *African Liberty*. https://www.africanliberty.org/2019/03/06/ghanas-deportation-of-nigerians-is-a-chapter-in-a-very-ugly-history-that-must-end/

United Nations. (2009). Achieving the Global Public Health Agenda: Dialogues at the Economic and Social Council. https://www.un.org/en/ecosoc/docs/pdfs/achieving_global_public_health_agenda.pdf

United Nations. (n.d.). Peace, dignity and equality on a healthy planet. https://www.un.org/en/sections/issues-depth/africa/index.html

Verbeke, J. (2018). What is it like to be a non-permanent member of the UN Security Council? http://aei.pitt.edu/94372/1/SPB96.pdf

Wambua-Soi, C. (2012, November 20). Rising Xenophobia against Somalis in Kenya. https://www.aljazeera.com/blogs/africa/2012/11/50161.html

CHAPTER 15

Freeing the Future from the Past: Redefining Soft Power and Cultural Diplomacy in a World of "Unequals"

Clemson Ayegbusi, Oluwafunke Folarin, Oluwakemi Udoh, and Sheriff Folarin

Conceptualizing Soft Power and Cultural Diplomacy

Soft Power

Over the years, there has been an increase in the usage of the term "soft power" among scholars and decision-makers alike in their attempt to discuss why and how states seek to get various forms of political and cultural attraction (Grix & Brannagan, 2016). In fact, "soft power" is

C. Ayegbusi
Babcock University, Ilisan-Remo, Ogun State, Nigeria

O. Folarin
Department of Leadership Studies, North Carolina A&T State University, Greensboro, NC, USA

S. Folarin et al. (eds.), *The United Nations and Sustainable Development Goals*, https://doi.org/10.1007/978-3-030-95971-5_15

constantly at the forefront when discussing state relations in the international system. This is because, according to the realists' vision of the global political system, the interactions of states are largely centred on (hard) power acquisition and power politics. Although power is an important and dominant concept in state relations, the landscape of international relations is changing continuously and this has led to the question of what stands as a country's power. Some scholars view power in terms of elements of national power. For instance, Mearsheimer (2001 cited in Gallaroti, 2011) opines that, "power is based on the particular material capabilities that a state possesses". Power, portrayed in terms of material capabilities, focuses on state possessions that, when combined, engender dominance and determine overall national power. These resources are the size of the nation's armed forces, size of territory and population, geographical location and gross national product (Raimzhanova, 2015). This notion of power is summarily termed "hard power".

Soft power on the other hand, focuses on a state's ability to shape the preference of others without using any form of force, coercion or aggression. Instead, it employs the tools of persuasion and co-option rather than military force and economic inducement in achieving desired outcomes (Nye, 1990). At the time the concept was coined by Joseph Nye, some scholars opined that the U.S. had become over-stretched as a result of its involvement in the war and its powers in international politics were bound to decline (Kennedy, 1987). Nye argued that although the U.S. might have lost its economic and military dominance, it still had the advantage of its attractive culture, foreign policy and political values and institutions over the rest of the world. This is what he refers to as "soft power". Therefore, engaging its attractive ideals and culture would further secure the hegemony of the U.S. (Nye, 1990). To him, if the U.S. military power increased, its capacity to persuade would decline and

O. Udoh (✉) · S. Folarin
Department of Political Science and International Relations, Covenant University, Ota, Ogun State, Nigeria
e-mail: oluwakemi.udoh@covenantuniversity.edu.ng

S. Folarin
e-mail: sheriff.folarin@covenantuniversity.edu.ng

would therefore, lose attraction. Soft power affects, appeals, entices, and induces others to believe and accept the rule, sense of value, lifestyle and social systems through moral conditions. Attraction is the key means for realizing goals rather than violence or temptation (Li & Lang, 2017) and attraction, more often than not, results in acceptance or acquiescence. In order to establish preferences, Nye identified culture, political ideology and attractive personalities as having moral authority and legitimacy.

Cultural Diplomacy

In any attempt at discussing the concept of cultural diplomacy, it is important to analyse the two terms that make up the concept: ***culture*** and ***diplomacy***. Tim-Tooney and Chung (2012, p. 16) define culture as a learned system that consists of patterns of traditions, beliefs, values, norms, meanings and symbols that are passed down from one generation to the next and are shared by varying degrees by the interacting members of a community. These patterns and manifestations of traditions, beliefs and values include arts, education, language, religion and food. In a similar vein, the UNESCO Universal Declaration on Cultural Diversity (2001) defines it as "the set of distinctive spiritual, material, intellectual and emotional features of society or a social group that encompasses in addition to art and literature, lifestyles, ways of living together, value systems, traditions and beliefs. Additionally, Czarnowski simply defines culture as 'the shared heritage, the fruit of the creative and processed efforts of countless generations". Matthes (2010) posits that culture is a wide range of learned human behaviour patterns, which are usually threatened by the popularity of other existing cultures.

On the other hand, diplomacy, which is a central activity that has evolved in inter-state relations over centuries, has been defined by Satow (2011) as the "application of intelligence and tact to the conduct of official relations between governments of independent states". Berridge (2010) gives an expanded meaning by explaining that diplomacy is essentially a political activity that is aimed at enabling states to secure the objectives of their foreign policy without resorting to force, propaganda or law. It consists of communication between officials designed to implement foreign policy.

For Pajtinka (2014), it refers to a set of activities that are either taken directly by states or their diplomatic representatives with the aim of promoting their foreign policies through the means of cultural exchange with other states.

In tracing the history of cultural diplomacy in inter-state relations, it is apposite to state that it is an old practice. Indeed, the trans-border movements of early explorers, traders and artists have all had an element of cultural transfers, which facilitated some form of cultural exchange. Stelowska (2015) argues that culture began to travel from one region to the other as far back as in ancient Greece. It travelled with migrations, trade and conquest. In this era, diplomats carried their own culture to foreign lands and came back home with foreign culture. Such interactions were also characterized by exchange of gifts, which was for establishing mutual trust. In modern times, precisely in the nineteenth century, cultural diplomacy continued as an activity that was kept in the realms of entrepreneurship, individual interest groups and art (Gienow-Hecht, 2010). France was the first European nation to develop an official programme of cultural diplomacy for the advancement of its image and cultural prestige abroad. In doing this, it created the *Alliance Francaise* in 1883 to spread the French culture by teaching the French language to its colonies (Einbinder, 2013). It is important to mention that historically, in the development and advancement of cultural diplomacy, nations adopted different strategies and methods. For France and Germany during the nineteenth century, it was the promotion of their indigenous language while Britain concentrated on education (Gienow-Hecht, 2010).

In the twentieth century, Germany used its culture as an instrument of propaganda towards Latin America when Hitler rose to power. This provoked a reaction from the U.S., which ultimately led to the adoption of the Convention for the Promotion of Inter-American Cultural Relations in 1936 in Buenos Aires (Stelowska, 2015). In addition, the Cold War between the U.S. and the Soviet Union motivated the use of culture as a weapon during the ideological war. In fact, the most exhibited instruments of cultural diplomacy during the war were the Russian ballet and American music. A series of activities took place during this period as the U.S. government institutionalized cultural diplomacy in the U.S.. The U.S. Information Agency (USIA) was established in 1953 to promote America's national interests abroad through cultural diplomacy and information programmes. The agency is called US Information Service (USIS) in other countries where it fosters mutual understanding between the U.S. and these countries (Stelowska, 2015). The Fulbright exchange programme came into existence while the Central Intelligence Agency organized the Advancing American Art Exhibition in 1946. However, with no ideological opponent at the end of the Cold War, the motivation for cultural diplomacy declined because there were no means of funding the initiatives during that era. The existence of USIA ceased in 1999 as a result of America's foreign affairs reforms and part of the agency was incorporated into the U.S. Department of State. After USIA was abolished, the Public Affairs Sections (PAS) of the U.S. Missions abroad under the Public Diplomacy and Public Affairs Office of the U.S. Department of State, assumed the responsibilities of America's cultural and public diplomacy. It was not until the September 9/11 attacks that the U.S. began to explore the possibilities of using culture as a means of politics (Stelowska, 2015). It is believed that constant interaction of people throughout history and exchange of their cultures have significantly improved relations between opposing groups.

Theory of National Power and National Interest

Power is a prominent concept in the field of international politics. However, there is no consensus among scholars on the role and nature of power in international relations. For this reason, Morgenthau (1948) opines that political power is one of the most controversial issues in Political Science. Waltz (1986) agrees that even though the concept of power is a major concept in realist theories of international politics, achieving a proper definition remains problematic and controversial. However, some scholars have attempted to offer some insights into the meaning of (national) power.

For Ahmad (2012), national power refers to the mix of strategic, military, economic, political and psychological strengths and weakness of a state. It is a state's "capacity to pursue strategic goals through purposeful action" (Tellis et al., 2000). Meanwhile, Boudon and Bourricaud (1989) define national power in terms of resources, strategies and outcomes. As national resources, power is the totality of the capabilities that are at the disposal of any state for the purpose of influencing others. These capabilities include its population, natural resources, armed forces and economy. Power, in terms of strategies, refers to the processes, relationships and situations through which states influence one another. Lastly, as outcomes, it focuses on the extent to which a state can achieve its desired goals or national interests.

Nations have interests and the foreign policy of every nation reflects its national interests. The pursuit and realization of these interests are the major reasons nations engage in any form of interaction with one another in the international system. In some circumstances, their interests could be incompatible and in others, they could harmonize. It is the reason nations go to war and seek cooperation with one another. As a matter of fact, realists argue that the concept of national interest "assumes continuous conflict and threat of war, to be minimized through the continuous adjustment of conflicting interests by diplomatic action" (Morgenthau, 1952). Indeed, national interests help nations to determine their priorities and chart their own course in international relations.

For Ajayi et al. (2015), national interest is a major explanatory instrument in analysing and understanding foreign policy. This is reinforced by the fact that by engaging in international politics, a state seeks its betterment, and power (which is both an end and, a means to an end). The methods that states adopt in a bid to secure their interests in the international community include; diplomacy; propaganda, alliances, coercion/aggression and economic means. Finally, the pursuit of national interest and power are central to inter-state relations as these two forces shape state behaviour beyond their borders.

Soft Power and Cultural Diplomacy in the Foreign Policies of America and China

Cultural diplomacy is an integral part of American diplomacy. It is at the centre of its foreign policy from the Second World War, which peaked during the Cold War. The Marshall Plan, through which neutral states and vulnerable allies received American economic boost, represented the height of American soft power in the Cold War to keep the Soviet Union and communist influence away from the countries (Bischof & Petschar, 2017). The Plan, enacted in 1948 was the European Recovery Programme, which provided aid to Western Europe after the devastation of Second World War II. It provided over $15 billion to help finance rebuilding efforts on the European continent. The U.S. claimed it was humanitarian, but it was extended to communist states with the aim of bringing them over to capitalist Europe (Bischof & Petschar, 2017). In a grand containment policy, Austria, Belgium, Denmark, France, West Germany, Great Britain, Greece, Iceland, Italy, Luxembourg, the Netherlands, Norway, Sweden, Switzerland and Turkey benefitted. These countries remained impenetrable for the Soviet Union throughout the Cold War.

A characteristic of American economic diplomacy is its cultural component or accompaniment. Countries that have benefited from American economic support or that have strong economic ties with the U.S. often also extend strong cultural ties. Before the end of the Cold War, the U.S. maintained USIS and cultural offices everywhere it has a significant presence. Interestingly, at the end of the super power rivalry, the U.S. has extended cultural influence to regions and countries that were traditional communist enclaves. Aside keeping cultural officers in their embassies, the U.S. has built, strategically and systematically, a huge and strong base of cultural ambassadors globally. Through its prestigious educational, cultural and professional exchanges such as the Fulbright programmes, Hubert Humphrey Fellowship programme, TechWomen, Fortune Department of State Women's Mentoring programme, Study of the U.S. Institutes, Secondary school teachers and students' exchanges, Youth exchanges, among others, the U.S. keeps its allies and other nations closer to Washington, DC (U.S. Department of State, 2020).

The American success in sustaining hegemonic dominance by cultural (and not by aggressive) means has been copied by other powers. These include Britain, France, Russia, Canada, Saudi Arabia, Qatar and China. While Saudi Arabia and few other Middle Eastern states have succeeded in replicating an America-style dominance in North Africa and the West African sub-region, China is by far more aggressive and successful in keeping most of the world in the wraps. China's cultural diplomacy is closely tied to the Chinese Yuan, technical aid, loans, agreements giving Chinese workers, companies and citizens unlimited access to operate freely in host countries (Mauldin, 2019). Chinese markets, stores, food courts, settlements (towns/villages), goods and services operate in major cities through these special agreements. These effectively build and eventually transfer the Mandarin culture to these countries.

Another feature of Chinese soft power and cultural diplomacy is the aggressive nature of pursuing exchange programmes with countries in the Global South. Conscious that the South is a fertile ground to start a global hegemony, particularly in the face of a freefall of American economic and cultural influence in the last four years, China has reached agreements with governments and companies. Among the accords are collaborations with governments of African, Middle East and South Asia in establishment of schools, exchange of scholars, expansion of trade and granting of loans and financial stimulus that have made China more attractive to deal with than the U.S.. More Chinese walk the streets of Lagos, Monrovia, Nairobi, Johannesburg, Algiers and Dakar, than Americans or the French, which is the hallmark of success of Chinese cultural diplomacy. China has promoted its culture through movies, festivals, music, religious forums, sports, tourism and of course, its numerous products in households around the world.

Aside social and economic means, China is also maintaining subtle control of the world through the Confucius Institute, established in educational institutions around the world, to export Chinese cultural elements and has tried to make the Chinese media global players. The aim of the Institute is to enhance China's soft power and project its image of peaceful rise. No wonder, China has seen a significant rise in its cultural profile in the world.

Excesses (and Hardness) of the Soft Power

Despite the apparent "softness" of a nation's soft power, it has been argued that it could be a strong tool that could be wielded in exerting hegemonic influence over other nations' values, culture and indeed their foreign policies. In such a situation, soft power becomes an intangible part of control that the hegemon employs to transfer ideas and values that are widely accepted by other states (Dirzauskaite & Ilinca, 2017). For instance, Brilmayer (1994 cited in Dirzauskaite & Ilinca, 2017) expresses that a hegemon could succeed in awakening the desire for political morality and respect for human rights in other nations, when the expectations of their population to be treated equally is violated. The hegemon redirects focus from itself towards shaping the behaviour of others in order to achieve its own underlying interests. Also, public diplomacy which is an instrument of soft power has been used over the years to communicate directly with foreign people, with the purpose of affecting their thinking and ultimately their governments' (Nisbet et al., 2004). The media, which is one of the most important channels for public diplomacy has been used to manipulate societies to satisfy the foreign policy goals of nations (Yukaruc, 2017). The Voice of America has played a vital role in spreading American values to the Middle East and other parts of the world; Turkey uses the Anatolia News Agency (AA) to publish news in Croatian Bosnian and Serbian languages through its office in Sarajevo (Yesil, 2015).

The hegemonic tendencies of a nation imply that it has the resources to influence the behaviour of lesser and competing powers. The American and western ideologies and values are considered the most attractive in the world and have been imbibed by many nations globally. These values have to a large extent shaped and conditioned the landscape of international relations among states and turned soft power into a theory of liberal hegemony. What this means is that for non-Western states to be considered successful vis-a-vis soft power, they must emulate the political and cultural values of the West. Hence, Nye's conception of soft power is inconsistent because it focuses essentially on the soft power of the U.S. without assessing its impact on the rest of the world. In conclusion, the resources of soft power are deployed by powerful states to create hegemonic systems that would shape the international system through non-coercive means.

A Case for New Soft Power and Cultural Diplomacy

Soft power is unarguably a pleasant alternative to hard power. Hard power (use of military might push national agenda) can be crude and can be the cause of conflicts and wars around the world, as experience has shown. But soft power has also been a subtle means of keeping vulnerable nations servile or subservient. Its component, cultural diplomacy, has been more of a smokescreen to maintain hegemonic influence. In power politics, hegemony, survival, preservation, or relevance or dominance is the ultimate goal of states. Therefore, if cultural diplomacy will actualize any or all of these, then it is not considered an oddity if it is being perfected.

However, at the rate China is going, determined to take over the world at all cost, applying the brakes is important if an implosion must not result in a major global explosion of conflict. A redefinition of cultural diplomacy is desirable. The United Nations pushes for equality and equity. With the consciousness that the world wars and multiple conflicts were caused by the absence of these, equality, equity and equal status in the global community have characterized UN agenda from 1945. For instance, France had through its cultural diplomacy in Africa created a master–servant configuration between it and the former colonies on the one hand; and caused disaffection on the other hand, between its affiliates and their Anglophone neighbours (Nwankwor, 2013). This has resulted in constant frictions and distrust leading to lack of cooperation between the two divides.

China's desperation to outdo the U.S. and western powers has been at a huge cost for the nations at its mercy. Its aggressive cultural diplomacy has redefined the context of cultural diplomacy. Nations are losing their identity and control over their own values. China wishes to see African states adopt the Mandarin language as a medium of communication and invests heavily in giving access to the linguistic value both in Africa and in metropolitan Beijing.

The idea of soft power in the first place, suggests inequality and cultural tool of diplomatic engagements as a tool suggests a relationship between two unequal cultures. The soft power shows military and economic might at the disposal of nation, which will use diplomatic instruments to subjugate, even by culture or public diplomacy. What this implies is that, the nation chooses not to use hard power to achieve the same objective. But dominance is still the crux and this is not the world that can guarantee justice, peace and order. It is against this backdrop that a "new soft power" (and cultural diplomacy) becomes necessary. A realist scholar will find it difficult to recommend a kind of power that will only help others and not fulfil national interest. But the reality, ironically, is that, this is one of the major factors that can promote and sustain a world of peace and order. In addition, powerful nations should promote a diplomacy of genuine exchange of ideas, values and people.

Conclusion

This chapter has been examining the contexts of soft power from the lens of one of its components—cultural diplomacy. Soft power is supposed to be a persuasive approach to international relations, typically involving the use of economic or cultural influence. But, this is changing. Powerful nations like China, France and some Arab powers (which use religion and promote religious fanaticism in some developing countries to establish cultural influence) seem to use an aggressive variant of soft power an obviously one-sided and firm cultural means to force their whims on other nations. This is tantamount to cultural imperialism and not "diplomacy".

If soft power is channelled towards taking less-developed nations along in meeting the 2030 Sustainable Development Goals, so that no country will be left behind in human development, soft power will have a whole new and tenable meaning. However, in a system of states where the gulf between the wealthy and poor countries is widening, any diplomacy or power that tends to further undermine the capacity or potential of other nations will only culminate in pet-up resentments and silent contempt, which are a recipe for international conflict.

References

Ahmad, A. (2012). Concept of national power. *Strategic Studies, 32*(2/3), 83–101.

Ajayi, L., Njoaguani, O., Olorunyomi, B., & Folarin, S. (2015). Nigeria's foreign policy and codification of national interest: A prescriptive analysis. *Covenant University Journal of Politics and International Affairs (CUJPIA), 3*(2), 68–81.

Berridge, G. (2010). *Diplomacy: Theory and practice* (4th ed.). Palgrave Macmillan.

Bischof, G., & Petschar, H. (2017). *The Marshall Plan: Saving Europe, rebuilding Austria.* University of New Orleans Publishing.

Boudon, R., & Borricaud, F. (1989). *A critical dictionary of sociology.* Translated and selected by Peter Hamilton. University of Chicago Press.

Dirzauskaite, G., & Ilinca, N. (2017). *Understanding "hegemony" in international relations theories.* Aalborg University.

Einbinder, M. (2013). Cultural diplomacy: Harmonising international relations through music. *A Master of Arts Thesis, Gallatin School of Individualised Studies, New York University.*

Gallaroti, G. (2011). Soft power: What it is, why it's important, and the conditions under which it can be effectively used. *Journal of Political Power*, Division II Faculty Publications. Paper 57.

Gienow-Hecht, J. (2010). What are we searching for? Culture, diplomacy, agents and the state. In M. Donfried & J. Gienow-Hecht, J. (Eds.), *In searching for a cultural diplomacy.* Berghahn Books.

Grix, J., & Brannagan, P. (2016). Of mechanisms and myths: Conceptualising states' "soft power" strategies through sports mega events. *Journal of Diplomacy and Statecraft, 27*(6), 251–272.

Ivor, R., & Satow, E. (Eds.). (2011). *Satow's diplomatic practice* (6th ed.). Oxford University Press.

Kennedy, P. (1987). *The rise and fall of the great powers.* Random House.

Li, L., & Lang, H. (2017). Joseph Nye's soft theory and its revelation towards ideological and political education. *Humanities and Social Science, 5*(2), 69–74. https://doi.org/10.11648/j.hss.20170502.13

Matthes, D. (2010). Culture, globalisation, and international relations. International Symposium on Cultural Diplomacy.

Mauldin, J. (2019). *China's grand plan to take over the world.* Retrieved on 14/10/2020 from https://www.forbes.com/sites/johnmauldin/2019/11/12/chinas-grand-plan-to-take-over-the-world/#65d87acc5ab5

Mearsheimer, J. (2001). *The tragedy of Great Power politics.*

Morgenthau, H. (1948). *Politics among nations: The struggle for power and peace* (3rd ed.). Alfred A. Knopf.

Morgenthau, H. (1952). Another "Great Debate": The national interest of the United States. *The American Political Science Review, 46*(4), 961–988. Retreived from https://doi.org/10.2307//1952108

Nisbet, E., Nisbet, M., Scheufele, D., & Shanahan, J. (2004). Public diplomacy, television news, and Muslim opinion. *The Harvard International Journal of Press/Politics, 9*(2), 11–37.

Nwankwor, M. (2013). French and cultural diplomacy—The African experience. *International Affairs and Global Strategy, 10.*

Nye, J. (1990). *Bound to lead: The changing nature of American power.* Basic Books.

Pajtinka, E. (2014). Cultural diplomacy in the theory and practice of contemporary international relations. *Politické vedy, 17*(4), 95–108. ISSN 1335–2741. Retrieved from https://www.researchgate.net/publication/269763112_Cultural_Diplomacy_in_Theory_and_Practice_of_Contemporary_International-Relations

Raimzhanova, A. (2015). Power in IR: Hard, soft, and smart. *Institute for Cultural Diplomacy and the University of Bucharest.*

Stelowska, D. (2015). Culture in international relations: Defining cultural diplomacy. *Public Journal of Political Science, 1*(3), 50–72.

Tellis, A. J., Bially, J., Layne, C., & McPherson, M. (2000). *Measuring national power in the post-industrial age.* Rand Corp.

Ting-Toomey, S., & Chung, L. (2012). *Understanding cultural communication.* Roxbury Publishing Co.

United States Department of State. (2020). *Exchange programs.* Retrieved 11/10/2020 from https://findit.state.gov/search?query=exchange+programs&affiliate=dos_stategov

Waltz, K. (1986). Reflections on theory of international politics: A response to my critics. In R. O. Keohane (Ed.), *Neorealism and its critics* (pp. 322–345). Columbia University Press.

Yukaruc, U. (2017). A critical approach to soft power. *Journal of Bitlis Eren University Institute of Social Science, 6*(2), 23–45.

Yesil, B. (2015). Transnationalization of Turkish dramas: Exploring the convergence of local and global market imperatives. *Global Media and Communication, 11*(1), 43–60.

PART III

Sustainable Health, Science and Technology

CHAPTER 16

Maximizing Olefins Production from Fluid Catalytic Cracking (FCC) Unit Using Zsm-05 Catalyst for the Nigerian Petrochemical Industry

Angela Mamudu, Francis Elehinafe, Felix Ishola, Emeka Okoro, and Gideon Ogunduyile

Introduction

Although Nigeria is ranked the largest crude oil producer in Africa and the sixth-largest oil-exporting country in the world, its petrochemical industry remains a significant source of concern (Ajee, 2015). Currently,

A. Mamudu (✉) · F. Elehinafe · G. Ogunduyile
Chemical Engineering Department, Covenant University, Ota, Nigeria
e-mail: angela.mamudu@covenantuniversity.edu.ng

F. Ishola
Mechanical Engineering Department, Covenant University, Ota, Nigeria

E. Okoro
Petroleum Engineering Department, Covenant University, Ota, Nigeria

S. Folarin et al. (eds.), *The United Nations and Sustainable Development Goals*, https://doi.org/10.1007/978-3-030-95971-5_16

Nigeria houses three petrochemical companies, namely: Warri Refinery and Petrochemical Company (WRPC), Kaduna Refinery and Petrochemical Company (KRPC), and Indorama Eleme Petrochemical Company (IEPC), which was formerly known as Eleme Petrochemicals Company Limited (EPCL). The similarity among these companies and any other petrochemical company at large is the need to use the by-products from the crude oil refineries as its feed. Though there have been different schools of thought towards the unproductiveness of the Nigerian petrochemical industry, the unavailability of primary raw materials is vital (Mamudu et al., 2019).

Petrochemicals, which are chemical products derived from petroleum, get their feed from different groups (Ji, 2015). These groups include olefins (ethylene, propylene, butylene, and butadiene), aromatics (benzene, toluene, and xylene), and synthesis gas (Balinga, 2015). Olefins, which are mostly used, are unsaturated aliphatic hydrocarbons with one or more double bonds in their chemical structures (Amghizar et al., 2017). Their derivatives are used directly as finished products or intermediates for further processing. Some of these petrochemical products include paint, brushes, socket covers, oil filters, tires, Teflon pots, pans, plastic bags, car seats, glasses, sporting equipment, cameras, shoes, tents, umbrellas, lamps, bandages, toys, tape measure, etc. (Mamudu & Chandler, 2019).

The crude oil refinery envelopes some set of processes (separation, conversion, upgrading, treatment, and blending) that converts the raw oil into valuable products. Atmospheric and Vacuum distillation units are standard separation processes that separate the crude oil based on the difference in boiling points into different distillates (Liquid Petroleum Gas, Naphtha, Kerosene, Diesel Atmospheric Gas Oil, Vacuum Gas Oil, Atmospheric Residue, and Vacuum Residue). The Atmospheric Distillation unit, which operates under atmospheric condition (101,325 kPa) with a maximum temperature of 370 °C, consists of a distillation column, heater, and sets of heat exchangers. The vacuum distillation unit has the same operating mechanism but accommodates a higher temperature with lower pressure (>101,325 kPa).

The gas oil coming from both the atmospheric and vacuum unit is broken down to lighter distillates via the conversion/cracking processes. Aside from the Fluid Catalytic Cracking Unit (FCCU) being the heart of the refinery, it is also the unit responsible for the cracking of the gas oil to lighter distillates, of which 80% are olefins (Vogt & Weckhuysen, 2015).

Presently the FCCU has successfully replaced the previously known steam and thermal cracking due to its ability to produce more octane gasoline and more olefins (Speight, 2006).

Fluid Catalytic Cracking Unit

The Fluid Catalytic Cracking Unit (FCCU) consists of a Catalytic Riser, Reactor, Regenerator, Fractionator and a Gas Recovery unit. The riser receives the feed, which could either be Light Vacuum gas oil (LVGO) or Heavy Vacuum Gas Oil (HVGO). Vacuum Gas Oil is a distillate product (370–550°c) from the vacuum distillation column which operates at vacuum (<101,325 kPa) or below atmospheric condition (101,325 kPa). As shown in Fig. 16.1, the feed at a temperature range of 315–430 °C is combined with slurry oil and injected into a catalytic riser. The catalyst in the riser cracks these feed into smaller molecules of vapour within 1–3 s. The catalyst to oil ratio should be within the range of 4:1 to 9:1 by weight (Rigutto et al., 2007). A batch reactor operating at 535 °C and 162 kPa separates the catalyst from the hydrocarbon vapour via cyclones. Steam stripping dissolves further traces of hydrocarbon vapour.

The regenerator helps to supply heat for feed cracking and restore the catalyst activity by burning off the deposited catalytic coke on the catalyst. At the same time, the flue gas passes through multiple sets of two-stage cyclones to remove the entrained catalyst. The regenerator operates at a temperature of 715 °C and pressure of 241 kPa and transfers the regenerated catalyst back to the catalytic riser. The fractionator helps to recover liquid products (fuel oil, petroleum naphtha, and off-gas) from the reactor vapours via condensation and re-vaporization of the hydrocarbon components (Rigutto et al., 2007). Slurry oil is the bottom product oil from the fractionating unit, which contains some amount of catalyst vapours. The gas recovery unit separates off-gas into lighter gases (propane, propylene, butanes, butylene, methane, ethylene, and ethane). The flue gas processing systems ensure complete combustion to CO_2 is achieved (Jones & Pajado, 2006).

FCCU Catalyst

Although Zeolite X or Zeolite Y are common catalysts used in crude refining operations, the ZSM-05 catalyst comes into play when more yield of olefin production is required. ZSM-05, which has a chemical

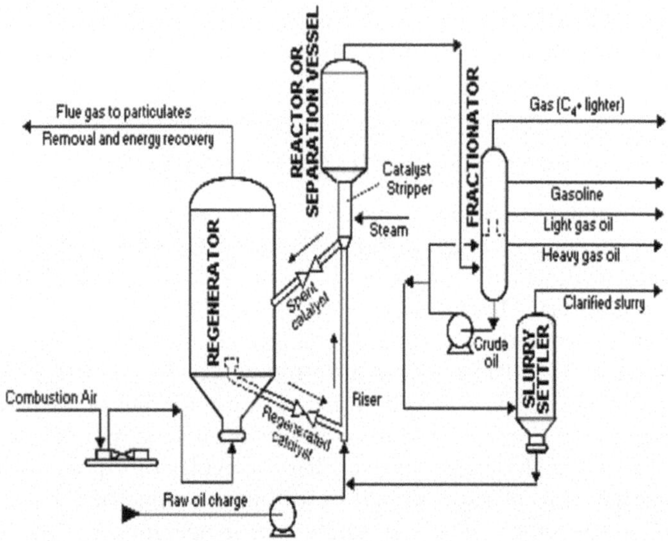

Fig. 16.1 Typical fluid catalytic cracking unit (Elamurugan, 2010)

formula of $Na_nAl_nSi_{96-n}O_{192}16H_2O$ $(0 < n < 27)$ was patented in 1975 by Mobil Oil (Banerjee et al., 2014). It is an aluminosilicate zeolite from the pentasil family of zeolite, also known as a heterogeneous catalyst for hydrocarbon isomerization reactions (Li et al., 2015). Apart from its better preference towards olefin production, it also helps in the conversion of heavier gasoline olefins to lighter olefins and reduces the production of coke during the process (Rostamizadeh & Taeb, 2015).

Previous Research

Although process variables collectively affect the olefin yield, Hutchinson and Roger (1996) proved that an increase in reaction temperature, re-cracking of cracked materials, and partial recycling of the catalyst leads to the production of more olefins. Amano et al. (2012) emphasized that the production of propylene needs a disproportionate share of hydrogen; therefore, more propylene production will take place from feed sources that are hydrogen-rich and low in contaminants because of the relative ease of conversion. Zhao and Hardley (1999) proved that an increase in hydrogen transfer index (ratio of paraffin to olefin ratio of C3, linear C4, and branched C4 species) determines the ability of the catalyst to generate secondary reactions, thereby resulting in a reduction in olefin production. Hu et al., (2008) stated that a rise in hydrocarbon partial pressure would increase the rate of all bimolecular reactions, thereby reducing olefin production while favouring gasoline range aromatics and paraffin.

Hamada and Watabe (2008) proved that the temperature in the riser where the catalytic cracking occurs should be in the range of 500–600 °C. Akah and Al-Ghrami, (2015) demonstrated that the contact time of the catalyst and the feed in the reactor should usually be less than 3 s; beyond this time, light olefins production becomes constant while secondary cracking occurs. In terms of ZSM-05 catalyst addition, Biswas and Maxwell (1990) highlighted that although the use of ZSM-05 results in a significant increase in propylene and butene associated with an approximately equivalent decrease in gasoline yield, it has a much lower potential to crack paraffin's in the C5–C8 range.

Aim of the Study

Previous works done, as stated above, show that although the incorporation of the ZSM-05 catalyst favours the production of more olefins, the efficiency of the catalyst productivity depends on other process variables. This study aims to determine the effects of four different types of Nigeria crude oil (Bonny Light, Bonny Medium, Escravos, and Qua Iboe crude) on the overall olefin yield. This study will also determine the best mixture of operating parameters (temperature, pressure, catalyst activity, riser length, and riser diameter) for maximum olefin production.

Methodology

Generally, a process design problem involves the evaluation of design parameters for a given process condition. In contrast, a typical process simulation problem consists of the assessment of output variables as a function of input variables and design parameters. In a standard binary distillation operation and a system of equations whose total number does not exceed 20, Mc–Cable Thiele Diagram is adopted for process design calculations. However, for multicomponent systems, assuming a graphical procedure is ruled out, Fenske, Underwood, and Gilliland (FUG) method can serve as an alternative. Alternatively, for the rigorous design of multicomponent distillation column, commercial process simulators (HYSYS) can be used to reduce the time and seems more reliable than the numerous calculations done by hand. It also allows for easy modification of operating conditions. It works via the different equations of states; notable ones include the Soave Redlich Kwong (SRK) and Peng Robinson Equation of States (PR-EOS).

Step 1: Oil Characterization at an atmospheric condition (101,325 kPa) of the different Nigeria crude assay (Qua Iboe, Bonny Light, Bonny Medium, and Escravos) using ASPEN HYSYS (version 10.0) was done based on their actual boiling point. Characterization evaluated the liquid volume fraction of the different distillates (Liquefied Petroleum Gas, Naphtha, Kerosene, Diesel, and Atmospheric Gas Oil) that came out from the crude oil at an ideal condition. Figure2 shows the process flow diagram.

- All crude oil has a flow rate of 250,000 kg/hr
- Peng Robinson fluid package was used due to its ability to handle pseudo-components (Hypothetical components). It is also more reliable and simpler to understand when compared to other equation of states. Its principles are expressed in the following equations [Peng & Robinson, 1976].

$$P = \frac{RT}{V_m - b} - \frac{a(T)}{V_m(V_m + b) + b(V_m - b)} \tag{16.1}$$

$$a(T) = 0.45724\frac{(RT)^2}{p_c} \tag{16.2}$$

$$a(T) = a(T_c)a(T) \tag{16.3}$$

$$a(T) = \left\{1 + m\left[1 - \frac{\sqrt{T}}{T_c}\right]\right\}^2 \tag{16.4}$$

Where

$$m = 0.3746 + 1.5423\omega - 0.2699\omega^2 \tag{16.5}$$

$$b = 0.07780\frac{RT_c}{P_c} \tag{16.6}$$

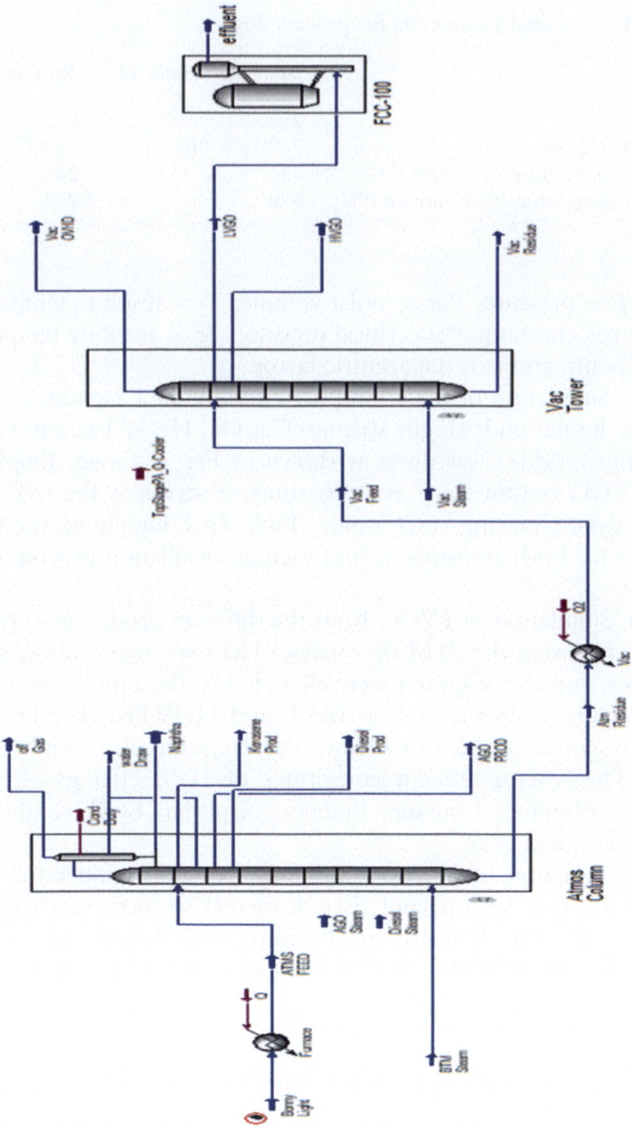

Fig. 16.2 Process flow diagram showing atmospheric distillation, vacuum distillation unit and the fluid catalytic cracking units (Authors)

Table 16.1 Essential parameters for process flow

Parameters	*Atmospheric Column*	*Vacuum Column*
Trays	29	9
Energy Flow (Kj/hr)	7.271e + 008	1.693 + 008
Inlet feed Ttemperature to furnace (°C)	15	288
Outlet feed temperature from furnace (°C)	370	800

where P = pressure, Vm = molar volume, T = absolute temperature, R = ideal gas constant, Pc = critical pressure, Tc = absolute temperature at critical point, and ω is the acentric factor.

Step 2: Simulation of the atmospheric residue in a vacuum condition to produce lighter ends (Light Vacuum Gas Oil, Heavy Vacuum Gas Oil, and vacuum residue) was done as shown in Fig. 2 above. Emphasis is laid on LVGO output since, for this study, it serves as the feed to the Fluid Catalytic Cracking (FCC) unit. Table 16.1 highlights the unique parameters for both atmospheric and vacuum distillation processes when converged.

Step 3: Simulation of LVGO from the different crude assays through the FCC unit using the ZSM-05 catalyst. The riser, regenerator, reactor, fractionator, and slurry splitter were all added to the simulation environment. (LVGO) enters the FCC at 165 C and 11.19 kPa. The FCC Unit catalytically converts the LVGO into smaller molecular weight hydrocarbons. The reactor effluent constitutes of H_2S, Fuel gas, propane, propylene, n-butane, I-butane, butenes, Naphtha, LCO (Light Cycle Oil), Bottoms, and coke.

Step 4: Variation of process conditions (reaction temperature, reaction pressure, riser length, and riser diameter) to increase Olefin yield using Aspen HYSIS. Temperature, Pressure, Riser length, and diameter were done within 480–580 °C, 260–520 kPa, 10-100 m, and 1–1.8 m, respectively.

Results and Discussion

Crude Oil Characterisation Based on Distillates True Boiling Point

For all crude oil that was passed through the atmospheric simulation process, off-gas, light naphtha, heavy naphtha, kerosene, light diesel,

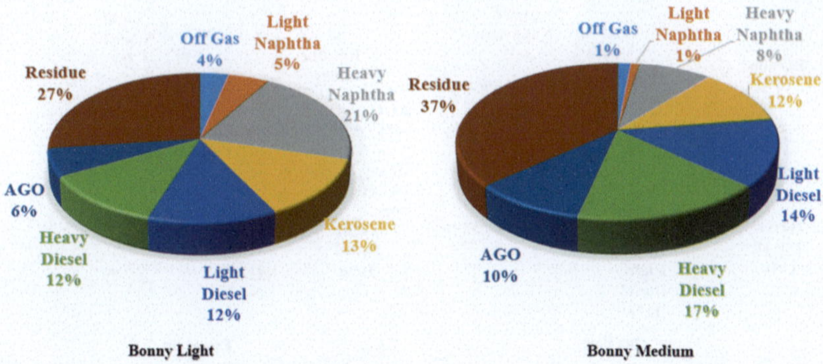

Fig. 16.3 Cut distributions for bonny light and bonny medium crude oil [Authors]

heavy diesel, atmospheric gas oil, and atmospheric residue came out at temperature 10, 70 , 180, 240, 290, 340, 370, and 1200 oC respectively. These values correspond to the standardized values (Hsu & Robinson, 2006). From Fig. 16.3 and 16.4, it is evident that bonny light favours more of the production of heavy naphtha (21%) more than any other distillates. This value accounts for 0.21 m^3 liquid volume fraction of the total oil. Generally, light crude oil tends to favour the distillation of more volatile products or more lightweight components. At the same time, the bulk, which comes out as residue, acts as the feed for the vacuum distillation process. Heavy Naphtha seems to be highly favoured by two (Qua Iboe–22%, Escravous–35%) out of the four samples of crude oil looked at. Bonny medium favours more of the production of heavy diesel with a value of 0.17m^3 liquid volume fraction of the total oil.

The atmospheric residue values are extensively analyzed since the output serves as the feed to the vacuum distillation column, which, when processed, provides proportions of olefins needed. From Fig. 16.3 and 16.4, it is noted that bonny medium, bonny light, Qua Iboe, and Escravous delivers 37, 27, 26, and 20%, respectively, of the residue, needed.

Conditions and Properties of Light Vacuum Gas Oil (LVGO)

Properties of LVGO from the Different Crude Oil

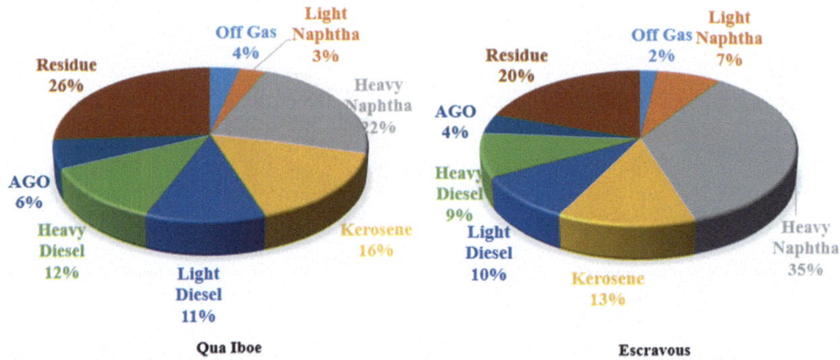

Fig. 16.4 Cut distributions for Qua Iboe and Escravos crude oil [Authors]

The mass flow rate for Light Vacuum Gas Oil (LVGO) coming out from bonny light, bonny medium, Escravos, and Qua-Iboe oil are 138,700 kg/hr, 128,100 kg/hr, 137,700 kg/hr, and 119,800 kg/hr respectively. Hence, the crude oil with the highest quantity of LVGO is Bonny light. Bonny light has the highest LVGO quantity relative to the other three crudes because; it is the lightest in terms of molecular weight, as shown in Table 16.2.

Table 16.2 Conditions of LVGO from the different crude oil

CONDITIONS	*Overall (Bonny Light)*	*Overall (Bonny Medium)*	*Overall (Escravous)*	*Overall (Qua- Iboe)*
Temperature: (C)	165	250.9	150.4	168.1
Pressure: (kPa)	11.19	11.19	11.19	11.19
Molar flow (kgmole/h)	654.6	355.8	679.8	558.3
Mass flow (kg/h)	138,700	128,100	137,700	119,800
Liq vol flow @Std Cond (m^3/h)	172	140.3	167.5	146.6
Molar enthalpy (kJ/kgmole)	−3.89e + 05	−5.84e + 05	−3.80e + 05	−3.92e + 05
Molar entropy (kJ/kgmole-C)	559.1	979.8	413.5	578.7
Molecular weight	211.9	360	202.6	214.6

Although all values shown in the table above were gotten from the HYSYS software when converged, the mass flow rates can be calculated manually using equation seven below (Uppaluri, 2010).

$MassFlowRate(M) = VolumetricFlowRtae(F) \times 42 \times 8.33 \times SpecificGravity$

The Output from the Fluid Catalytic Cracking Unit Using ZSM-05 Catalyst

At a temperature, pressure, riser length, and diameter of 530°c, 340 kPa, 50 m, and 1.3 m, respectively, Table 16.3 below shows the individual constituents that come out from the fractionator as described in Fig. 16.1. The HYSYS software gives these values as when converged. Generally, all crude possesses a low amount of hydrogen sulfide (<1wt %), which indicates that they all fall under the range of sweet crude oil (Demirbas, 2015). Table 16.3 shows that ethylene and butadiene were not produced from all crude oil samples, while propylene and butylene were produced in a large quantity. Simultaneously, naphtha distillate also came out in large amounts, which, when passed through a hydro skimming or catalytic cracking unit, produces Gasoline. In respect to propylene and butylene, Escravous has the largest amount (25.206 wt. %) followed by bonny medium (10.445 wt. %), bonny light (10.274 wt. %), and Qua-Iboe (9.562 wt. %).

Effects of Varying Parameters on Olefin Yield in FCCU

Although Escravous crude oil produced the largest amount of olefins at temperature, pressure, riser length, and diameter of 530°c, 340 kPa, 50 m, and 1.3 m respectively, as given by HYSYS software, this section aims to vary these parameters within some theoretical range to highlight the effects on the olefin yield.

Effects of Reactor Temperature

With a pressure of 340 kPa, catalytic riser length of 50 m and riser diameter of 1.3 m, the reactor temperature was varied between 480–580°C to determine the effect on olefin production. Figure 16.5 shows that for all crude oil samples, an increase in temperature resulted in a corresponding rise in olefin yield. This trend is similar to the work carried out by Amano

Table 16.3 Yield of FCCU effluent components from the different crude oil

Components	*Products wt. % (Bonny Light)*	*Products wt. % (Escravous)*	*Products wt. % (Bonny Medium)*	*Products wt. % Qua Iboe*
H_2s	0.583889916	0.501775547	0.588869074	0.576366117
Fuel gas	2.320759226	3.028118171	2.200741983	2.06567013
Propane	1.878489017	1.745355335	2.280009773	1.644313127
Propylene	4.368768988	4.448116829	13.45006817	4.03322192
Nbutane	1.997382274	1.400553875	1.889108986	1.828927057
Ibutane	3.870012667	3.067415968	5.85612581	3.515168683
Butenes	5.909670182	5.997019231	11.75650439	5.529746985
Naphtha	57.52711525	46.56318128	37.96021253	55.20055866
Gas oil	10.1378921	15.80681876	11.81949926	12.52775394
Bottoms	4.564573691	10.91400574	5.568900451	6.458794386
Coke yield	6.841446683	6.527639257	6.629959565	6.619478996
Total	100	100	100	100

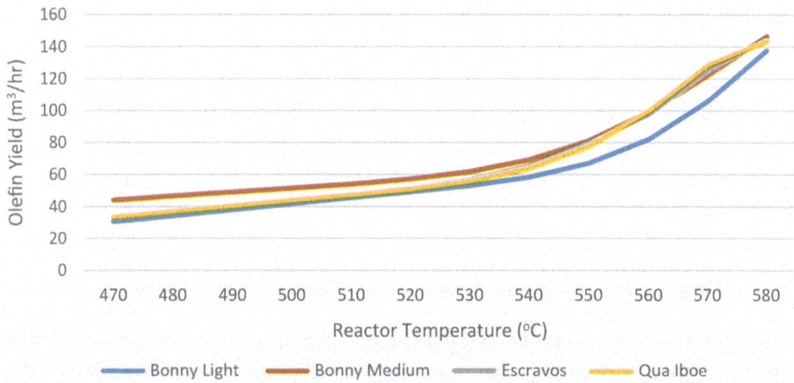

Fig. 16.5 Graph of Olefin yield versus reactor temperature for all crude oil samples

et al., (2012) and Hamada and Watabe (2008), though they stopped at 540 °C. Bonny medium, Qua Iboe, and Escravous crude fell within the range of 147–148 m^3 /hr while Bonny light crude had the lowest olefin yield with a value of 140 m^3 /hr.

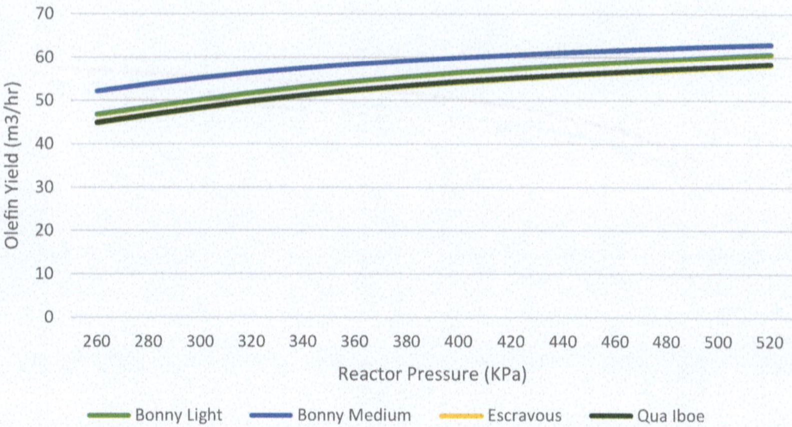

Fig. 16.6 Graph of Olefin yield versus reactor pressure for all crude oil samples

Effect of Reactor Pressure

With a temperature of 530 °C, catalytic riser length of 50 m, and riser diameter of 1.3 m, the reactor pressure was varied between 260–520 kPa. Figure16.6 also shows an increase in the pressure leads to a direct increase in olefin yield with bonny medium recording the highest value (62 m^3/hr) while Qua Iboe & Escravous crude oil having the same amount of 58 m^3 /hr. Hu et al., (2008) carried out similar work, but it was the hydrocarbon partial pressure that was measured. Their work proved that an increase in the partial pressure decreases olefin production.

Riser Length

With a pressure of 340 kPa, a temperature of 530 °C, and a catalytic riser diameter of 1.3 m, the riser length was varied between 10–100 m. Fig. 16.7 also showed that an increase in the catalytic riser length results in an immediate rise in olefin yield for all crude oil. This trend is similar to the work carried out by Fuyiyama et al., (2010) and Knight and Mehlberg (2011), although they used the Zeolite X catalyst and also recorded an increase in olefin yield.

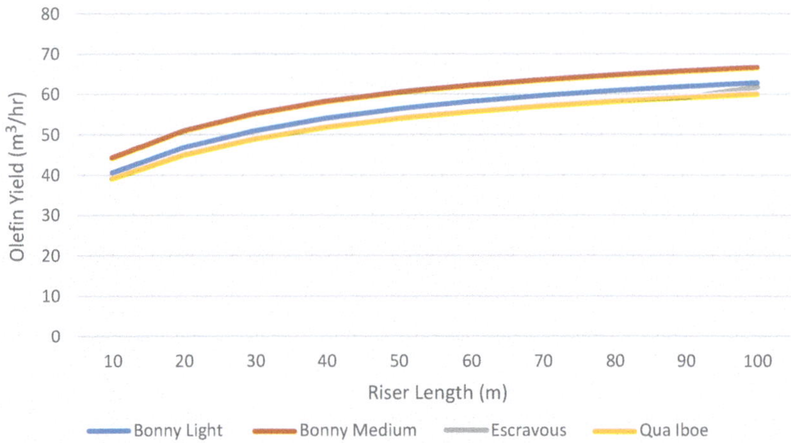

Fig. 16.7 Graph of Olefin yield versus riser length for all crude oil samples

Riser Diameter

Variation in riser diameter (1 to 1.8 m) was carried out for all crude oil samples keeping other variables constant (530 °C, 340 kPa, and riser length of 50 m). The increase in riser diameter results in a consecutive rise in Olefin yield, as shown in Fig. 16.8. Therefore, the Olefin yield is directly proportional to the riser length.

Conclusion

Temperature, Pressure, Riser length, and diameter were varied within 480–580 °C, 260–520 kPa, 10–100 m, and 1–1.8 m respectively to determine the best operating parameter mix for optimum olefin yield. Bonny medium crude oil produced the largest amount of olefins (22.206 wt. %). For all factors considered, variation in process parameters favoured bonny medium crude as it also recorded the highest olefin yield in terms of temperature (142 m^3/hr), pressure (62 m3/hr), and riser length (68m3/hr). Escravous crude oil recorded the highest olefin yield value (159 m^3/hr) when the riser diameter was varied. Bonny medium crude oil is more favoured because of its higher density value when compared to the rest crude oil samples.

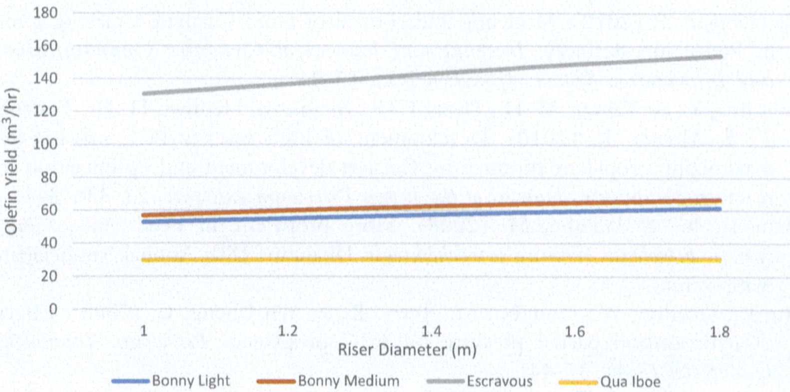

Fig. 16.8 Graph of Olefin yield versus riser diameter for all crude oil samples

References

Ajee, M. (2015). Aligning the Nigerian Petrochemical Industry to Oil and Gas Industry needs. *American Journal of Chemical Engineering, 3*(2–1), 18–24.

Akah, A., & Al-Ghrami, M. (2015). Maximizing propylene production via FCC technology. *Applied Petrochemical Research, 5*(4), 377–392.

Amano, T., Wilcox, J., Pouwels, C., & Matsuura, T. (2012). Process and catalysis factors to maximize propylene output. *Petroleum Technology Quarterly, 3*(2), 17.

Amghizar, I., Vandewalle, L. A., Geem, V., & K. M & Marin, G. B. (2017). New trends in Olefin production. *Engineering, 3*(2), 171–178. https://doi.org/10.1016/J.ENG.2017.02.006

Balinga, J. (2015). *The IGBT Device. Physics, Design, and applications of the insulated gate bipolar transistor*. William Andrew Applied Science Publishers. Page 583. https://doi.org/10.1016/B978-1-4557-3143-5.00018-3

Banerjee, P. C., Woo, R. P., Grayson, S. M., Majumder, A., & Raman, S. R. (2014). Influence of Zeolite coating on the corrosion resistance of AZ91D Magnesium Alloy. *Materials, 7*(2), 6092–6104.

Barrer, R. (1981). Zeolites and their synthesis. *Zeolites, 1*(3), 130–140.

Biswas, J., & Maxwell, I. E. (1990). Octane enhancement in fluid catalytic Cracking: Role of ZSM-05 addition and reactor temperature. *Applied Catalysis, 58*(1), 1–18.

Demirbas, H., Alidrisi, H., & Balubaid, M. A, (2015). API gravity. *Sulfur Content, and Desulfurization of Crude Oil, Petroleum Science, and Technology, 33*(1), 93–101. https://doi.org/10.1080/10916466.2014.950383

Elamurugan, P. (2010). Modeling and control of Fluid Catalytic Cracking Unit in Petroleum Refinery. *International Journal of Computer Communication and Information System (IJCCIS), 2*(1), 13–24.

Fujiyama, Y., Al-Tayyar, M. H., Dean, C. F., Aitani, A., Hedhwi, H. H., Tsutsui, T., & Mizuta, K. (2010). Development of high severity FCC process for maximizing propylene production: Catalyst development and optimization of reaction conditions. *Journal of the Japan Petroleum Institute, 23*, 336–341.

Hamada, R., & Watabe, M. (2008). More propylene in FCC units. *Catalysts in petroleum refining petrochemicals.* Dhahran: 18th Annual Saudi-Japan Symposium.

Hu, R., Gordon, W., Hongbo, M., Terry, R., & Wu-Cheng, C. (2008). Effect of hydrocarbon partial pressure on FCC propylene. *Petroleum Technology Quarterly, 13*(4), 37–44.

Hutchinson, D., & Roger, H. (1996). Catalytic cracking to maximize light olefins. *Petrole et techniques*, 29.s

Ji, Y. (2015). Membrane technologies for water treatment and reuse in the gas and petrochemical industries. Materials, Processes, and Applications. Woodhead Publishing Series in Energy pp. 519–536. https://doi.org/10.1016/B978-1-78242-121-4.00016-2

Jones, D. S., & Pajado, P. P. (2006). *Handbook of Petroleum Processing.*, *23*, 12–20.

Knight, J., & Mehlberg, R. (2011). Maximizing propylene from your FCC. *Hydrocarbon processing* .Special report

Li, Y., Sun, H., Feng, R., Wang, Y., Subhan, F., Yan., Z., Zhang, Z & Liu, F. (2015). Synthesis of ZSM-5 zeolite from diatomite for fluid catalytic cracking application. *Applied Petrochemical Research, 5*, 347–353.

Mamudu, O. A & Chandler, H. (2019). *A review on solids separation, disposal, and handling system for the petroleum refining industry.*

Mamudu, O. A., Igwe, G. J., & Okonkwo, E. (2019). Process design evaluation of an optimum modular topping refinery for Nigeria crude oil using HYSYS Aspen Software. *Cogent Engineering, 6*, 1659123. https://doi.org/10.1080/23311916.2019.1659123

Peng, D. Y. and Robinson, D. B. (1976). A new two-constant equation of state, *Industrial and Engineering Chemistry, 15*(1), 59–64.

Rigutto, S. M., Veen, R. V & Huve, L. (2007). Zeolite in hydrocarbon processing. *Studies in Surface Science and Catalysis, 168*(23), 855–913, XXIII–XXVI

Rostamizaseh, M & Taeb, A. (2015). Synthesis and reactivity in inorganic, *Metal-Organic, and Nano-Metal Chemistry, 46*(5).

Speight, J. G. (2006). *The chemistry and technology of petroleum.* CRC Press.

Uppaluri, R. (2010). Refinery process design (Lecture Notes): Department of Chemical India. Page 183

Vogt, E. T. C., & Weckhuysen, B. M. (2015). Fluid catalytic cracking: Recent developments on the grand old lady of zeolite catalysis. *Chemical Society Review, 44*(20), 7342–7370. https://doi.org/10.1039/c5cs00376h

Zhao, X., & Hardley, R. H. (1999). ZSM-5 additive in fluid catalytic cracking. 2. Effect of hydrogen transfer characteristics of the base cracking catalysts and feedstocks. *Industrial and Engineering Chemical Research, 38*(10), 3854–3859.

CHAPTER 17

Modelling Energy Poverty and Energy Inequality into India's Energy Policy

Sovik Mukherjee and Asim K. Karmakar

Introduction

In the last five hundred years, the human civilisation has been continuously expanding their technological limits manifold, increasingly drawing in huge amounts of energy resources from Mother Nature. To the extent, humans have overdrawn; the unsustainability issue became prominent in terms of risk of disruptions to energy supply, environmental damage on account of energy production and generation followed by persistent energy poverty, to which India is no exception (Birol, 2007).

Energy is the most crucial in determining the pace of economic development and impact of stress created by an economy on the ecosystem as measured by the carbon footprint part of the ecological footprint (see

S. Mukherjee (✉)
St. Xavier's University, Kolkata, India

A. K. Karmakar
Department of Economics, School of Professional Studies, Netaji Subhas Open University, Nadia, India

S. Folarin et al. (eds.), *The United Nations and Sustainable Development Goals*, https://doi.org/10.1007/978-3-030-95971-5_17

Sengupta, 2015; Pachauri, 2010). The notion of energy poverty in India entails two conflicting issues, i.e., one of ensuring equity in distribution and the other of energy development given the dualistic nature of the society. This brings us to the specific context of energy policy for India,—(a) energy security at the macro level so that there is always an adequate supply and equitable accessibility of energy either in primary or final forms; (b) the energy use should also meet the efficiency and cleanliness criteria before ensuring that there is no energy poverty resulting from demand–supply mismatch of electrical energy (Kyagusuz, 2011).

Given such a scenario, the question is how an economy ends up in a situation of energy poverty? The UN's Millennium Development Goals (UN, 2000)—its objective is to eradicate extreme poverty, improve living conditions and facilitate progress towards a sustainable development path—initially did not include any mention of access to energy. Subsequently, energy was included as a goal among Sustainable Development Goals (SDGs); Goal 7 reads: "Ensure access to affordable, reliable, sustainable, and modern energy for all." (Lu et al., 2015). Though energy poverty is very well documented in the literature across the globe (Bouzarovski & Petrova, 2015; Chakravarty & Tavoni, 2013; Liu et al., 2019; Zubi et al., 2019; among others), integrating energy poverty and energy inequality in the energy policy and thereby discussing the feasibility of use of new renewables remains an unexplored area. The recent literature in the Indian context (Bhide & Monroy, 2011; Gupta et al., 2020; Pachauri, 2010) is yet to quantify the rural–urban breakup of energy poverty and energy inequality. Herein, lies the contribution of the present paper. This paper aims at putting an intuitive explanation for energy poverty and energy inequality by integrating it in India's energy policy context to motivate the feasibility of the use of new renewables. Since the proportion of people lying below the poverty line is comparatively higher than the developed ones, affordability issue arises (Lanjouw, 2001). The income distribution of the households and fuel prices have to be such that there is universal access to cleaner cooking fuel (e.g. LPG) and lighting at the household level. The income position puts a hindrance in terms of accessing such a clean energy fuel which in turn pushes the poor households to go in for an alternative fuel (poor in terms of energy efficiency) leading to high energy bills and further sucking these households into the trap of energy poverty (Dhara, 2017).

The thrust of research in science and technology is now for the discovery and development of a carbon-free renewable resource to move the world out of the fossil fuel-driven second industrial revolution effects, i.e. basically a focus on shifting away from fossil fuels to renewable energy resources, including, solar, wind, thermal, biomass, water, etc. (González-Eguino, 2015; Rifkin, 2011). The other question which remains unanswered in the literature is how the optimal fuel mix should be like if India has to come out of this energy poverty trap. The rest of the paper has been organised as follows. Section "Measuring Energy Poverty and Energy Inequality: Indian Context" develops the theoretical model and looks into the rural–urban energy-poverty/energy-inequality scenario using NSSO household unit-level data from 68th rounds survey (between July 2011–June 2012). In view of the energy poverty and inequality issue, in Sect. "Measuring Energy Inequality", the paper tries to justify that why completely shifting to new renewables-based power generation is not feasible at this point in India, given the shortfall in resource rent extraction to meet up the financing requirements for the same. The paper ends with a conclusion.

Focus Objectives

This study aims at the issue of energy poverty, in particular, the rural–urban magnitude of energy poverty in India by graphing the Specific Concentration Curve (SCC) using National Sample Survey (NSSO) household unit-level data from the 68th round (between July 2011 and June 2012) and also looks at a crude measure of inequality in the distribution of fuels. In line with the issue of taking an economy out of energy poverty or addressing the inequality in the distribution of fuels, the paper tries to show that completely shifting to new renewables-based power generation is not feasible at this point in India given the shortfall in resource rent extraction.

Measuring Energy Poverty and Energy Inequality: Indian Context

Measuring Energy Poverty

In the Indian context, energy poverty in this study is defined in the following perspective. We consider a household to be cooking energy poor in the following analysis if its principal fuel of use for cooking is biomass while the other households have been considered as non-poor

Table 17.1 Rural Household Energy Poverty

Decile Class of MPCE	*Cumulative Share of Population*	*Cumulative Share of total Population falling in the respective decile group and primary cooking fuel as biomass*	*Cumulative Share of total Population falling in the respective decile group and principal fuel for lighting as electricity*
2	20	0.181	0.096
4	40	0.359	0.216
6	60	0.525	0.357
8	80	0.679	0.522
10	100	0.788	0.733
Poverty ratio for cooking energy (rural) **0.79**; Poverty ratio for lighting energy (rural) **0.27**			

Source Authors' derivations

in terms of cooking energy. Similarly, any household which declares electricity to be its primary lighting fuel would be considered as a case of non-poor and the other households would be treated as poor. The household's consumption data of 68th round of NSSO for 2011–12 shows the cooking poverty ratio to be around 79% in rural India and 18% in urban India as per such definition (see Table 17.1). Similarly, it was found that in rural area the lighting poverty ratio is 27% while the same is only 5% in urban area (see Table 17.2).

With reference to Tables 17.1 and 17.2, note that— (i)Households with principal fuel as biomass for cooking are poor for cooking energy; (ii)Households with principal fuel other than electricity for lighting are poor in terms of lighting energy.

Where India Stands Globally

India's energy poverty is highlighted more by the fact of low per capita electricity production and use which is less than one-third of world average, one-fourth of China and less than 7.5% of USA. Going by World Bank 2018 data, 85% of India's population has access to electricity while it has been 87.3% at the global level, and 100% for the people of USA and China. Besides, an issue of major concern has been that most of the CO_2 emission in the energy sector takes place from the fuel combustion in the

Table 17.2 Urban household energy poverty

Decile class of MPCE	*Cumulative share of population*	*Cumulative share of total population falling in the respective decile group and primary cooking fuel as biomass*	*Cumulative share of total population falling in the respective decile group and principal fuel for lighting as electricity*
2	20	0.103	0.173
4	40	0.154	0.365
6	60	0.178	0.560
8	80	0.179	0.756
10	100	0.182	0.954
Poverty ratio for cooking energy (rural) **0.18**; Poverty ratio for lighting energy (rural) **0.05**			

Source Authors' derivations

electricity and the transport sector both of which are heavily dependent on fossil fuel in India and as a result, Indian power generation has been more dependent on fossil fuels and less sustainable compared to other large economies like China, USA and global average.

One of the major problems of India with regard to energy security is her high dependency on imports for energy supply. Net import of energy in India had a share of 46.13% of total energy use in India in 2018–19 which has grown over time from a relatively low level of 8% in 1990–91. The shares of import in the total apparent consumption of coal, oil and natural gas had risen over time in the period since 1990–91 and reached a level of 23%, 79% and 28% respectively in 2018–19 due to the growth of demand outpacing their respective supplies from domestic sources. The import prices of all the three fossil fuels had also grown in nominal dollar and rupee terms as well as in real rupee terms in the two decade period 1989–90 to 2010–11 to 2010–2020. While the growth of net imports of all fossil fuels together in oil equivalent terms has been 9% per annum over the period under reference (its share in the total apparent consumption of energy increasing at the rate of 3.25% per annum), the unit price of the fossil fuel in oil equivalent unit increased in nominal dollar and rupee terms at the rates of 15% and 20% respectively (Sengupta, 2015). This led to a situation of growth of net import bill of India at an unsustainable high rate of 19.5% per annum, leading to almost 95 times increase in

2019–20 over the base of 1990–91 (see Sengupta, 2020). Price volatility of a large energy importing country like India gives rise to the conditions of such uncertainties which result in both energy insecurity and macroeconomic unsustainability of development as may arise from its pressure on the balance of payments situation due to its deficit. This has become an added reason for India's special thrust on switching to new renewable energy resources replacing fossil fuels.

Energy poverty is regarded as one of the aspects of income poverty. Provision of energy services in form of electricity, motive power, etc., facilitate industrial and agricultural growth in the country. Such growth and development enhance the livelihood opportunities in terms of greater level of employment and entrepreneurial opportunities (Sengupta, 2020). This shall further translate into higher income of the households and subsequent reduction in poverty levels. But with nearly 50 million people lying below the poverty line, an approximate 6%, there is a big question mark for the households to have access to clean energy given their high capital cost and hence, the issue of energy poverty becomes all the more relevant.

Measuring Energy Inequality

The specific concentration curve plots the cumulative share of the total use of a given cooking or lighting fuel against the cumulative share population from the lower end of the scale of per head or per household income or consumption expenditure. Its position vis-a-vis the 45° line is indicative of inequality in sharing the fuel for cooking and lighting vis-a-vis inequality of similar distribution of total consumption expenditure on all items together. The comparative position of the Lorenz curve and the specific concentration curve indicates whether the concerned fuel may be considered as a necessity or luxury item by the concerned segments of the households. If the specific concentration curve lies between 45° line and the Lorenz curve it is considered by households in the concerned range of income or per capita expenditure variation as a necessity, while it would be considered as a luxury item if it lies below the Lorenz curve (refer to Fig 17.1 and 17.2). Based on the values of SCI, we have LPG for cooking and electricity for lighting vis-a-vis the Lorenz curve to be luxury goods in rural areas and those of kerosene for rural lighting and LPG, electricity in urban areas to be considered as necessities depending upon the preference structure of the households in different income-expenditure classes

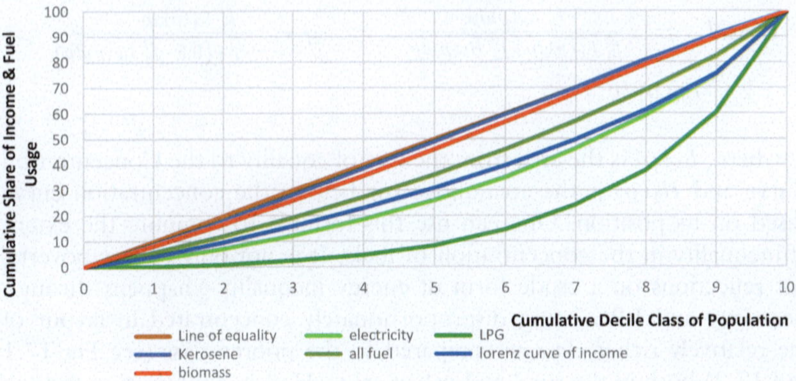

Fig. 17.1 Specific concentration curve for fuels & Lorenz curve for income (rural)*

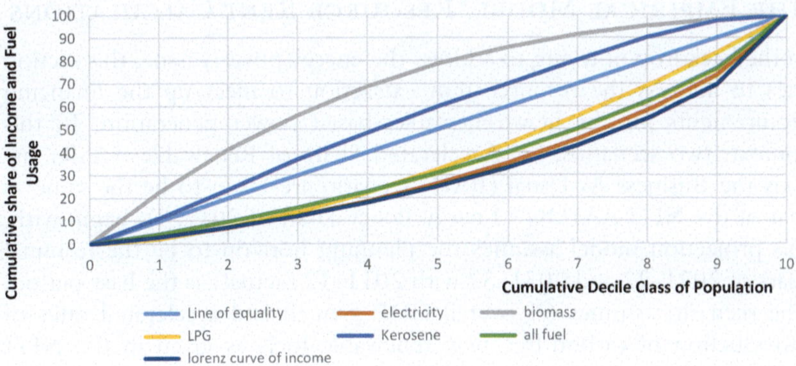

Fig. 17.2 Specific concentration curve for fuels & Lorenz curve for income (urban)*

(Sen, 1997). Formally, the form of the specific concentration curve the authors use in this context is actually derived from the standard health inequality concentration index (see Kakwani et al., 1997). The formula for the computation of the Specific Concentration Index (SCI) is given below,

$$1. \ SCI = \frac{\int_0^1 L_h(p)dp}{\int_0^1 L_h(p)dp + \int_0^1 H_h(p)dp} = \frac{\int_0^1 L_h(p)dp}{\int_0^1 L_h(p)dp + \left(0.5 - \int_0^1 L_h(p)dp\right)} = 2\int_0^1 L_h(p)dp$$

where, $L_h(p)$ is the area from the line of equality to the Concentration Curve and $H_h(p)$ is the area above (or below) the concentration curve based on its position. One can use this formula to compute the extent of inequality in the concentration of fuels. It is not only energy poverty, but reflections on a crude form of energy inequality—happens through electricity and LPG being disproportionately concentrated in favour of the relatively richer class as compared to the poorer class (see Fig 17.1 and 17.2) both in the rural and urban areas. Hence, a motivation to look into the optimal fuel mix in the following section and encourage the use of new renewables-based clean fuels being accessible to all.

The Empirical Model: Resource Rent Calculations

In the backdrop of trying to address the energy poverty issue, this section tries to address the resource rent extraction to meet up the financing requirements for the new renewables-based power generation. In this context, two scenarios, i.e. Accelerated Share of Renewables (ASR) vis-à-vis the Business As Usual (BAU) scenario are taken to be the same as that of the NITI AAYOG's Energy Policy Draft of 2017. To begin with, this projection model assumes the planning horizon to be the terminal years of 2021–22 and 2031–32 with 2011–12 (actual) as the base period. The scenario assumes 6% overall GDP growth and accelerated rates of introduction of carbon-free new renewable fuels as given in the NITI AAYOG's Energy Policy Draft 2017.

Moving on to the estimation of resource rents, a few years back there existed a coal cess imposed by the Government of India at the rate of Rs. 400/- per tonne. This was originally introduced in 2010 at the rate of Rs. 50/- per tonne and later enhanced in 2016 to the level of Rs. 400/- per tonne. This was imposed as a carbon tax on the production and importation of coal, lignite and peat whose proceeds were to directly flow to National Clean Energy and Environment Fund. This was supposed to be a non-lapsable fund, the unutilised portion of the cess revenue being transferable to the following year in the same fund for utilisation (Rajan, 2017). This will be routed through the Consolidated Fund of India but earmarked for clean energy development initiative. The fund was supposed to be utilised for financing research and innovative development projects in clean energy technologies. The cess thus had dual objective of penalising production and import of coal and its variants and encouraging a shift towards renewables. Since this is thus supposed to serve the purpose of resource rent which we propose to be imposed as a resource rent tax to be mobilised for financing clean energy development, we give our observations and comments on the adequacy of this cess and discuss in that context the required rate and form of resource taxation required for the development of new renewables-based green power as envisaged in the era of the Third Industrial Revolution.

However, after the introduction of GST in 2017 (Goods and Services Tax) in India, a GST cess has been introduced on some luxury or demerit goods for compensating revenue loss of states which suffer from the shift to GST from the earlier tax regime. The coal cess was abolished when this new GST cess was introduced and was supposed to be subsumed by it. This was followed by a transfer of the accumulated fund of the unutilised coal cess to the Consolidated Fund of India out of which most of the government expenditure is made. Although the fund of coal cess is supposed to be made available for the purpose for which it is set up, the actual historical record of fund utilisation for this cess has been very poor. First of all, only a mere 37% of the total coal cess collected has been transferred to the National Clean Energy and Environment Fund. Out of this 81% has been used for financing projects for clean energy development. It is thus only a share of 30% of coal cess has been applied for the purpose for which it has been meant.

It is really an issue if the Government of India is serious about using coal cess fund for the objective of developing new technologies for clean energy. This is particularly important as the coal cess has been now subsumed under the GST cess and there has been siphoning of the unused money of the National Clean Energy and Environment Fund to fund the GST compensation to industrially advanced states of the past to placate their disgruntlement over the loss of revenue due to the regional redistributive impact of GST reforms. Such diversion of use of fund of coal cess is surely immoral if not illegal.

However, one may raise the issue if the current coal cess of Rs. 400/- per tonne is adequate as an eco-tax either for the purpose of internalising the environmental external cost of use of coal in the context of power sectors' use. Such coal cess would imply hike in the cost of power

(Rs./KWh) only by INR 0.30 in 2011–12 which will come down to Rs. 0.26 in 2021–22 and Rs. 0.23 in 2031–32 due to improvement in thermal power's generation efficiency as per the estimates in NITI AAYOG's Energy Policy Draft 2017. Table 17.3 shows, on the other hand, how coal cess at the rate of Rs. 400/- per tonne would generate cumulative revenue of INR Billion 3094 for the time horizon up to 2021–22 and 8322 up to 2031–32, assuming a linear phasing of growth of cess revenue over time between the terminal years of any decade according to the baseline BAU. When these are compared with the requirement of financial resources for the cumulative generation capacity build-up from the same base year 2011–12 as projected for the same scenario we find the cumulative coal cess revenue will meet only 43.66% of the capital requirement of creation of generation capacity in new renewables-based power up to 2021–22, such coverage declining to 37.29% in 2031–32 and to 22.53% in 2041–42 (2041–42 we have not reported). For ASR, the level of adequacy of cess revenue is even lower for the different time horizons as compared to the BAU scenario (see Table 17.3).

Table 17.3 Coal cess revenue @INR 400.00 per tonne of coal and its adequacy

BAU. business as usual scenario with respect to energy efficiency and fuel mix				
Period	*Coal cess revenue (current) INR Billion*[a]	*Cumulative cess revenue from base year 2011–12 (INR Billion)*[b]	*Cumulative capacity resource requirement for new renewables up to the current year INR Billion* [c]	*Cess finance availability/capacity resource requirement for new renewables) in %*
2011–12	216.268	216.268		
2021–22	402.636	3094.520	7087.796	43.660
2031–32	723.452	8322.322	22,320.449	37.286
ASR. High energy eff. Cum Accld. Intro. of New Renewables				
2011–12	216.268	216.268		
2021–22	349.605	2829.364	6429.161	44.008
2031–32	540.507	6930.319	24,759.739	27.990

[a]based on projected tonnes of coal required (in tonnes), i.e. 6% growth factor from the base year.
[b]linear growth factor of 5% per year taken into consideration for calculation of coal cess revenue after adjusting for the efficiency factor.
[c]adopted from Sengupta (2020)
Source Authors' own estimates

One may however argue that the coal cess was imposed with the limited objective of capital financing for only development of new technology and innovations possibly through R&D, and not for financing the building up of the entire new generative capacity embodying the new technologies. Besides, the adequacy of resource rent estimates as shown in Table 17.3, is not considering the transmission and distribution investment required for setting up new capacities in the new renewables and also resource rents extracted through gas. So bringing in gas might raise the coverage to a certain extent. However, the focus here is on the importance of complementarity of fossil fuel-based power and the backstop technology (new renewables) based power from the viewpoint of meeting the challenge of financing the new technology-based development in the power industry.

Conclusion and Recommendation

In a country where almost 25% of the global population is without electricity and 31% is without clean cooking fuel (Sengupta, 2015), the question the paper addresses is can we use the new renewables sources of electric power generation to meet the needs of an accessible and clean energy on a large scale? Like biomass (under other renewables) does not have the potential to shoulder the chunk of electricity generation unlike coal and gas. Thus, the answer depends on how much should be the rent domestically extracted from either coal or gas to finance these capacity requirements from solar or wind or other renewables? There are studies in the literature which consider roughly 20% of the oil-linked price of coal or gas to be the resource rent component of the fuel price. The paper herein presents a case with coal. But, is this sufficient based on the funds requirement reported in Table 17.3? The paper establishes that the answer is a big no even if we include the resource rents from gas.

The projections of investment requirement as presented in Table 17.3 for the build-up of the new renewables-based power system capacity should not as such pose any big constraint in these days of globalisation when global capital is crossing national boundaries with much greater ease. The real challenge would however arise in attracting entrepreneurship and fund in particular choice option of generation technology due to low credit rating of many of such projects in India at least, to begin with. Such rating may be affected not only by the risk involved due to technology and business environment of that particular project, but also by the macroeconomic and country-level policies in the context of attracting foreign capital. The alternatives would be to develop new initiatives for finance like—regional infrastructural banks, multilateral banks or the resource rent based climate fund like the one proposed here. Given the importance of new renewables in power generation, of late, the central government is investing in the development of green corridors in renewable energy-rich states to evacuate power from solar parks or wind parks where particularly there is no pre-existing regular grid connectivity (work is being carried out by the POWER GRID of India) and simultaneously subsidising the cost of rooftop installations of solar PVs and the grid cost of distributing both solar and wind energy.

The most important feature of this composition of mix for the overall energy system or the electricity generation in India has been the dominance of fossil fuel with high carbon footprint. The driving force behind the observed pattern of growth of India's power sector, which provides the major opportunity of fuel substitution, has been energy security to provide support to India's high growth of GDP and to provide energy security to the households in terms of availability, access to electricity and efficiency in view of the energy poverty and inequality concerns. Cleanliness criteria, most of the times, have taken a back seat. The relative endowments of availability of the alternative fuels and their cost competitiveness have been the principal determinants of such choice of fuel composition. The environmental unsustainability arising out of ignoring the cleanliness criteria (no control on CO_2 emissions), has however, driven the search for alternative to fossil fuel which has led to the present policy thrust on the accelerated introduction of new renewables as alternative energy resources. But as pointed out in the study, challenges exist not only with regard to the feasibility part (in terms of resource availability, accessibility and efficiency) but also on the financing part (through extracting resource rents or through other forms like the creation of clean energy development funds through international cooperation) for financing such form of power generation based on new renewables as have been discussed—this is an area that has to be taken up for future research.

Summing up, the study elaborates here that it is not an *either-or* approach in our fuel choice during the transition from fossil fuel to green energy regime. These should include both the optimum use of fossil fuel for generating the resource rent arising from their exploitation and their mobilisation for investment in the development of the backstop technology of renewables-based energy as well as in various energy conservation technologies across the CO_2 intensive sectors of the economy through their modernisation. We propose the conversion of the fossil fuel assets into clean energy resource developing asset not by stopping altogether extraction of fossil fuel but by using the capital fund created out of their resource rent arising from their extraction for the purpose of development of the new renewables. There should of course be every effort of converting the existing fossil fuels through beneficiation and other technical measures into cleaner ones for particularly the generation of electrical energy.

References

Bhide, A., & Monroy, C. R. (2011). Energy poverty: A special focus on energy poverty in India and renewable energy technologies. *Renewable and Sustainable Energy Reviews, 15*(2), 1057–1066.

Birol, F. (2007). Energy Economics: A Place for Energy Poverty in the Agenda?. *The Energy Journal,28*(3), 1–6.

Bouzarovski, S., & Petrova, S. (2015). A global perspective on domestic energy deprivation: Overcoming the energy poverty–fuel poverty binary. *Energy Research & Social Science, 10*, 31–40.

Chakravarty, S., & Tavoni, M. (2013). Energy poverty alleviation and climate change mitigation: Is there a trade off? *Energy Economics, 40*, S67–S73.

Dhara, S. (2017). The central role of surplus energy in human development and a class-divided unsustainable society. In P. Mukhopadhyay, N. Nawn, & K. Das (Eds.), *Global ghange, ecosystems, sustainability: Theory, Methods, Practice* (pp. 82–97). Sage.

Gupta, S., Gupta, E., & Sarangi, G. K. (2020). Household energy poverty index for India: An analysis of inter-state differences. *Energy Policy,144*, 111592.

González-Eguino, M. (2015). Energy poverty: An overview. *Renewable and Sustainable Energy Reviews, 47*, 377–385.

Kakwani, N., Wagstaff, A., & Van Doorslaer, E. (1997). Socioeconomic inequalities in health: Measurement, computation, and statistical inference. *Journal of Econometrics, 77*(1), 87–103.

Kaygusuz, K. (2011). Energy services and energy poverty for sustainable rural development. *Renewable and Sustainable Energy Reviews, 15*(2), 936–947.

Lanjouw, J. O. (2001). Demystifying poverty lines. *Series on Poverty Reduction (New York, UNDP, 1997).* Retrieved from http://siteresources.worldbank.org/PGLP/Resources/LanjouwDemystifyingPovertyLines.pdf

Liu, Z., Wu, D., He, B. J., Wang, Q., Yu, H., Ma, W., & Jin, G. (2019). Evaluating potentials of passive solar heating renovation for the energy poverty alleviation of plateau areas in developing countries: A case study in rural Qinghai-Tibet Plateau, China. *Solar Energy, 187*, 95–107.

Lu, Y., Nakicenovic, N., Visbeck, M., & Stevance, A. S. (2015). Policy: Five priorities for the UN sustainable development goals. *Nature, 520*(7548), 432–433.

NITI Aayog. (2017). *Draft National Energy Policy*. Retrieved from https://niti.gov.in/writereaddata/files/new_initiatives/NEP-ID_27.06.2017.pdf

Pachauri, S. (2010). The energy poverty dimension of energy security. *The Routledge Handbook of Energy Security* (pp. 209–222). Routledge.

Parikh, J., & Parikh, K. (2011). India's energy needs and low carbon options. *Energy, 36*(6), 3650–3658.

Rajan, A. (August 3, 2017).*Diversion of clean energy funds to GST is a problem—But a bigger problem is the coal cess itself.* Retrieved from https://scroll.in › *India › Counterview*

Rifkin, J. (2011). *The third industrial revolution: How lateral power is transforming energy, the economy, and the world*. Macmillan.

Sengupta, R. (2020). *Entropy law, sustainability, and third industrial revolution.* Oxford University Press.

Sengupta, R.P. (2015). Role of new renewables in the sustainable energy development of India: Environmental aspects and other drivers. In Rahul Tongia (Ed.), *Blowing hard or shining bright? Making renewable power sustainable in India* (insert page number). Brookings India Publications.

Sen, A. K. (1997). From income inequality to economic inequality. *Southern Economic Journal, 64*(2), 384–401.

UN. (2000). *United Nations millennium declaration, RES/55/2.* United Nations.

UN. (2015). *United Nations millennium declaration, RES/55/2.* United Nations.

Zubi, G., Fracastoro, G. V., Lujano-Rojas, J. M., El Bakari, K., & Andrews, D. (2019). The unlocked potential of solar home systems: An effective way to overcome domestic energy poverty in developing regions. *Renewable Energy, 132*, 1425–1435.

CHAPTER 18

Adolescents' Self-Esteem and the Attainment of Sustainable Development Goal of Good Health and Well-Being

Olusolami Okunlola, Abiodun Gesinde, and Jonathan Odukoya

Introduction

The United Nations (UN) Sustainable Development Goals (SDGs) are a set of 17 goals with 169 target areas set to be achieved within the years 2016 and 2030 (UNICEF, 2017). The SDGs are follow-up initiatives to the Millennium Development Goals (MDGs) which were set for the years 2000 to 2015 (Hwang & Kim, n.d.). While the MDGs focused

O. Okunlola (✉) · A. Gesinde · J. Odukoya
Department of Psychology, Covenant University, Ota, Ogun, Nigeria
e-mail: olusola.okunlola@stu.cu.edu.ng

A. Gesinde
e-mail: abiodun.gesinde@covenantuniversity.edu.ng

J. Odukoya
e-mail: adedayo.odukoya@covenantuniversity.edu.ng

S. Folarin et al. (eds.), *The United Nations and Sustainable Development Goals*, https://doi.org/10.1007/978-3-030-95971-5_18

particularlyon low-income nations, the SDGs are more global in focus (UNICEF, 2017; Hwang & Kim, n.d.). The SDGs are a compendium of sharedvision of the UN member nations carved within a framework that can be supported, maintained in order to achieve improved lives for all people everywhere (GBD, 2016 SDGCollaborators). With the UN's global ambition not to "leave anyone behind inits sustainable development agenda, active contributions and collaborations at all levels were engaged andindeed, adolescents and youths were not left behind" (Hwang & Kim, n.d.). They were includedas priorities in the SDG agenda as contributions through an online survey were taken from over 8million adolescents and youths from different countries. The majority of the respondents were under 30 years old (23% under 15 and 54% between the ages 16–30) (Hwang & Kim, n.d.).With adolescents as key players inthe achievement of the SDGs, issues that concern them such as their standard ofliving, health,and well-being are important factors to consider in this discourse.

The SDG3 is a pivotalgoal among the 17 SDGs, as it focuses ongood healthand well-being. It reads "ensure healthy lives andpromote well-being for all at all ages" (The Commonwealth, 2017; United Nations Development Programme [UNDP], n.d.), and more specifically, target 3.4 of the SDG3 seeks to reduce mortality through non-communicable diseases and promotemental healthand well-being. Indeed it takesgood health and a sound mind toachieve education, poverty alleviation,gender equality, and other SDGs. According to United Nations International Children's Emergency Fund (UNICEF, 2017),mental health is one of the five areasof healthand well-beingthat the SDGs seek to address. More specifically, childand adolescentmental health are important for the kind of society that is desired through the SDG 2030 agenda (UNICEF, 2017; World Health Organization [W.H.O.], 2019). To attain it, a lot has to be done to create awareness so that care formental health becomes the reality of all people and the World Health Organization (WHO) appears to be spearheading this (International association for Community Development [IACD], 2019; W.H.O., 2014, 2019).

Although there has been a substantial increase in global attentionto adolescent health, it's been arguedthat adolescent health in low and middle-income countries, including Nigeria, has been neglected (Kapungu et al., 2017). This neglect appears to be taking a negative toll on thementalhealth andoverall well-beingof adolescents in developing-nations. Adolescents who are persons transitioning between childhood and adulthood have been said to be faced with several stressful situations which affect theirmental health (W.H.O., 2015). Adolescentmental health has been associated with self-harm and suicidal behavior (W.H.O., 2014, 2015). About67,000 adolescent deaths annually are due to self-harm and suicide (Kapungu et al., 2017; W.H.O., 2015), and key contributors to this reality include anxiety, depression,low self-esteem, and behavior problems (W.H.O., 2017). UNICEF had noted that the action of listing-mental health as an agendafor Sustainable Development is a crucial step toward reducing preventable deathsamong adolescents (Bleidorn, 2016).

In today's mental health research, self-esteem has been recognized as an important factorin adolescenthealthand well-being (UNICEF, 2017, W.H.O, 2014, 2015). Self-esteem refers to self-liking, self-respect, and a person's perception of his self-worth (Rosenberg, 1965). It is a subjective and personal assessment of a worthiness of a person (Harris & Orth, 2019). Theoretically, the underpinnings of Abraham Maslow (Maslow, 1987), present self-esteem as a very important need of notonly adolescents but all humanbeings. Adolescents are at a phase of life where they are coping with identity formation issues, quest for independence, and interdependence. Based on their realities, they tend to view themselves positively ornegatively. Self-esteem is often defined aslow self-esteem, orhigh self-esteem (Harris & Orth, 2019), some also add a third,moderate self-esteem (Rosenberg, 1965).

High self-esteem is synonymous with healthy self-esteem and the role ofhealthy self-esteem in the livesof adolescents cannot be overemphasized as it is very critical to their functionality (Okunlola et al., 2020).High self-esteem has been associated with positive life outcomes (Robins et al., 2012) such as healthy physical and mental health, as well as enhancedeconomic well-being based on their excellent academic grades (Orth & Robins, 2014).Low self-esteem on the other hand tends to engender negative outcomes (Orth & Robins, 2014) such as poor academic grades (Robins et al., 2012), depression, and suicidal ideation (Batchman et al., 2011; Orth & Robin, 2014; Chinawa et al., 2015), among others. A number of factors have been reported to be contributory to the varying levelsof adolescent self-esteem. They include age (Bachman et al., 2011), gender (Bachman et al., 2011; Chinawa et al., 2015), social class (Okonkwo, 2013), family contexts (Klarin et al., 2012), and childhood experiences such as child abuse (Okunlola et al., 2021). This paper focuses on age and gender factors that contributeto adolescent self-esteem. This is because the SDG 3 prioritizes various ages along the human life span as well as gender (UNICEF, 2019).

Predictors of Adolescent Self-Esteem

Several factors have been identified as predictorsof self-esteemin adolescents and they include; age, gender, family factors (e.g. Parenting Style), ethnicity, socioeconomic status, and personality traits, among others. This paper discusses two of these factors.

- Age as a predictorof self-esteem

It has been well established in literature that age predictshuman self-esteem (Bachman et al., 2011; Orth & Robins, 2014; Bleidorn et al, 2016). Discussions on the flowof self-esteem across the human lifespan have also been discussed in literature (Erol & Orth, 2011). As discussed earlier in thispaper, self-esteem tends to wax high in childhood and wanes from late childhood through adolescence. Asthe adolescent approaches young adulthood, however, increasein self-esteem is experienced through middle adulthood, and peaks between 50 and 60 years old until a general decline is observed again in late adulthood (Orth & Robin, 2014).

A growing body of research exists on the trajectoryof self-esteem across the human lifespan. While some had focused on the entire lifespan (Robins & Trzesniewski, 2005; Trzesniewski, et al, 2003), others concentrated on the flow between late adolescence and early adulthood (Erol & Orth, 2011; Hutteman et al., 2015). Some others also focusedon self-esteem across early and middle adolescence (Erol & Orth, 2011; Harris et al., 2017). Suffice it to say that there is paucity of literature on studies that covered the trajectory of self-esteem in the entire period of adolescence (early, middle, and late altogether).

Early adolescence, which occurs between 10 and 14 years old (Williams, 2017), has been noted to be the time when cognitive shifts occur. The adolescents begin to show higher-order reasoning about self and its characteristics (Harter, 1999); in other words, they engage in more abstract and conceptual thinking about the self. Hencetheir self-esteem becomes multidimensional in structure and is influenced by a complex, interdependent set of individual and contextual factors, as against self-conception as a simple unidimensional system in childhood (Brinthaupt & Lipka, 2002; DuBois & Hirsch, 2000; Rosenberg, 1986).

As adolescent cognition advances, so do the strong effects of social relations (Brinthaupt & Lipka, 2002). Early adolescents tend to form tight bonds with their friends and the sense of how others approve or disapprove them tends to be internalized. This internalization which begins from middle childhood finds expression on their view of themselves in early adolescence. Furthermore,the adolescents' interactions with their peers often make them form cliques which become their source of self-appreciation (Brinthaupt & Lipka, 2002). In other words, it is what their peers and others around them say or feel about them becomes what they internalize as who they are.

Apart from the cognitive and social aspects, the physical changes that characterize early adolescence, also tend to predicttheir self-esteem. Pubertal changes occur, leading to rapid growth spurt andthe development of sexual characteristics in the individual (Muntean, 2006). These body changes tend to interfere with the sense of self and identitythe adolescent is already internalizing and they tend to introspect a lot (Brinthaupt & Lipka, 2002). Harter (1999) in his study, however, observed that even thoughearly adolescents make attempts to organize and integrate their self-systems, they are unable to form a whole, coherent, realistic, and internally consistent system. This fact may be responsible for why fluctuations intheir self-esteem peaks (Demo & Savin-Williams, 1992) producing a general declinein self-esteem at this stage.

Simmons (1987) in his study observedlow self-esteem inearly adolescents. This he reported was due to the difference in the timing of individual biological transitions; according tohim, self-esteem ofearly adolescents tends to be negatively affected once a different timing is observed in their peers [especially with girls] (Simmons, 1987). Simmons thus considered this fact as a greater cause forlow self-esteem inearly adolescents than the actual experiences of puberty itself and it takes positive factors aroundthe adolescent, such as home and school factors, to enhance his orher self-esteem (Brinthaupt & Lipka, 2002).

- Gender as a predictorof Self-esteemin Adolescents

A large bodyof research supports gender as a predictorof self-esteemin adolescents (Bachman et al., 2011; Bleidorn et al, 2016; Chinawa, et al, 2015; Polce-Lynch, et al, 2001; Quatman & Watson, 2001; Schwalbe & Staples, 1991). These studies present empirical evidence to show that male andfemale adolescents tend to differ strongly intheir self-esteem. This difference however indicates girls to exhibitlower self-esteem than boys; and the reason has been largely attributed to girls' dissatisfaction with their physical appearance and body image (ACT for Youth Upstate Centre of Excellence, 2003; Chinawa et al., 2015; Harter, 1999), as well as their weight (Rumpel & Harris, 1994).

Oyefeso and Zacheaus (1990) in their study investigated the influence of gender differenceon adolescentself-esteem among Yorubas. With a sample of 60 girls and 60 boys, their result indicatedhigher self-esteem in boys than in girls. The authors concluded that the difference in the process of socialization for males and females in Yoruba communities may be responsible for their findings.

In a similar study from the United States, Polce-Lynch et al. (2001) sampled 209 adolescents in an attempt to examine age and gender patternsin self-esteem. They found that while girls reportedlower self-esteem than boys in early adolescence; boys reportedlower self-esteem in late adolescence than the younger boys. Again, Bleidorn et al (2016) conducted an internet-based systematic cross-cultural examination of gender dimensionsof self-esteem among a large sample size (985,937)of adolescents.These adolescents represented forty-eight nations of the world and the results revealed that males consistently reportedhigher self-esteem scores than females. They found associations with cultural differences in socioeconomic and sociodemographic indicators, as the basis for gender differencein adolescentself-esteem. Conversely, however, Okonkwo (2013) did not find gender toinfluence self-esteem in his study of 38 males and 46 females. To him, small sample size in his study may have limited the outcomes of the study.

Role of Adolescent Self-Esteem in Attaining SDG 3

This paper has established the importance of self-esteem inenhancing adolescent mental health. Good mental health on the other hand is required for adolescent psychological well-being. It appears that the onus for achieving SDG3, lies more withthe government of member nations than with UNs asa body. The UN has not only presented a platform but it has also supported nations in various ways to achieve all goals at all levels. The promotion ofmental health in childrenand adolescents then becomes an important task for all countries (W.H.O., 2014, 2017).

Implications for Counseling Psychologists

Self-esteem has been said to be one of the mostwidely researched constructs in the social sciences due to its import on thepsychological well-being of individuals, including adolescents. This has great implications for counseling psychologists and they include:

1. It helps them know how to counsel parents on various ways they can support their children toward healthy self-esteem.
2. School counselors can help to intervene for students withlow self-esteem either due to sexual abuse, or other experiences.

Conclusion and Recommendations

This paper has been an attempt to present a conceptual discourseon self-esteem among adolescents. The self-esteem of adolescents has been discussed in the light of its meaning, development, and its dimensions across adolescent stages of development. The role of self esteem in attaining the UN's SDG3, which seeks to ensure that every person of all ages obtainsgood healthand well-being by the year 2030, has also been discussed. In spite of the laudable goal of the UN, however, it appears the world is not on track in terms ofthe attainment of the SDGs (The Commonwealth, 2017). While a significant progress has been made in developed countries, there appears to be unevenness at country, social class,and health and even gender levels to the attainment of SDG3 in developing countries such as Nigeria (The Commonwealth, 2017). It the light of this, this paper recommends that the government of nations, including Nigeria, must demonstrate the political and financial will to enhancethe health of her population, especially childrenand adolescents. We also recommend that the government should take the lead in creating awareness of the importance of mental health among adolescents. Constant education of the populace appears to be a major tool to achieve SDG 3 and in turn all the other SDGs. People need constant awareness through multiplechannels, about what the SDGs are, and how everyone should be a part. Apart from these, we underscore the need for psychologists and counseling practitioners in Nigeria, who are professionally saddled with the task of helping individuals maintain ahealthy well-being, to make use of their skills in improving thementai health of people around them in schools, hospitals, etc. This will be very helpful in bringing the targets of the SDG3 to reality.

References

ACT for Youth Upstate Center of Excellence. (2003). *Research facts and figures; adolescent self-esteem.*

Batchman, J., O'Malley, P., Freeman-Doan, P., Trzesniewski, K., & Donnellan, M. (2011). Adolescent self esteem: Differences by race/ethnicity, gender, and age. *Self and Identity, 10*(4), 445–473.

Bleidorn, W., Arslan, R., Denissen, J., Rentfrow, P., Gebauer, J., Potter, J., & Gosling, S. (2016). Age and gender differences in self-esteem—A cross-cultural window. *Journal of Personality and Social Psychology, 111*(3), 396–410.

Brinthaupt, T. M., & Lipka, R. P. (2002). *Understanding early adolescent self and identity: Applications and interventions*. State University of New York Press. Project MUSE.

Chinawa, J., Obu, H., Manyike, P., Obi, I., Odetunde, O. I., & Chinawa, A. (2015). Self esteem among adolescents in Nigerian secondary schools: A neglected issue. *British Journal of Medicine & Medical Research, 5*(1), 98–106.

Demo, D., & Savin-Williams, R. (1992). Self-concept stability and change during adolescence. In T. M. Brinthaupt & R. P. Lipka (Eds.), *Understanding early adolescent self and identity: Applications and interventions* (pp. 1–21). State University of New York Press. Project MUSE.

DuBois, D., & Hirsch, B. (2000). Self-esteem in early adolescence: From stock character to Marquee attraction. *Journal of Early Adolescence, 20*(1).

Emam, M., & Abu-Serei, U. (2014). Family functioning predictors of self-concept and self-esteem in children at risk for learning disabilities in Oman: Exclusion of parent and gender contribution. *International Education Studies, 7*(10), 89–99.

Erol, R., & Orth, U. (2011). Self-esteem development from age 14 to 30 years: A longitudinal study. *Journal of Personality and Social Psychology, 101*(3), 607–619.

GBD 2016 SDG Collaborators. Measuring progress and projecting attainment on the basis of past trends of the health-related Sustainable Development Goals in 188 countries: An analysis from the Global Burden of Disease Study

2016. Lancet 2017, 390, 1423–59. http://dx.doi.org/10.1016/S0140-6736(17)32336-X

Harris, M., Wetzel, E., Robins, R., Donnellan, M. & Trzesniewski, K. (2017). The development of global and domain self-esteem from ages 10 to 16 for Mexican-origin youth. *International Journal of Behavioural Development.*

Harris, M. A., & Orth, U. (2019). "The link between self-ssteem and social relationships: A Meta-analysis of longitudinal studies". Journal of Personality and Social Psychology. *Advance Online Publication, 2019*, 1–19. https://doi.org/10.1037/pspp0000265

Harter, S. (1999). *The construction of the self: A developmental perspective.* Guilford Press.

Hutteman, R., Nestler, S., Wagner, J., Egloff, B., & Back, M. D. (2015). Wherever I may roam: Processes of self-esteem development from adolescence to emerging adulthood in the context of international student exchange. *Journal of Personality and Social Psychology, 108*, 767–783. https://doi.org/10.1037/pspp0000015

Hwang, S., & Kim, J. (n.d.). *United nations and sustainable development goals: A handbook for youth.* Retrieved from https://www.unescap.org/sites/default/files/UN%20and%20SDGs_A%20Handbook%20for%20Youth.pdf.

International association for Community Development (IACD) (2019). *Sustainable development goal 3.* Retrieved from https://www.iacdglobal.org/2019/10/10/world-mental-health-day-and-sdg-3-good-health-and-well-being/

Kapungu, C., Petroni, S., Allen, N., & Zeck, W. (2017). Gendered influences on adolescent mental health in low-income and middle-income countries: Recommendations from an expert convening. *Lancet Child & Adolescent Health*, https://dx.doi.org/10.1016/S2352-4642(17)30152-9

Klarin, M., Šimić Šašić, S., & Proroković, A. (2012). The contribution of family and peer interaction to the understanding of selfesteem in adolescents—Gender and cultural similarities and differences. *International Journal of Humanities and Social Science, 2*(21), 1-12.

Maslow, A. H. (1987). *Motivation and personality* (3rd ed.). Harper & Row.

Muntean, A. (2006). *Psychology of human development.* Polirom Publishing House.

Okonkwo, E. (2013). Dual income family, gender and adolescents' self-esteem. *Ife Psychologia, 21*(1), 127–138.

Okunlola, O. B., Gesinde, A. M., & Odukoya, J. A. (2020). Proceedings of INTCESS 2020—7th International Conference on Education and Social Sciences 20–22 January, 2020—Dubai (UAE).

Okunlola, O. B., Odukoya, J. A. & Gesinde, A. M. (2021). Outcomes of sexual abuse on self-esteem among adolescents: A systematic review. *Cogent Social Sciences, 7*, 1, https://doi.org/10.1080/23311886.2020.1856296

Orth, U., & Robins, R. (2014). The development of self esteem. *Current Directions in Psychological Science, 23*(5), 381–387.
Oyefeso, A., & Zacchaeus, A. (1990). Self-esteem as determined by gender differences among Yoruba adolescents in Ibadan, Nigeria: A research note. *Journal of Child Psychology, Psychiatry and Allied Disciplines, 331*, 461–463.
Polce-Lynch, M. Myers, B., Kliewer, W., & Kilmartin, C. (2001). Adolescent self-esteem and gender: Exploring relations to sexual harassment, body image, media influence, and emotional expression. *Journal of Youth and Adolescence, 30*(2), 225–244.
Quatman, T., & Watson, C. M. (2001). Gender differences in adolescent self-esteem: An exploration of domains. *The Journal of Genetic Psychology, 162*, 93–117.
Robins, R., Trzesniewski, K., & Donnellan, M. (2012). A brief primer on self esteem. *The Prevention Researcher, 19*(2), 1–7.
Robins, R. W., & Trzesniewski, K. H. (2005). Self-esteem development across the lifespan. *Current Directions in Psychological Science, 14*, 158–162. https://doi.org/10.1111/j.0963-7214.2005.00353.x
Rosenberg, M. (1965). *Society and the adolescent self-image* (p. 1965). Princeton University Press.
Rosenberg, M. (1986). Self-concept from middle childhood through adolescence. In J. Suls & A. G. Greenwald (Eds.), *Psychological perspectives on the self* (pp. 107–136). Erlbaum.
Rosenberg, M. (1989). *Society and the adolescent self-image*. Princeton University Press.
Rosenberg, M., Schooler, C., Schoenbach, C., & Rosenberg, F. (1995). Global self-esteem and specific self-esteem: Different concepts different outcomes. *American Sociological Review, 60*(1), 141–156.
Rumpel, C., & Harris, T. B. (1994). The influence of weight on adolescent self-esteem. *Journal of Psychosomatic Research, 38*(6), 547–556.
Schwalbe, M., & Staples, C. (1991). Gender differences in sources of self-esteem. *Social Psychology Quarterly, 54*(2), 158–168.
Simmons, R. (1987). Self-esteem in adolescence. In T. M. Brinthaupt & R. P. Lipka (Eds.), *Understanding early adolescent self and identity: Applications and interventions* (pp. 1–21). State University of New York Press. Project MUSE.
The Commonwealth. (2017). *A curriculum framework for the sustainable development goals*. https://www.thecommonwealth-educationhub.net/wp
Trzesniewski, K. H., Donnellan, M. B., & Robins, R. W. (2003). Stability of self-esteem across the life span. *Journal of Personality and Social Psychology, 84*, 205–220. https://doi.org/10.1037/0022-3514.84.1.205

UNICEF. (2017). *Comparing child-focused sustainable development goals (SDGs) in high- income countries: Indicator development and overview*. https://www.unicef-irc.org/publications/pdf/IWP_2017-08.pdf

UNICEF. (2019). *Mental health*. Retrieved from https://data.unicef.org/topic/child-health/mental-health/#more--6569

United Nations Development Programme (UNDP). (n.d). *Sustainable development goal 3*. https://www.undp.org/content/undp/en/home/sustainable-development

WHO. (2014). *Preventing suicide: A global imperative*. World Health Organization.

WHO. (2015). *Mental health atlas 2014*. World Health Organization. Retrieved from http://apps.int/iris/bitstream/10665/178879/1/9789241565011_eng.pdf

WHO. (2017). *Global accelerated action for the health of adolescents (AA-HA!): Guidance to support country implementation*. World Health Organization.

Williams, Y. (2017). What is adolescence?—Definition, stages & characteristics. *Lifespan Developmental Psychology*.http://study.com/academy/lesson/what-is-adolescence-definition-stages-characteristics.html

World Health Organization. (2019). *Mental health*. Retrieved from https://www.who.int/mental_health/world-mental-health-day/en/

CHAPTER 19

Biodegradation of Waste Papers: A Sustainable Technology for a Clean Environment

Modupe Ojewumi, Olawole Olanipekun, Oyinlola Obanla, Adedoyin Abinusawa, and Oluwatobi Kolawole

Introduction

Agricultural (biomass) and household wastes can be very useful if properly recycled (Adeyemo et al., 2013; Jabir & Jabir, 2016; Kim et al., 2016; Saxena & Singh Chauhan, 2017; Wyk & Mohulatsi, 2003; Wyk et al., 1999). Presently, used paper products are not well recycled and they are eventually dumped or burnt, thus further increasing environmental pollution. The process of bioconversion of waste promises to be impressive in controlling solid waste, and the generation of bio-products from leftovers

M. Ojewumi (✉) · O. Obanla · A. Abinusawa · O. Kolawole
Department of Chemical Engineering, Covenant University, Ota, Ogun, Nigeria
e-mail: modupe.ojewumi@covenantuniversity.edu.ng

O. Olanipekun
Department of Chemical Engineering, UNILAG Akoka, Lagos, Nigeria

S. Folarin et al. (eds.), *The United Nations and Sustainable Development Goals*, https://doi.org/10.1007/978-3-030-95971-5_19

can be achieved and maintained by measures that include the action of microorganisms and enzymes (Varotkar et al., 2016). Various metabolic activities of microbial enzymes and in particular, their ability to interact with organic (complex) and inorganic substrate is now being used in the treatment of solid wastes (Wani & Rao, 2013). As a result, the biodegradation of waste papers to reducing sugars using enzymes/microorganisms as a catalyst is a crucial step to be looked into in the production of sugars using an environmentally friendly process (Ojewumi et al., 2014; Wani & Rao, 2013). There has been an increase in the bioconversion of wastepaper materials due to wastepaper pretreatment (Ojewumi, Emetere, et al., 2019). Thus, pretreatment is a crucial step because fermentation and Saccharification processes depend solely on it. Major goal of pretreatment is to improve carbohydrates enzymatic hydrolysis and bioconversion efficiency overall increment for the production of sugars. In order to achieve this goal, various methods of pretreatment, mostly involving chemical pretreatment, have been proposed, with multiple catalysts and reagents for different substrates developed (Ojewumi, Obanla, et al., 2020).

Methods such as grinding/milling, steam/steam explosion, hot water/autohydrolysis, acid treatment, alkali treatment, and so on have been reported (Ojewumi, 2016c). One of the most frequently used methods is the alkaline pretreatment due to the desirable features it possesses. Alkaline pretreatment utilizes mostly nonpolluting and noncorrosive chemicals and are carried out under milder conditions than those needed for acid pretreatment. Since Alkaline reagents effectively interact primarily with lignin, they are mostly used for lignin removal (Ojewumi et al., 2018a; Ojewumi, Oyekunle, et al., 2019).

Deinking is usually carried out in order to remove the ink particles present in the papers. This is because the ink particles hinder effective hydrolysis, since paper contains high ash content with inorganic fillers such as calcium carbonate and clay which is been added to improve the printing properties (Kim et al., 2016; Wani & Rao, 2013; Wyk & Mohulatsi, 2003). It is now a common process carried out in paper mills where newsprint is recycled. This involves an appreciable quantity of chemicals and usually resulting in a high pollution load. Enzymatic and physical methods of deinking have a valuable approach because of their high efficiency and environmentally friendly nature. In paper recycling processes, enzymatic deinking reduces chemical consumption, thereby reducing the load on the wastewater treatment system and environmental pollution (Ojewumi, Kolawole, et al., 2019; Ojewumi, Ogele, et al., 2019).

Fermentable/reducing sugars are sugars that can be broken down by yeast to produce bio-ethanol. It is an alternative to the use of fossil fuels, and is more environmentally friendly, as combustion of fossil fuels leads to the emission of greenhouse gases which causes global warming (Wyk & Mohulatsi, 2003).

Experimental Procedures

Source of Raw Materials

Waste Papers: Waste foolscap, newspapers, and brown envelop used for this research were collected from the Covenant University environs.

Microorganisms: *Rhizopus* (fungi) clinical isolate were sourced from Applied Biology and Biotechnology Unit Laboratory of Covenant University, Ota, Ogun State.

Preparation of Cellulase: The preparation of cellulose used was done using the method of (Ojewumi et al., Ojewumi, Oyekunle, et al., 2019). The fungi isolates were Standardized using 0.5 Mcfarland, and 1 ml of each isolate was dispensed into the already pretreated substrates and were mixed to make a homogenous mixture, and then they were incubated at 37^0C at room temperature (Saxena & Singh Chauhan, 2017; Ojewumi, Oyekunle, et al., 2019; Ojewumi, Obielue, et al., 2018; Ojewumi et al., 2016b).

Pretreatment of Paper Materials: The waste papers were sorted and cut into smaller sizes of 2 cm by 2 cm, which is the physical pretreatment carried out for efficient conversion (Ojewumi et al., 2019b; Ojewumi, Ezeocha, et al., 2020).

Deinking and Alkaline Pretreatment: Method of (Ojewumi, Obielue, et al., 2018; Ojewumi, Oyekunle, et al., 2019) was used.

Enzymatic Hydrolysis: The pretreated paper substrates were mixed with the *Rhizopus* solution (1 mL) and incubated for 7 days at temperatures 37, 40, and 45°C. Paper samples were collected daily and analysed using the Dinitrosalicylic acid method for analysis of fermentable sugars.

Proximate Analysis Determination: The determination of moisture content, crude fibre, and ash content were analysed using the standard AOAC method 2000 (Ojewumi et al., 2016a; Ojewumi, 2016c; Ojewumi et al., 2018c). While the carbohydrate content was determined using the Anthrone method (Ojewumi, Obielue, et al., 2018).

Determination of Reducing Sugars Content: The concentrations of sugars were determined by the Dinitrosalicylic acid method which is popularly known as the DNS method and absorbance was recorded for each sample that was collected (Ojewumi, Obielue, et al., 2018; Ojewumi, Oyekunle, et al., 2019) (Figs. 19.1, 19.2, 19.3, 19.4, 19.5, 19.6 and 19.7).

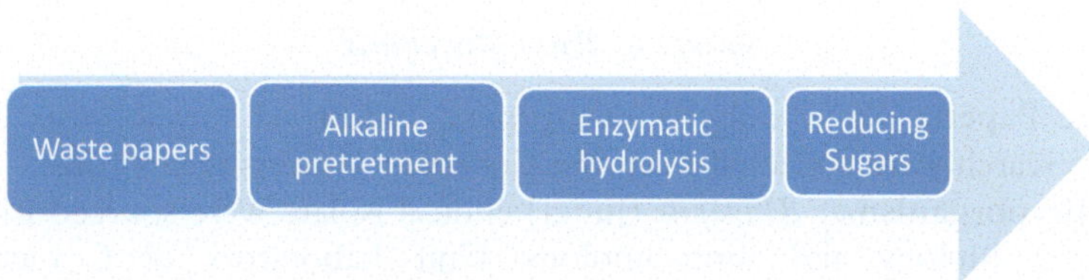

Fig. 19.1 Bioconversion process

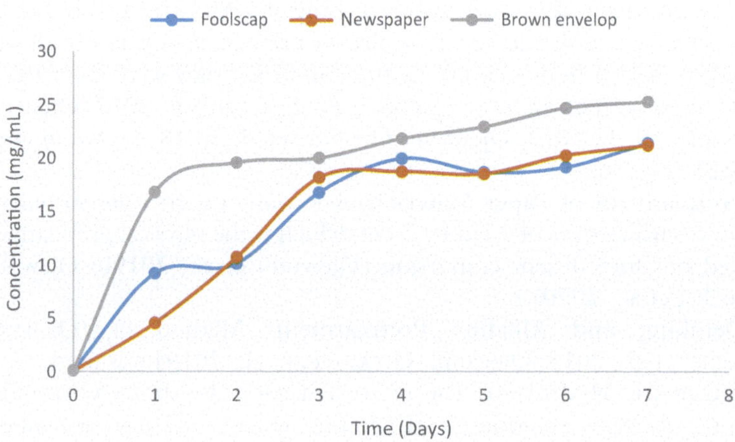

Fig. 19.2 Concentration of reducing sugar against time at 37°C using *Rhizopus*

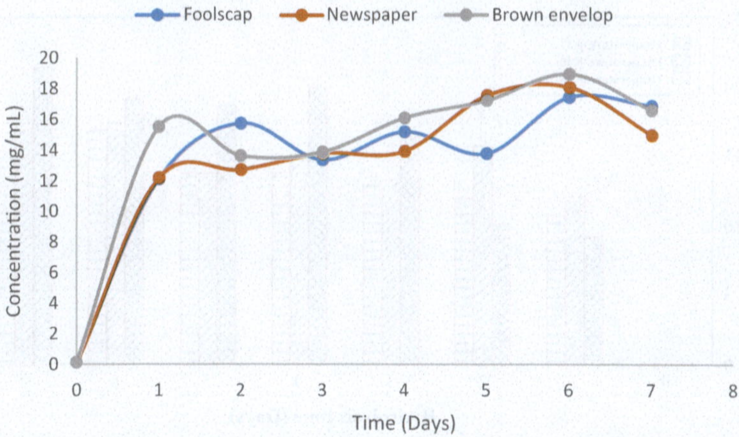

Fig. 19.3 Concentration of reducing sugar against time at 40°C using *Rhizopus*

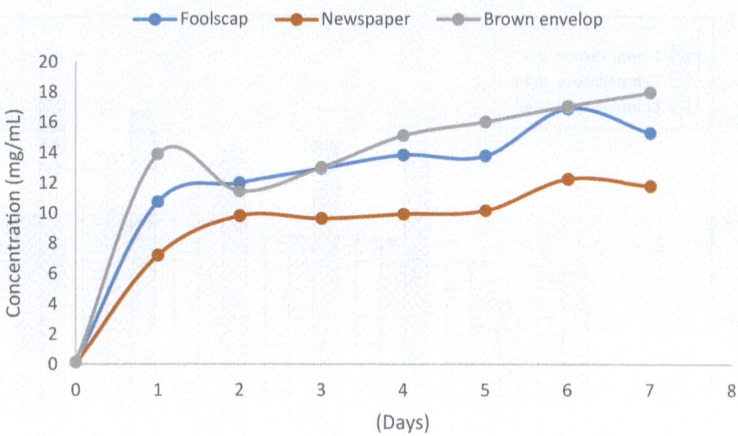

Fig. 19.4 Concentration of reducing sugar against hydrolysis time at 45°C using *Rhizopus*

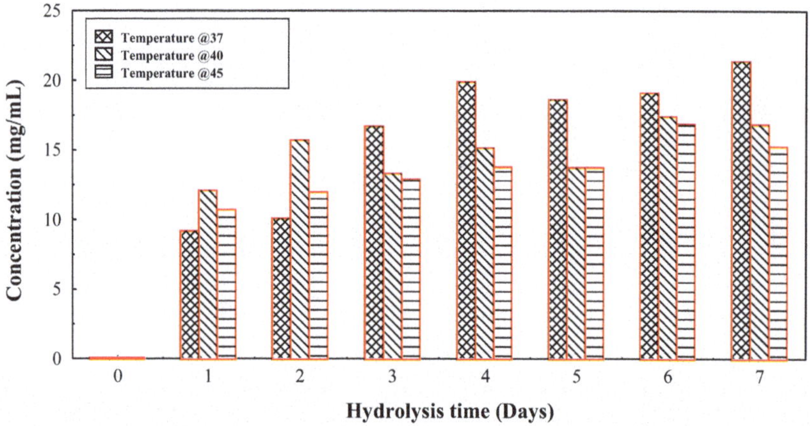

Fig. 19.5 Different temperature effects on the yield of reducing sugar using Foolscap paper as substrate

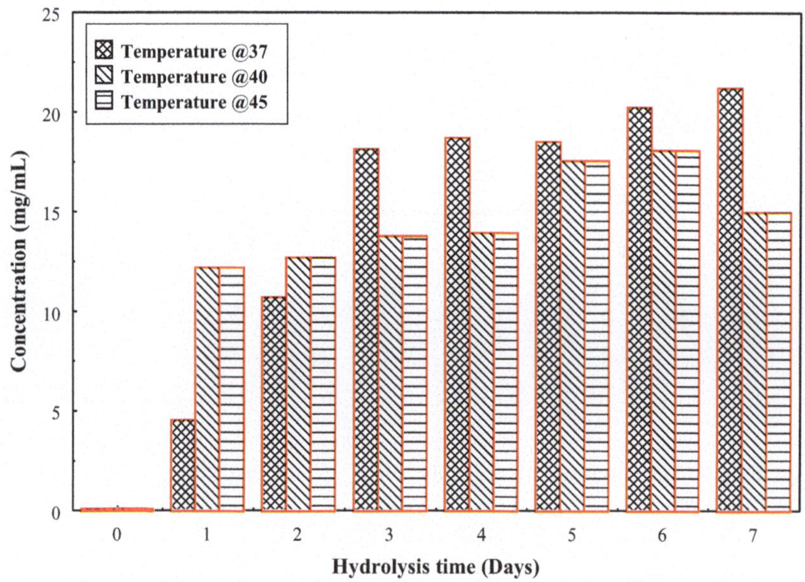

Fig. 19.6 Different temperature effects on the yield of reducing sugar using Newspaper as substrate

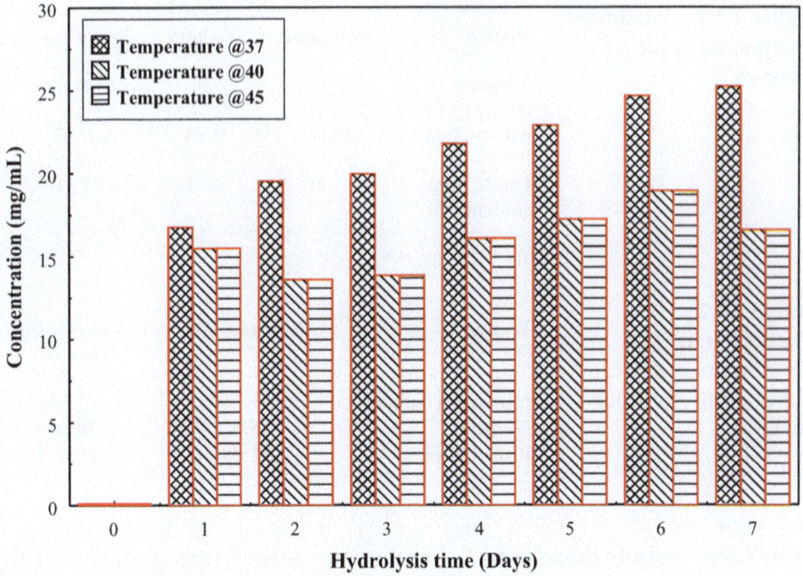

Fig. 19.7 Different temperature effects on the yield of reducing sugar using Brown envelop as substrate

Results and Discussion

With the use of the Dinitrosalicylic acid test method, the standard glucose calibration curve was plotted and all calculations were done with Microsoft Excel 2018 with a line equation [$y = 13.623x + 0.1254$].

where y = Concentration in mg/ml

x = Absorbance

Table 19.1 shows the proximate analyses of the three paper samples used. The newspaper had the highest moisture composition, this might probably be due to the fact that the newspapers used were collected from the Library where the air conditioner is always on. Crude ash composition was discovered to be highest in the foolscap paper sample with a value of 9.8%; the crude ash composition informs the presence of mineral and sand in the sample. The crude ash content also informs the contamination of the samples with the soil. Brown envelop sample had the highest percentage crude fibre of about 2.7%, this can be due to the thickness and colour of the paper sample compared to others. Table 19.2

Table 19.1 Proximate analyses on waste samples

Analysis	*Newspaper*	*Foolscap*	*Brown envelop*
Moisture content (%)	6.00	5.30	5.60
Ash content (%)	9.00	9.80	7.00
Crude fibre content (%)	1.00	0.52	2.70

Table 19.2 Carbohydrate concentration in treated paper using Anthrone method

Samples	*Absorbance (Abs.)*	*Concentration (mg/mL)*
Newspaper sample	31.210	41.011
Foolscap	15.022	20.010
Brown envelop	21.885	28.872

shows the carbohydrate composition of the waste paper samples using the Anthrone method. Newspaper was obtained as the sample with the highest percentage Carbohydrate composition of about 41.011 mg/mL (Ojewumi, Oyekunle, et al., 2019).

After enzymatic hydrolysis for 7 days (1 week) at 37, 40, and 50°C, the concentration of reducing sugar was monitored for 24 h (daily) to observe the trend of the process (increase or decrease) and the results were recorded. Generally, the trend of the concentration of the reducing sugar was on the increase from the 1st day to the 7th day as shown in Figs. 19.2, 19.3, 19.4 at the stipulated temperatures with Brown envelop having the highest concentration of reducing sugar on the 7th day. Although slight distortions occurred in certain days which could be due to reduction in microbial activities with the aqueous solution of the mixtures.

Enzymes are generally known to be specific in action and are active in operation at specific conditions which are popularly known as optimum conditions. The general optimum conditions for *Rhizopus* are within the range of 35–50°C, although analysis was focussed within the range of 37–45°C. At 37°C, *Rhizopus* produced the highest yield on all the paper samples used. Brown paper sample had the highest concentrations with 25.261 mg/ml. From research study carried out by (Wyk & Mohulatsi, 2003) Brown paper samples, the polysaccharide constituent of the sample is about 70–76% of the dry weight, and the enzymatic hydrolysis susceptibility of the sample to liberate fermentable sugars is largely increased with pretreatment method or pre-hydrolysis; with proper pretreatment method on the Brown paper sample involving physical pretreatment in reduction of the size to 2 cm by 2 cm, deinking with 4% sodium hypochlorite and alkaline pretreatment using sodium hydroxide, hence the high concentration yield of the Brown paper after the enzymatic treatment at 37°C for 7 days. The best yield obtained from the *Rhizopus* after 7 days at 40°C also was on the foolscap sample with a concentration of 16.909 mg/ml, while for 45°C Brown paper.

The comparative analysis carried out with the varying temperature of 37°C, 40°C, and 45°C, it was deduced that the yield of reducing sugars liberated decreased with an increase in temperature. Enzymes have peculiar optimum temperature where they function at their best. Considering the temperature rise from optimum condition, their functional state could either reduce or become inactive. This might be due to conformational changes also that enzymes or other essential proteins do not function well and hence bacteria dies. Other reasons might be due to the cell walls that are protecting the bacteria; those proteins also get affected because of temperature change. Hence there are chances of bacteria dying. Although bacterial enzymes such as the ones used for this work have an optimum range of temperature that aid their microbial activities (37°C–45°C). However, the comparative analysis of both temperature and the metabolites shows that 37°C is a more optimum temperature in the production of reducing sugar from waste paper substrates and also that *Rhizopus* has very good effects in the bioconversion on the paper samples. The Brown envelops and the office paper samples were the most susceptible of all the paper samples analysed.

Conclusion

This work confirmed *Rhizopus* to have the ability to degrade papers into fermentable sugars. Highest concentration of reducing sugar as recorded on Brown envelope sample (25.260 mg/ml) which poses to have the highest susceptibility rate among the other waste paper samples, followed by the foolscap paper samples. The temperature ranging from 37, 40 to 45°C is an optimum temperature range for proper bacterial actions on the substrate which are waste paper materials. Temperature at 37°C was recorded to be a better Saccharification temperature than 40 and

45°C. The enzymatic hydrolysis of waste paper is of major interest, seeing it could be an alternative solution for solid waste material treatment and corresponding glucose and ethanol production. The bioconversion process of waste papers to fermentable sugars is an "environmentally friendly" one since no harmful side products were released during the process, also the demand for energy during the process is very low (as the highest temperature was 45°C).

References

Adeyemo, I. A., Adetoyi, O. E., Oni, M. O., Ayodele, M. J., & Olayemi, A. B. (2013). Studies on degradation of waste papers using microflora/microbial consortia isolated from refuse dumpsites in Ilorin metropolis. *International Journal of Biotechnology and Food Science, 1*(1), 13–22.

Kim, J. S., Lee, Y., & Kim, T. H. (2016). A review on alkaline pretreatment technology for bioconversion of lignocellulosic biomass. *Bioresource Technology, 199*, 42–48.

Jabir, M., & Jabir, M. M. (2016). A study of biodegradation of paper wastes by using bacteria isolated from the soil. *Asian Journal of Microbiology and Biotechnology Environmental Sciences, 18*(3), 225–229.

Ojewumi, M. E., Ayomide, A. A., Obanla, O. M., & Ojewumi, E. O. (2014). Pozzolanic properties of waste agricultural biomass-african locust bean pod waste. *World Journal of Environmental Biosciences, 6*(3), 1–7.

Ojewumi, M. E., Omoleye, J., & Ajayi, A. A. (2016a). Optimum fermentation temperature for the protein yield of parkia biglobosa seeds (Iyere). *3rd International Conference on African Development Issues (CU-ICADI)*, 584–587. ISSN: 2449-075X.

Ojewumi, M. E., Omoleye, J., & Ajayi, A. A. (2016b). The effect of different starter cultures on the protein content in fermented African Locust Bean (*Parkia biglobosa*) seeds. *International Journal of Engineering Research & Technology (IJERT), 5*(4), 249–255.

Ojewumi, M. E., (2016c). Optimizing the conditions and processes for the production of protein nutrient from *Parkia biglobosa* Seeds, A Ph.D. thesis submitted to the Department of Chemical Engineering, Covenant University, Ota, Nigeria.

Ojewumi, M. E., Odubiyi, A. O., & Omoleye, J. (2018a). Bio-conversion of sweet potato peel waste to bioethanol using saccharomyces cerevisiae. *International Journal of Pharmaceutical and Phytopharmacological Research, 8*(3), 46–54.

Ojewumi, M. E., Obielue, B. I., Emetere, M. E., Awolu, O. O., & Ojewumi, E. O. (2018b). Alkaline pre-treatment and enzymatic hydrolysis of waste papers to fermentable sugar. *Journal of Ecological Engineering, 19*(1), 211–217.

Ojewumi, M. E., Odubiyi, A. O., & Omoleye, J. (2018c). Effect of storage on protein composition of fermented soybean (*Glycine Max*) Seed by *Bacillus subtillis. Novel Techniques in C Nutrition and Food Science, 2*(4), 1–5.

Ojewumi, M. E., Emetere, M., Amaefule, C. V., Durodola, B. M., & Adeniyi, O. D. (2019a). Bioconversion of orange peel waste by *Escherichia coli* and *Saccharomyces cerevisiae* to Ethanol. *International Journal of Pharmaceutical Sciences and Research, 10*(3), 1246–1252.

Ojewumi, M. E., Oyekunle, D. T., Amaefule, C. V., Omoleye, J. A., & Ogunbiyi, A. T. (2019b). Investigation into alternative energy sources from waste citrus peel (Orange): Approach to environmental protection. *Journal of Physics: Conference Series* 1378 022066, IOP Publishing. https://doi.org/10.1088/1742-6596/1378/2/022066

Ojewumi, M. E., Ogele, P. C., Oyekunle, D. T., Omoleye, J. A., Taiwo, S. O., & Obafemi, Y. D. (2019c). Co-digestion of cow dung with organic kitchen waste to produce biogas using Pseudomonas aeruginosa. *Journal of Physics: Conference Series*. 1299 012011, IOP Publishing. https://doi.org/10.1088/1742-6596/1299/1/012011

Ojewumi, M. E., Kolawole, O. E., Oyekunle, D. T., Taiwo, O. S., & Adeyemi, A. O. (2019d). Bioconversion of waste foolscap and newspaper to fermentable sugar. *Journal of Ecological Engineering, 20*(4), 35–41.

Ojewumi, M. E., Obanla, O. R., Ekanem, G. P., Ogele, P. C., & Ojewumi, E. O. (2020a). Anaerobic decomposition of cattle manure blended with food waste for biogas production. *International Journal of Recent Technology and Engineering (IJRTE), 9*(2), 357–365. ISSN: 2277–3878.

Ojewumi, M. E., Ezeocha, C. R., Alagbe, E. E., Obanla, O. R., & Omodara, O. J. (2020b). Optimization of bleaching of crude palm oil using activated groundnut hull. *4th International Conference on Engineering for a Sustainable World (ICESW)*. IOP Conference series. In Press.

Saxena, A., & Singh Chauhan, P. (2017). Role of various enzymes for deinking paper: A review. *Critical Reviews in Biotechnology, 37*(5), 598–612.

Van Wyk, J. P. H., Mogale, M. A., & Moroka, K. S. (1999). Bioconversion of waste paper materials to sugars: An application illustrating the environmental benefit of enzymes. *Biochemical Education, 27*(4), 227–228.

Van Wyk, J., & Mohulatsi, M. (2003). Biodegradation of wastepaper by cellulase from Trichoderma viride. *Bioresource Technology, 86*(1), 21–23.

Varotkar, P., Tumane, P. M., & Wasnik, D. D. (2016). Wasnik, Bioconversion of waste paper into bioethanol by co-culture of fungi isolated from lignocellulosic waste. *International Journal of Pure Applied Bioscience, 4*, 206–215.

Wani, K., & Rao, R. (2013). Bioconversion of garden waste, kitchen waste and cow dung into value-added products using earthworm Eisenia fetida. *Saudi Journal of Biological Sciences, 20*(2), 149–154.

CHAPTER 20

Fog Computing Technology: A Review of Current Trends

Isaac Odun-Ayo and Oladapo Alagbe

Introduction

The advent of Cloud computing has brought about lots of advantages to consumers and end users such as accessibility to infrastructure, flexibility and elasticity (Hajibaba & Gorgin, 2014). These computing services which are scalable, on-demand, elastic, multi-tenant and virtualized, are provided to customers over the internet by Cloud Service Providers (CSPs), which makes up the concept of Cloud Computing (Odun-Ayo, Ajayi, et al., 2018). There has been an upward trend in the connection of Internet-of-Things (IoT) devices to Cloud Computing, as data generated by these devices are analyzed in the Cloud. This has heightened the application of technologies such as Big Data/Data Analytics, which are supported by cloud computing (Odun-Ayo, Okereke, et al., 2018). Data is currently being produced at an astronomical rate, and this has led to an

I. Odun-Ayo (✉) · O. Alagbe
Department of Computer and Information Sciences, Covenant University, Ota, Nigeria
e-mail: isaac.odun-ayo@covenantuniversity.edu.ng

S. Folarin et al. (eds.), *The United Nations and Sustainable Development Goals*, https://doi.org/10.1007/978-3-030-95971-5_20

explosion in the demand for high computing capacity based on this data increase, and also the evolution of other enterprise information systems (Chao et al., 2018).

The increased use of cloud computing has led to it being rife with various challenges such as network latency and privacy-related concerns, as there is an increase in the need for real-time and near real-time data analytics. Technologies such as Edge and Fog computing serve as the conduit between the data sources such as IoT and end user devices, and the cloud computing infrastructure, as they operate at the fringes of the network. Such technologies lead to savings in bandwidth by ensuring that not all traffic is sent to the core cloud (Odun-Ayo et al., 2019).

Fog computing has been described as a "decentralized computing architecture whereby applications, compute, data, and storage are located somewhere between the source of the data and the cloud, thereby bringing closer to the data source, the advantages and capabilities of the cloud" (*What Is Fog Computing?—Definition from WhatIs.com*, n.d.). The terminology "Fog Computing" was formed by Cisco, as the next wave of innovations directed at bringing computing capabilities closer to the users and the "things" that generated the data, thereby achieving greater compliance, efficiency and security, unlike what was obtainable through cloud computing.

According to Varghese and Buyya (2018), "fog computing is used to leverage the existing compute resources on edge nodes, such as mobile base stations, routers and switches, or integrate additional computing capability to such (network) nodes along the entire data path between user devices and a cloud datacenter". A typical mock-up of the Fog Computing Structure in the Device-Cloud relationship is as depicted in Fig. 20.1.

IoT devices are increasingly being utilized in Industries. These are known as Industrial Internet-of-Things (IIoT) devices, and they led to the "Industry 4.0" concept based on Cyber-Physical Systems (CPS), which then led to the creation of more types of data that originally would have been processed in the Cloud. These data types include data generated from sensors, data as a result of Operating Technology and Information Technology (OT-IT) integration, data generated from connected smart devices and data that is generated from robots in cloud-based systems. These data require content perception, real-time computing and parallel processing which can be handled effectively by Fog Computing (Zhang et al., 2018).

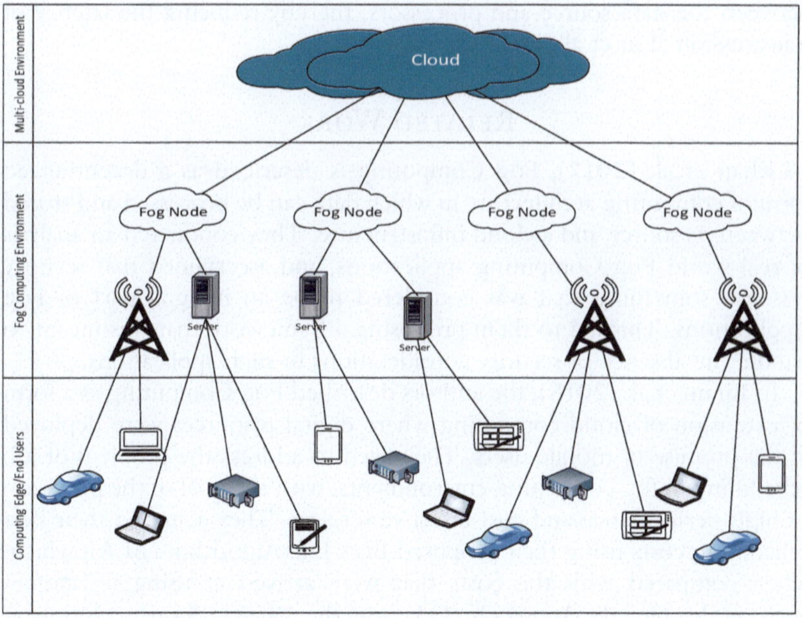

Fig. 20.1 Fog computing structure (*Source* Patil 2018)

Fog computing is not meant to replace cloud computing, rather it is meant to work collaboratively with the cloud thereby extending the traditional cloud-based computing model to a scenario where iterations of the architecture can be found in various layers of a network's topology (Byers & Swanson, 2017). Fog computing is meant to bridge the gap between the traditional cloud computing architecture, and the individual IoT devices that serve the end users directly, through the provision of computing, storage, networking and data management on the network nodes, within a close distance from the IoT devices (Basir et al., 2019). Unlike Ubiquitous Computing though, Fog Computing is targeted at complicated computing tasks, that can utilize a collection of inexpensive and low specs hardware that collectively can make up a high-performance platform (Yousefpour et al., 2019). Fog computing is meant to address the problem of latency in sensitive computing activities as fog computing makes use of local computing resources for data processing, instead of remote cloud resources. This ensures that there is geographical proximity between the data source and processors, thereby reducing the latency of transmission (Liu et al., 2017).

Related Work

In Khan et al. (2017), Fog Computing is described as a decentralized form of computing architecture in which data can be processed and stored between its source and a cloud infrastructure. They conducted an analysis of real-world Fog Computing applications, and ascertained that security was not something that was considered to be an integral part of Fog Applications. This led to them proposing a framework that was meant to handle the absence of security considerations in such applications.

In Bitam et al. (2018), the authors described Fog Computing as a form of extension of cloud computing where digital resources were deployed at the premise of mobile users. They tried to address the problem of job scheduling in fog computing environments, with the goal of the provision of high-performance and cost-effective services. They achieved their best scheduling costs using their proposed Bees Life Algorithm (BLA), which, when compared with the costs that were arrived at using techniques such as the Greedy Approach (GA) and the Particle Swarm Optimization approach, performed much better. The BLA is a population-based approach that is based on the collaborative behaviors of the individuals of the population. Furthermore, they observed that when executing the mutation operation, local optima escape was observed.

In Neto et al. (2018), the authors presented a Fog-Framework for Intelligent Public Safety in Vehicular Environment (FISVER) laboratory testbed. They created a prototype, and also performed extensive evaluations in a real testbed. This framework was then utilized to apply fog computing to smart video surveillance-based Smart Transportation Safety (STS). This supported autonomous and real-time crime detection on public bus services using in-vehicle and fog infrastructure.

The authors in You et al. (2019) evaluated the performance of conventional communication systems via Cloud/Centralized Radio Access Networks (C-RAN) alongside the performance of Fog Computing-based Radio Access Networks (F-RAN). They suggested various service scenarios which reflected the characteristics of immersive media such as Augmented Reality and Virtual Reality. Furthermore, the authors identified the technologies that are necessary for the proposed service scenarios to be supported adequately.

In Venčkauskas et al. (2019), the authors presented a new lightweight Secure Self-Authenticable Transfer Protocol (SSATP) that can be used for communications between Edge nodes and Fog nodes. This protocol utilized modified header fields of standard User Datagram Protocol (UDP) packets to transfer additional protocol handling and dataflow management information, and also authentication information for user data. The authors also presented two modifications of this protocol, and they determined that their modifications were marginally faster than the Datagram Transport Layer Security (DTLS) protocol that was used for transport in the Constrained Application Protocol (CoAP) which was commonly used.

The authors of Aleisa et al. (2020) extensively discussed the Fog Computing model and Access Control models. They presented a state-of-the-art Access Control model that is meant to address the Access Control needs of Fog Computing. The authors also identified the access control requirements of Fog Computing, and they used them to present a state-of-the-art Fog Access Control Evaluation System that addressed all the identified Access Control needs. Furthermore, the authors identified and discussed the various security and privacy-related issues of Fog Computing Access Control.

In Goethals et al. (2020), the authors addressed the near real-time optimization of Fog Service placement through the creation of a service scheduling algorithm which they labeled as "Swirly". This algorithm is capable of incorporating changes in network conditions and connected devices. They presented a large-scale fog service scheduler, which is capable of functioning on a scale of hundreds of thousands of edge devices, while theoretically being able to handle changing network conditions on topologies.

Materials and Method

To perform this review paper, it was pertinent that the various aspects of Fog Computing were reviewed according to various publications. This included a review of the architecture of Fog Computing, the various communication protocols that are utilized in Fog Computing, the characteristics of Fog Computing, and the advantages and disadvantages of Fog Computing. These are all addressed in the following sections.

Fog Computing Architecture

According to Liu et al. (2017), Fog Computing is split into two parts, computing and networking. Computing takes care of the traditional compute and storage needs of the IoT devices, while the networking deals with communication between the nodes, the devices and the cloud computing infrastructure. These two parts are generally determined by the activities that are undertaken to achieve the fog computing concept, namely

- Partitioning of data into sizeable chunks
- Allocation of the chunks to participating nodes
- Queueing and transmission of the chunks
- Due to the queues, channel allocation occurs, thereby leading to some chunks being sent to idle channels for processing
- Processed chunks are sorted according to their finishing time
- The chunks are then transmitted back to their source via the channel allocation concept
- Chunks are then reconnected to form their wholes, at their initial source

The architecture of the typical fog computing environment is made up of the following layers (Aleisa et al., 2020):

1. **Physical Layer**
   This layer is made up of all the hardware that participate in sending and receiving data, to and from IoT devices and the Cloud, and could be made up of either physical or software-based appliances. These appliances are responsible for Network Function Virtualization (NFV) and Software-Defined Networking (SDN) services which enable the Fog Computing environment to function effectively.
2. **Monitoring Layer**
   Detection and logging of performance-related issues and events are conducted in this layer. Metrics such as latency, throughput, bandwidth and congestion are measured in this layer. Furthermore, the detection of security events occurs in this layer, alongside the security layer of the IoT environment.
3. **Processing Layer**

A cardinal use of the Fog Computing architecture is the processing of data closer to the end devices, such as on LAN gateways and other Fog computing servers. This layer is responsible for the types of processing that occur, thereby minimizing the quantity of data that should be transmitted to the cloud environment for intensive data processing.

4. **Storage Layer**

   Data that is generated from the IoT devices are typically stored in this layer of the Fog Computing environment. This storage is characterized by greater sizes than is present in the IoT devices, but still less than what is obtainable from cloud environments, and usually serves as a short to medium-term storage space, unlike the cloud that is for long-term storage.

5. **Security Layer**

   The security layer is used to achieve and maintain the confidentiality, integrity and availability of all the nodes in the fog. It works in close collaboration with the monitoring layer in achieving these objectives and is also where technical and administrative controls are placed.

6. **Application Layer**

   This layer consists of all the applications and protocols that are used to achieve communication between the devices, nodes and cloud. It is similar to the applications layer of the OSI model in computer networking (Fig. 20.2).

Fog Computing Communication Protocols

Since the bulk of Fog Computing is resident in the application and service management layers of the communication stack, it is important to review the types of communication protocols that can be used to achieve node-to-node communication, node-to-cloud communication and node-to-device communication. These protocols are based on the communication protocols that are utilized by IoT devices. A non-exhaustive list of such protocols include:

Constrained Application Protocol (CoAP)

The CoAP is a lightweight protocol that is ideal for implementing communication between sensors in cloud computing environments.

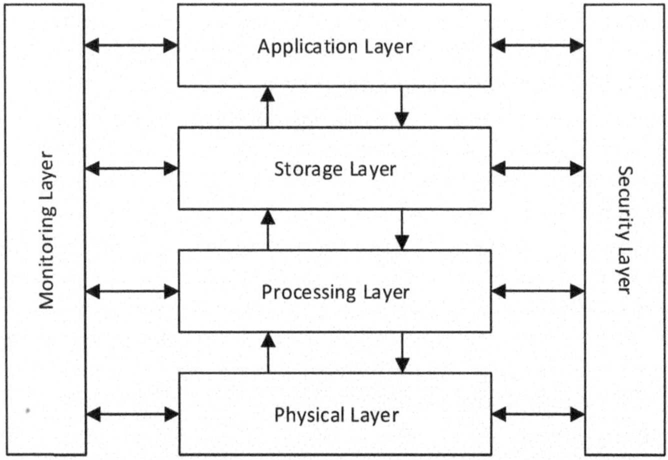

Fig. 20.2 Fog computing layers' intercommunication (*Source* Aleisa et al. 2020)

It adopts the UDP and uses efficient XML Interchanges (EXI) format for data transfer. It consumes less storage and compute resources and is used in several domains such as smart homes and industrial uses (Alhaidari & Alqahtani, 2020).

Message Queue Telemetry Transport (MQTT)

The MQTT protocol utilizes publish/subscribe architectural patterns, with a central broker that mediates between both layers, providing communication and information storage. This protocol is ideal for scenarios where reliability is not a critical requirement, and low bandwidth utilizations exist. Various forms of this protocol exist such as RabbitMQ, IBM MessageSight and Mosquitto, which also implement additional features (Butterfield, 2016).

Advanced Message Queuing Protocol (AMQP)

The AMQP is an open standard protocol. It relies on TCP and is used primarily for the provision of interoperability between servers. This protocol tracks messages and guarantees their transmission from one server to the other, regardless of node failure along the way. It is a robust protocol that is heavyweight and more established than others and is mostly utilized where message reliability is required.

Data Distribution Service (DDS)

This protocol was primarily developed for communication between machines (M2M), and was developed to address the needs of big data application that utilize the publish/subscribe model. This protocol is used in situations where fault tolerance and reliability are very important. It was created by the Object Management Group (OMG), and it is a data-centric model that focuses on ensuring that the data that is presented by one node, is known by all other nodes quickly and accurately (Butterfield, 2016).

Characteristics of Fog Computing

The major characteristics of Fog Computing, according to Saharan and Kumar (2015) include the following:

Mobility: Devices that make up the fog computing environment are usually characterized by mobility. They are usually not fixed to a particular location.

Freedom: Fog Computing infrastructure is used to reduce the amount of computing activities that are conducted on the core cloud infrastructure by offloading these activities to the Fog nodes (Edge Servers), thereby increasing the degree of freedom and independence of end devices, away from the cloud.

Cost: The equipment that makes up Fog Computing infrastructure is usually low-powered, and inexpensive, unlike what is needed for cloud computing infrastructure. This leads to an overall cost that is much lower than what is obtainable in cloud computing. Furthermore, the resources of the infrastructure are such that they can be easily increased, should the need arise.

Computation Ability: Fog computing devices usually have their own computing, storage and networking services and can fully function autonomously. Fog systems can be installed on low specification devices like IP cameras, and low-power processors like ARM processors can easily serve the computing needs.

Low Latency: There is a reduction in the number of hops that data packets have to travel for computation and processing to occur on them. This is due to the proximity between the data source and the cloud node that the data processing will occur. This leads to a minimization of data transmission overheads, thereby improving the performance and responsiveness of the applications that require such processed data at the edge.

Advantages of Fog Computing

- Reduces the quantity of data that is transferred to the cloud
- Ensures that network bandwidth is conserved
- Improves response time of systems
- Ensures that security is improved by keeping data close to the edge
- Supports mobility
- Reduces latency in the local network and internet

Disadvantages of Fog Computing

- Physical locations take away from anytime, anywhere data benefit of the cloud
- Security issues such as IP address spoofing, and man-in-the-middle attacks
- Issues of privacy
- Availability/cost of fog equipment/hardware
- Raises concerns with trust and authentication
- Raises concerns with respect to the security of wireless networks

Results and Discussion

Fog Computing has been found to be applicable to a number of scenarios based on the advantages it presents. These application areas can be split into real-time and near real-time use-cases, depending on the latency requirements of their functions (Osanaiye et al., 2016), which is usually higher than what cloud computing can guarantee. These application areas include:

1. **Smart Cities**: Smart homes, smart offices, smart institutions, smart transportation systems, smart agriculture and smart healthcare services all combine to form the Smart City concept. These usually make use of IoTs, Edge computing, Fog computing and Cloud Computing technologies for the generation of data and its analysis thereby enabling real-time and near real-time operations and

decision-making actions. Edge computing, in collaboration with fog computing is used to transfer some of the compression-related tasks to other edge and fog nodes, thereby reducing the burden of data transmission to cloud infrastructure (Bilal et al., 2018; Patil, 2018).

2. **Smart Manufacturing (Industry 4.0)**: Fog computing is used to achieve the critical requirement of Industry 4.0, namely real-time services with high data processing, maximum capacity and scalability (Basir et al., 2019). Fog computing ensures that transmission delay is eliminated by the provision of data storage on network edge nodes, instead of the remote locations of cloud storage, data is analyzed and processed much faster than what the IIoT applications can do by themselves, the transmission of irrelevant information over the network is avoided through the use of cache-enabled nodes, and filtered and required interaction is provided between CSPs and end devices.
3. **Self-driving cars, drones and airplane systems**: Advanced Driver Assistance Systems (ADAS) can be utilized to allow cars leverage on systems that can deliver better experiences for the users, when combined with Fog Computing, as there is only so much that a car can do in terms of data analysis, and the latency between cloud infrastructure and the cars do not make such analytics feasible as the information from such analytics is needed for both real-time and near real-time operations (Neto et al., 2018). These will help the self-driving vehicles to react to environmental conditions in a much faster manner, thereby making them safer. Fog Computing achieves the democratization of ADAS (Meng et al., 2020).
4. **Remote monitoring for Oil and Gas operations**: Meng et al. (2020) presents how Oil and Gas operations can benefit from Fog Computing based on how near-instant rules could be set up at the various operations sites, where they can analyze data that is generated by sensors at the site, to see signs of events and take the necessary steps to prevent disasters, even before they occur.
5. **Mobile augmented reality (AR), networked gaming**: Immersive Media services such as augmented reality and virtual reality (AR/VR) require massive data storage, ultrahigh computing power and ultralow latency, which their end devices cannot provide adequately. F-RAN have been determined to be massive enablers for these services as they provide the necessary resources for these services to function adequately, over the C-RAN (You et al., 2019).

6. **Mobile eCommerce**: Meng et al. (2020) stated that Fog Computing could be utilized in the retail industry to analyze how customers shop and also place items in their shopping carts, thereby using such information to improve customer engagement and also reduce the tendency for customers to abandon their carts. The data could be generated from sources like images, coupons, etc., and can help the retailers in improving target merchandise and also sales and promotions activities.
7. **Physical security and surveillance systems**: Fog computing has been applied to the "STS in Smart Cities", and via the FISVER to perform autonomous and real-time crime detection on public bus services (Neto et al., 2018).
8. **Virtual assistants**: Smart home assistants such as Google Nest and Amazon Echo are beginning to see further processing and data analytics be performed closer to the end devices through technologies such as fog computing and federated learning.

Conclusion

Due to the ubiquitous nature of IoT devices in both Industrial scenarios and their proliferation in everyday objects, their importance requires compute, storage and applications to be brought closer to end users and data sources, unlike what was previously obtainable when analytics was being migrated to the cloud. This and many more use-cases will lead to increasing use of Fog and Edge computing technologies, alongside the maturing cloud computing technology. Therefore, there is bound to be increasing relevance and importance of Fog computing in how technology is generally used. This seminar touches the concept of Fog Computing and shows that a considerable amount of research is presently ongoing in this aspect of computing. This paper focuses on the current state of Fog Computing, and the advances that have been recorded since its inception. However, there still needs to be improvements in how security is handled in Fog Nodes, how power management is achieved, and how compute can be scaled in a heterogeneous environment like is obtained from various vendors that make up the Fog Computing environment. Further research should also be targeted toward improving the performance of fog computing beyond networking activities such as routing, switching and packet forwarding. In addition, interoperable fog nodes architecture from various vendors still needs to be evaluated and enhanced.

Acknowledgements We appreciate Covenant University's sponsorship and support through its Center for Research, Innovation and Discovery (CUCRID).

References

Aleisa, M. A., Abuhussein, A., & Sheldon, F. T. (2020). Access control in fog computing: Challenges and research agenda. *IEEE Access, 8*, 83986–83999. https://doi.org/10.1109/ACCESS.2020.2992460

Alhaidari, F. A., & Alqahtani, E. J. (2020). Securing communication between fog computing and IoT using constrained application protocol (CoAP): A survey. *Journal of Communications, 15*(1), 14–30. https://doi.org/10.12720/jcm.15.1.14-30

Basir, R., Qaisar, S., Ali, M., Aldwairi, M., Ashraf, M. I., Mahmood, A., & Gidlund, M. (2019). Fog computing enabling industrial internet of things: State-of-the-art and research challenges. *Sensors (Switzerland), 19*(21), 1–38. https://doi.org/10.3390/s19214807

Bilal, K., Khalid, O., Erbad, A., & Khan, S. U. (2018). Potentials, trends, and prospects in edge technologies: Fog, cloudlet, mobile edge, and micro data centers. *Computer Networks, 130*(2018), 94–120. https://doi.org/10.1016/j.comnet.2017.10.002

Bitam, S., Zeadally, S., & Mellouk, A. (2018). Fog computing job scheduling optimization based on bees swarm. *Enterprise Information Systems, 12*(4), 373–397. https://doi.org/10.1080/17517575.2017.1304579

Butterfield, E. H. (2016). *Fog computing with Go: A comparative study.* Claremont McKenna College.

Byers, C., & Swanson, R. (2017). *The OpenFog consortium reference architecture: Executive summary* (pp. 1–10). https://www.openfogconsortium.org/wp-content/uploads/OpenFog-Reference-Architecture-Executive-Summary.pdf

Chao, H. C., Hu, B., & Chen, C. Y. (2018). Fog computing and internet of everything for emerging enterprise information systems. *Enterprise Information Systems, 12*(4), 371–372. https://doi.org/10.1080/17517575.2017.1405076

Goethals, T., De Turck, F., & Volckaert, B. (2020). Near real-time optimization of fog service placement for responsive edge computing. *Journal of Cloud Computing, 9*(1). https://doi.org/10.1186/s13677-020-00180-z

Hajibaba, M., & Gorgin, S. (2014). A review on modern distributed computing paradigms: Cloud computing, jungle computing and fog computing. *Journal of Computing and Information Technology, 22*(2), 69–84. https://doi.org/10.2498/cit.1002381

Khan, S., Parkinson, S., & Qin, Y. (2017). Fog computing security: A review of current applications and security solutions. *Journal of Cloud Computing, 6*(1). https://doi.org/10.1186/s13677-017-0090-3

Liu, Y., Fieldsend, J. E., & Min, G. (2017). A framework of fog computing: Architecture, challenges, and optimization. *IEEE Access, 5*, 25445–25454. https://doi.org/10.1109/ACCESS.2017.2766923

Meng, Y., Naeem, M. A., Almagrabi, A. O., Ali, R., & Kim, H. S. (2020). Advancing the state of the fog computing to enable 5g network technologies. *Sensors (Switzerland), 20*(6), 1–26. https://doi.org/10.3390/s20061754

Neto, A. J. V., Zhao, Z., Rodrigues, J. J. P. C., Camboim, H. B., & Braun, T. (2018). Fog-based crime-assistance in smart IoT transportation system. *IEEE Access, 6*, 11101–11111. https://doi.org/10.1109/ACCESS.2018.2803439

Odun-Ayo, I., Ajayi, O., & Misra, S. (2018). *Cloud computing security: Issues and developments*. Lecture Notes in Engineering and Computer Science, 2235.

Odun-Ayo, I., Goddy-Worlu, R., Bogle, S., & Geteloma, V. (2019). A systematic mapping study of cloud, fog, and edge/mobile devices management, hierarchy models and business models. *Advances in Science, Technology and Engineering Systems Journal, 4*(2), 91–101. https://doi.org/10.24507/icicelb.10.09.797

Odun-Ayo, I., Okereke, C., & Orovwode, H. (2018). Cloud computing and internet of things: Issues and developments. *Proceedings of the World Congress on Engineering, 1*, 6.

Osanaiye, O., Chen, S., Yan, Z., Lu, R., Choo, K.-K. R., & Dlodlo, M. (2016). From cloud to fog computing: A review and a conceptual live VM migration framework. *IEEE Access: Special Section on Recent Advances in Cloud Radio Access Networks*, 5(d). https://doi.org/10.1109/ACCESS.2017.2692960

Patil, P. V. (2018). Fog computing. *International Journal of Computer Applications, 60*(1), 68–74. https://doi.org/10.4018/ijghpc.2017100107

Saharan, K. P., & Kumar, A. (2015). Fog in comparison to cloud: A survey. *International Journal of Computer Applications*, *122*(3), 10–12. https://doi.org/10.5120/21679-4773

Varghese, B., & Buyya, R. (2018, September). Next generation cloud computing: New trends and research directions. *Future Generation Computer Systems*, *79*, 849–861. https://doi.org/10.1016/j.future.2017.09.020

Venčkauskas, A., Morkevicius, N., Jukavičius, V., Damaševičius, R., Toldinas, J., & Grigaliūnas, Š. (2019). An edge-fog secure self-authenticable data transfer protocol. *Sensors (Switzerland), 19*(16), 1–19. https://doi.org/10.3390/s19163612

What is fog computing?—Definition from WhatIs.com. (n.d.). Retrieved August 22, 2020, from https://internetofthingsagenda.techtarget.com/definition/fog-computing-fogging

You, D., Doan, T. V., Torre, R., Mehrabi, M., Kropp, A., Nguyen, V., Salah, H., Nguyen, G. T., & Fitzek, F. H. P. (2019). Fog computing as an enabler for immersive media: Service scenarios and research opportunities. *IEEE Access, 7*, 65797–65810. https://doi.org/10.1109/ACCESS.2019.2917291

Yousefpour, A., Fung, C., Nguyen, T., Kadiyala, K., Jalali, F., Niakanlahiji, A., Kong, J., & Jue, J. P. (2019). All one needs to know about fog computing and related edge computing paradigms: A complete survey. *Journal of Systems Architecture, 98*(December 2018), 289–330. https://doi.org/10.1016/j.sysarc.2019.02.009

Zhang, J., Chen, B., Zhao, Y., Cheng, X., & Hu, F. (2018). Data security and privacy-preserving in edge computing paradigm: Survey and open issues. *IEEE Access*, *6*(Idc), 18209–18237. https://doi.org/10.1109/ACCESS.2018.2820162

CHAPTER 21

Conclusion

Aderemi Atayero, Sheriff Folarin, and Esther Akinlabi

The chapters in this book have addressed local and global human development issues with a multidisciplinary and interdisciplinary approach. Scholars and professionals from various academic and ideological backgrounds in the nineteen previous chapters have taken stock of and analysed issues that have affected the world in the last decades with

A. Atayero (✉)
Department of Electrical and Information Engineering, Covenant University, Ota, Nigeria
e-mail: atayero@cu.edu.ng

S. Folarin
Department of Political Science and International Relations, Covenant University, Ota, Nigeria
e-mail: sheriff.folarin@covenantuniversity.edu.ng

E. Akinlabi
Department of Mechanical Engineering Science, University of Johannesburg, Johannesburg, South Africa
e-mail: etakinlabi@uj.ac.za

Pan African University Life and Earth Sciences Institute, Ibadan, Nigeria

S. Folarin et al. (eds.), *The United Nations and Sustainable Development Goals*, https://doi.org/10.1007/978-3-030-95971-5_21

the view to providing medium and long-term solutions and have by extension, expanded the frontiers of knowledge.

The issues captured in the preceding chapters include conflict–ethnicity, xenophobia, race; poverty, human security, education, climate change, water and food security, diplomacy, gender, and good governance. Other topics of discourse range from science and technology to engineering, architecture, and health (COVID-19 in particular). The issues are topical and central to the focus of the United Nations, which, in the last seventy five years, have sought an end to the perennial crises of the international community. Some of the issues addressed are critical to the UN Sustainable Development Goals (SDGs) and its forbear, Millennium Development Goals (MDGs).

In fact, several of the chapters are inspired by the ingenuity of the idea and challenges of the SDGs, which may encumber its actualisation in some countries and the rest of the world. The discussions thus provide insights to troubleshooting the encumbrances, x-raying, and unearthing the hidden impediments, with the view to setting a robust agenda and stimulating new thoughts on how to create a desirable future and building a more results-oriented United Nations.

The division into three sections is for the purpose of thematic approach to looking at the issues, which are critical areas that occupy the centrepiece of narratives on moving the global system forward. The thematic approach in organising the chapters will guarantee that no value is lost. The sequence is to also allow a flow—from the human social and economic needs as well as community relations and organisation, to the world of science and technology, which has become a defining moment for the future.

This book does not pretend to address all the critical issues of the world. Global problems are multifaceted, copious, and diverse. For instance, the challenges for actualising the SDGs are multiple and inexhaustive. In UN report of 2017, difficult global environment, sluggish growth and humanitarian crises are identified as a major inhibitor to individual and collective efforts, which have created many implementation gaps (UN, 2017). Thus, there was the Addis Agenda framework to provide a broad framework for individual actions and international cooperation to increase sustainable development investments. This is with the hope that its rapid implementation can stimulate global growth and advance the world toward achieving the SDGs. The Addis Agenda, reached in Etiopia, "seeks to mobilize public finance, to set appropriate frameworks to unlock private finance, trade opportunities and technological development, ensure debt sustainability and align the international financial, monetary and trading system with economic, social and environmental priorities" (UN Report, 2017). The approach entails both domestic actions and a commitment to create an enabling international environment that supports national efforts.

According to the report,

> At its heart are two main elements: integrated national financing frameworks to underpin coherent and nationally owned sustainable development strategies; and supportive global trade, monetary and financial systems. The national frameworks and strategies address country-specific needs and circumstances, and provide coherence to the many policy actions across the Addis Agenda action areas. Their implementation is what will drive progress toward the sustainable development goals and targets. (UN Report, 2017)

The UN avers further that SDGs face other challenges, which include difficult macroeconomic conditions, a large drop in commodity prices, decelerating trade growth and volatile capital flows; natural disasters, environmental, humanitarian and security crises. These difficulties could be further exacerbated if the international community retreats from its commitment to multilateral cooperation for sustainable development. A renewed commitment and concrete actions by member-states to create and preserve an enabling international economic environment will therefore remain a priority.

In spite of the concerted efforts to realise the SGDs and promise of same, it is pertinent to note that there are reservations in some quarters. One of the concerns not captured in this book is that investment in decent population growth is the best approach to actualising SDGs, which has not been the case. According to populationmatters.org:

> The United Nations' 17 Sustainable Development Goals (SDGs) aim to achieve decent lives for all on a healthy planet by 2030. As things stand, most of them are likely to be missed. This is partly because they fail to address human population growth. Positive, empowering population solutions are key to meeting the SDGs. (Population Matters, 2020)

A study on the SDGs will span multiple volumes of scholarly outputs. This particular study thus looks at a few of the angles from which the

UNSDGs can be x-rayed. This enterprise thus constitutes just one of those scholarly, but practical efforts to bring stakeholders together to look at issues from multidisciplinary angles. The book, on its own, is thus a conference. It is expected that discourses from this text should stimulate thinking in such a way that scholarly submissions can further be interrogated, investigated and examined. This, in our view, is how to grow the bank of knowledge and expand the knowledge economy.

The editors wish to thank Covenant University and United Nations Information Centre (UNIC) for the initiative to have the UN@75 international conference and the fruitful venture of producing a book to preserve the knowledge shared at the conference. Palgrave Macmillan is especially appreciated for accepting to publish the book. The collaborative efforts among the organisers, publishers and authors are indeed the kind of future desirable to build a better world. It is hoped that the book will translate to productive social interfaces in reality.

References

Population Matters. (2020). *Population and the sustainable development goals*. Retrieved on February 12, 2020 from https://bit.ly/33zAwEt

United Nations. (2017). *Financing for development: Progress and prospects*. Retrieved on February 10, 2020 from https://bit.ly/359OpcQ

Appendix One: Keynote Address by General Chikadibia Obiakor (Rtd)—October 23, 2020

United Nations (UN) and the Evolution of Peace Support Operations (PSOs)

Introduction

1. On this auspicious occasion commemorating the 75th anniversary of the UN, it is indeed my privilege to be invited by Covenant University to make a presentation on the United Nations and the evolution of Peace Support Operations (PSO). This topic is apt not only because it is central to our collective effort to preserve world peace but also because UNPSOs remain the primary tool through which the UN imparts through multilateralism. I will attempt to expound on PSOs, its history, basic principles, issues in contemporary PSOs, emerging threats and my thoughts on the future of UN PSOs.

2. Since recorded history, attempts have been made to minimize the impact of violent conflict and disasters upon people. Churches, governments and alliances of governments have all had a hand in this attempt at conflict reduction or resolution. The interventionist attempts have not always been benign, indeed many interventions have been conducted in order to impose a peace, or at least what the intervenor thought was peace. Peace is an order with justice. The elegance of this definition lies in the sequence of the prerequisites. Order with Justice. One can impose order on society in many ways. Again history is full of regimes that have imposed order—Papa Doc, the Third Reich, Kim Jong-Un of

S. Folarin et al. (eds.), *The United Nations and Sustainable Development Goals*, https://doi.org/10.1007/978-3-030-95971-5

North Korea and Bashar Al-Assad of Syria. That order was imposed is not in question, what is in question is the peacefulness of these societies. Obviously, the justice component is key.

3. It is this effort at finding an acceptable means of mitigating the effect of wars or prevent the same that led to the birth of the United Nations on 24 October 1945.[1] The purpose is to bring all nations of the world together to work for peace and development, based on the principles of justice, human dignity and the well-being of all people. It affords the opportunity for countries to balance global interdependence and national interests when addressing international problems. In synch with the political correctness of the post-world-war days the UN charter established multiple ends for the vision of "a better world". The charter identified the purposes of the United Nations being the maintenance of international peace and security; development of friendly relations among nations; creation of cooperation in solving international economic, social, cultural and humanitarian problems and the promotion of respect for human rights and fundamental freedoms and to be a centre to harmonize the actions of nations in attaining these ends. Consequently, the UN, after approval by the Security Council, sends peacekeepers to regions where armed conflict has recently ceased or paused to enforce the terms of peace agreements and to discourage combatants from resuming hostilities.

Understanding PSOs

4. Peace Support Operations (PSOs) are multifunctional operations in which impartial military activities are designed to create a secure environment and to facilitate the efforts of the civilian elements of the mission to create a self-sustaining peace. Other elements of peace support operations include:

a. **Peace-making**
b. **Peace-enforcement**
c. **Peace-building**
d. **Peace-keeping**

[1] https://www.un.org/en/sections/history/history-united-nations/index.html.

History and Evolution of Peace Support Operations

5. Peace support operations (PSOs) have been an instrument of foreign and security policy since the early nineteenth century, but gained real importance, legitimacy and institutional basis with the end of the Second World War, after the establishment of the United Nations. From modern perspective, history of peacekeeping counts 72 years. The first peacekeeping operation was conducted by the United Nations in June 1948 in the form of military observer mission.[2] It was called United Nations Truce Supervision Organization in Palestine (UNTSO) and was originally mandated to supervise the truce ordered by the Security Council to end the first Arab–Israeli war. Later, similar missions were set up in Kashmir and other conflict areas.

6. It is necessary to observe that the concept of 1 peace support operations (PSOs) is not clearly defined in the UN Charter. For example, Peacekeeping operations are practical mechanisms devised to contain armed conflicts and facilitate their resolution by peaceful means. This mechanism was developed by the UN at the initial stage of the Cold War, because its original collective security and peace enforcement system, based on the authority of the Security Council and major power consensus, became unworkable as a result of the disagreement between the two superpowers. It was developed progressively.

7. Between the tasks of conflict prevention and peacekeeping lie the attempts of handling existing disputes by bringing disputing parties to agreement by peaceful means. As parties to the UN Charter, member states are under an obligation to resolve their disputes peacefully. Article 33 (probably the most important article in Chapter VI) enumerates a number of dispute settlement methods from which parties can choose—negotiations, mediation, conciliation, arbitration, judicial settlement, resort to regional arrangements or other peaceful means—states have to choose something in order to fulfil their obligation to settle the dispute. If the parties fail to settle it by the means indicated in Article 33, they are under an obligation to refer it to the Security Council. And if they fail to reach a peaceful solution, with a resulting armed conflict, they are under a customary law obligation to end the armed conflict as soon as possible, essentially through the methods and means described in Article 33.

[2] https://www.un.org/en/sections/history/history-united-nations/index.html.

8. Chapter VI gives a prominent role to the Security Council in seeking solutions to international disputes.[3] The council shall, when it deems necessary, call upon the parties to settle their dispute by the means referred to in Article 33. The obligation of Article 33 would thereby be reinforced and the corresponding demand of the Security Council would be of no less binding on a nation than Article 33 itself. The Council may also recommend appropriate procedures or methods of adjustment. If the Council deems that continuance of the dispute is likely to endanger the maintenance of international peace and security, it may recommend specific terms of settlement. In practice, however, only those means and methods of dispute settlement which are accepted by the parties have a chance of being successful. Although Chapter VI contains legal obligations for states, its peacemaking strategy is based upon the consent of parties in dispute.

As earlier indicated, PSOs are not from a strict point of view foreseen under either Chapter VI or Chapter VII of the UN Charter; they fall somewhere in between and not surprisingly the unwritten Chapter VI$^{1/2}$ has been suggested as their legal basis.

Basic Principles of Traditional Peacekeeping Operations

9. The basic principles applied to traditional UN peacekeeping operations may be summarized under three headings:

a. **Consent.** Peacekeeping operations are based on the consent of the parties to the conflict. Their deployment in an area of conflict required the consent of the host government and the other main parties concerned. The principle of consent also applied to the troop-contributing governments, which have been supplying the required military personnel on a voluntary basis;
b. **Impartiality.** UN peacekeepers sent to the area of conflict are obliged not to take sides in the conflict and support the interests of one of the parties against those of the other;
c. **Non-use of force**. The UN peacekeepers are not authorized to use force except in self-defence. They have to act with restraint at all times and seek to carry out their mission by negotiation and suasion and not by coercion.

[3] https://www.un.org/en/sections/un-charter/chapter-vi/index.html.

Mixed Operations—From Peacekeeping to Peace Enforcement

10. New developments in the concept of the PSOs could be said to have emerged in Bosnia and Somalia, namely operations that started as peacekeeping but were later mixed with elements of peace-enforcement. In 1992, the United Nations Protection Force (UNPROFOR) peacekeeping operation in Bosnia was given some specific Chapter VII authority to assist in the delivery of humanitarian relief and the protection of "safe areas". In 1993, the Security Council decided to give UNPROFOR some additional enforcement authority, this time in the context of the protection of its own personnel. Also, in dealing with deepening crisis in Somalia, the Security Council established in May 1993 the UN peacekeeping force endowed with enforcement power under Chapter VII of the UN Charter, United Nations Operation in Somalia (UNOSOM II). In addition to ensuring a secure environment for the delivery of humanitarian assistance, the UN operation in Somalia was mandated to promote national reconciliation, rehabilitation and the disarming of various Somali militias, by force if necessary. The UN operation in Somalia failed and was withdrawn in March 1995, with its mandate largely unfulfilled. The one in Bosnia was also terminated in 1995, after accords had been concluded between the warring parties at Dayton under US auspices. A much smaller civilian police mission and a NATO-led Peacekeeping force took over the task in December 1995.

11. The setbacks in Somalia, Bosnia and Rwanda ushered in a period of retrenchment of UN peacekeeping activities. The total number of UN peacekeepers had declined from more than 70,000 as of December 1994 to about 14,500 as of July 1998.[4] The retrenchment in UN peacekeeping operations was due mainly to failure in performance occasioned by the application of the principle of Peacekeeping designed for international conflict to intrastate conflicts. In order to deal with this difficulty, at the initial stage, the UN made attempts to change the mandate of some peacekeeping operations in action—legally, if the mandates for enforcement are given under Chapter VII of the UN Charter, the operations by definition don't require the consent of the parties concerned. From the first look, this could solve mentioned problem upon dealing with interstate types of conflicts. However, such "mixed" operations and immediate change of mandate from peacekeeping to peace-enforcement created new

[4] Analysis of the Different Models of Peace Support Operations and Forms of NATO Involvement, as a Part of a New Security Architecture by Dr. David BAKRADZE.

problems. Since Chapter VI is consent-based and Chapter VII is not, mixed operations run into difficulties due to the loss of impartiality—an essential requirement for obtaining the co-operation of the parties to a conflict. As a result, UN peacekeeping forces were not able to prevent and stop tragedies in Bosnia and Somalia. In drawing lessons from the UN experience in Somalia and Bosnia, in his 1995 "Supplement to an Agenda for Peace", the then-Secretary-General made the following important remark: "In reality, nothing is more dangerous for a peacekeeping operation than to ask it to use force when its existing composition, armament, logistic support and deployment deny it the capability to do so. The logic of peacekeeping flows from political and military premises that are quite distant from those of enforcement; and the dynamics of the latter are incompatible with the political process that peacekeeping is intended to facilitate. To blur the distinction between the two can undermine the viability of the peacekeeping operation and endanger its personnel".

12. The ability of the UN Security Council to define mandates properly subsequently has led to an explosion in the amount of peacekeeping troops from 14,500 in 1998 to 90,750 in 2018, i.e., a time frame of 20 years.[5]

[5] https://peacekeeping.un.org/en/military.

Model of Peace Support Operations

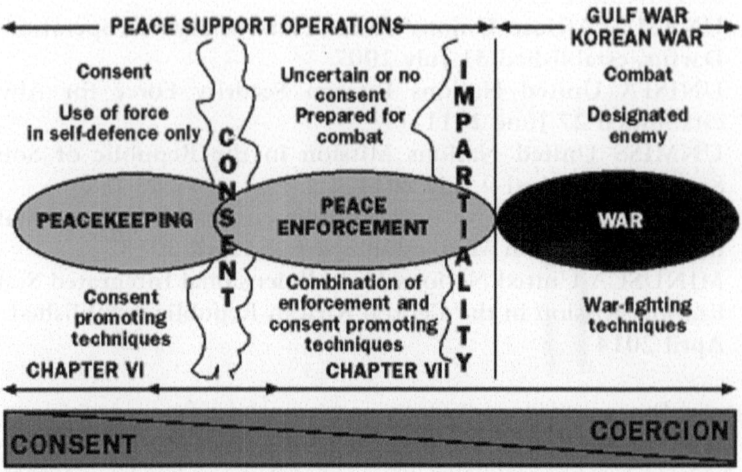

Current Peacekeeping Operations

13. There are presently thirteen UN Missions located around the world[6]:

> **UNTSO United Nations Truce Supervision Organization, Jerusalem, established 29 May 1948**
> **UNMOGIP United Nations Military Observer Group in India and Pakistan, established 24 January 1949**
> **UNFICYP United Nations Peacekeeping Force In Cyprus, established 1964**
> **UNDOF United Nations Disengagement Observer Force, Golan, established 31 May 1974**
> **UNFIL United Nations Interim Force In Lebanon, established 19 March 1978**
> **MINURSO United Nations Mission for the Referendum in Western Sahara, established 24 April 1991**
> **UNMIK United Nations Interim Administration Mission in Kosovo, established 10 June 1999**

[6] https://peacekeeping.un.org/en/where-we-operate.

MONUSCO United Nations Organization Stabilization Mission in the Democratic Republic of the Congo, established 30 November 1999
UNAMID African Union/United Nations Hybrid operation in Darfur, established 31 July 2007
UNISFA United Nations Interim Security Force for Abyei, established 27 June 2011
UNMISS United Nations Mission in the Republic of South Sudan, established 9 July 2011
MINUSMA United Nations Multidimensional Integrated Stabilization Mission in Mali, established 25 April 2013
MINUSCA United Nations Multidimensional Integrated Stabilization Mission in the Central African Republic, established 10 April 2014

Regional Organizations in PSO

14. The challenge of the proliferation of new types of regional conflicts has been so overpowering that the United Nations has been stretched to the limit by the responsibility of finding solutions for complex emergencies. The UN Charter provides a role for regional organizations in the maintenance of the peace and security in their respective regions. In fact, Article 33(1) contains the provision that parties to any dispute endangering international peace and security should seek a solution by resort to regional agencies or arrangements, as one of the peaceful means. Concerning the enforcement action by regional organizations and/or arrangements, Article 51 of the UN Charter recognizes the inherent right of individual or collective self-defence, including the right to self-defence in a regional context. Article 53(1) states that the Security Council shall utilize such regional arrangements and agencies for enforcement action under its authority. However, it stipulates that no enforcement action should be taken by regional entities without the authorization of the Security Council. In addition to that, Article 54 provides that the Security Council shall at all times be kept fully informed of activities undertaken by regional arrangements for the maintenance of international peace and security.

Issues in Contemporary PSOs

15. Some of the challenges to effective peace support operations are considered largely conceptual. In the past, peacekeepers were merely

expected to separate hostile forces and observe cease-fire or truces. For the operation to be successful, it was essential that the parties to the conflict offered collaboration and support. However, in recent conflicts involving ethnic-based disputes, intervention without the clear consent of the parties to the conflict has resulted in an environment for peace-keeping that is no longer benign. Peacekeepers increasingly work in a climate of continuing armed conflict, sometimes in places where there are poorly defined borders or cease-fire lines and no guarantees of respect for their safety or role. This new and complex environment, together with the ambitious objectives of the United Nations and ever-growing pressure on scarce resources, has made it more imperative than ever to think clearly about when and how the UN should become involved in peacekeeping operations.

16. **Protection of Civilians (POC)**[7]**:** The report of the High-Level Independent Panel on UN Peace Operations (HIPPO), released in June 2015, noted a growing gap between what is expected of peace operations and what they delivered. The HIPPO report particularly recognized this gap in the protection of civilians (POC), which it describes as a "core obligation" of the UN. That report reiterates that the core mandate of UNPSOs is the Protection of Civilians (POC) which previously was just one of the mandates given for establishing PSOs.

It recommends **phased and sequenced mandates which** could allow missions to focus their efforts and resources on POC when protection threats are highest, and to avoid undertaking activities that could undermine protection objectives. However, phased and sequenced mandates are only likely to succeed if they provide strategic objectives for missions to achieve, rather than detailed lists of tasks for missions to implement. Moreover, the adoption of phased and sequenced mandates can only lead to effective prioritization of POC on the ground if it is tied to reform in three additional areas.

a. Effective prioritization of POC depends on a **political strategy** that identifies whether and how POC is envisioned to contribute towards the mission's political goals.

[7] https://www.ipinst.org/2019/11/poc-in-peace-ops-un-policies-into-national-frameworks.

b. It depends on how POC is approached in mission **planning analysis.**
c. It depends on **timely deployment** in response to protection crises.

17. **SMART peacekeeping (use of technology)**[8]: The United Nations has adopted a strategy for technology and innovation for peacekeeping. More importantly, it is showing the will and the means to implement this strategy. Furthermore, the emergence of the technology-contributing country (TechCC) concept offers new possibilities to complement the traditional notion of the troop-contributing country (TCC) and police-contributing country (PCC). TechCCs can greatly assist not only the UN directly but also the developing world, which currently supplies the large majority of uniformed peacekeepers but whose militaries are more low-tech. The days of peacekeepers patrolling buffer zones between two conflict parties has since ended instead, they face ever more complicated large-scale situations, with diverse and fragmented actors, both state and non-state, while at the same time receiving more complex multi-layered mandates. Technological advances cover all areas of peacekeeping, from communication devices to weapons systems. And the scope of reasons why these technologies are not (yet) being used for missions is similarly wide: from the simple question of cost, to developed nations' fears about exporting advanced technologies to developing nations, who usually supply the troops on the ground, to more complex legal and ethical concerns about certain equipment.

18. **Safety and Security of peacekeepers**[9]: 2017 saw the highest number of peacekeeper fatalities through violent acts in over two decades, with 56 peacekeepers killed. In an effort to reverse this trend and improve the safety and security of UN peacekeepers, the Secretary-General in November 2017 appointed Lieutenant General (Retired) Carlos Alberto dos Santos Cruz (Brazil) to carry out an in-depth review of peacekeeping fatalities and injuries due to hostile acts. This resulted in the Improving Security of United Nations Peacekeepers report also known as the Santo Cruz report. The report states "that the United Nations and Troop- and Police-Contributing Countries need to adapt to a new reality: The blue

[8] http://www.providingforpeacekeeping.org/project/smart-peacekeeping-toward-tech-enabled-un-operations/.

[9] https://www.un.org/en/unpdf/report-on-improving-security-of-peacekeepers.shtml.

helmet and the United Nations flag no longer offer "natural" protection. Peacekeeping environments now feature armed groups, terrorists, organized crime, street gangs, criminal and political exploitation, and other threats. If the United Nations and T/PCCs do not change their mindset, take risks and show a willingness to face these new challenges, they will be consciously sending troops into harm's way."

19. **Conduct and Discipline**: The United Nations Charter requires that all UN personnel must maintain the highest standards of integrity and conduct.[10] The UN is committed to ensuring that all its personnel deployed globally serve with professionalism, courtesy and dignity. Over 100,000 civilian, military and police personnel are currently deployed in the various UN peacekeeping operations and special political missions around the world. The UN expects that all peacekeeping personnel adhere to the highest standards of behaviour and conduct themselves in a professional and disciplined manner at all times.

UN personnel are required to:

- Respect local laws, customs and practices.
- Treat host country inhabitants with respect, courtesy and consideration.
- Act with impartiality, integrity and tact.[11]

Unfortunately, there are cases of misconduct involving peacekeeping personnel. In response, the UN and Member States ensure that all credible allegations are investigated and that appropriate action is taken when allegations are substantiated. The UN has a zero-tolerance policy with respect to sexual exploitation and abuse. The UN has a three-pronged strategy to address all forms of misconduct including sexual exploitation and abuse: prevention of misconduct, enforcement of UN standards of conduct and remedial action.

20. **Political will**[12]: The lack of political will of Western nations to engage in peacekeeping missions especially under the auspices of the United Nations has been identified as one of the challenges facing PKOs in the current context. However, this unwillingness has been attributed to

[10] https://www.un.org/en/ethics/.

[11] https://peacekeeping.un.org/en/standards-of-conduct.

[12] https://cpr.unu.edu/the-politics-of-action-for-peacekeeping.html.

their involvement in other theatres like the Balkans, Afghanistan and Iraq. Russia and China are showing a new willingness to cooperate and the US is learning the inadequacy of unilateralism. In light of the weakening political will on the part of developed countries, developing countries have stepped up and are now assuming the burden by contributing the majority of peacekeepers. This new dimension of developing countries embarking on PKOs has been due to their desire to assume greater responsibility in the area of peace and security. The monetary incentives for countries to contribute troops, which can add up to a significant windfall for a developing economy, have also been identified as one reason for this increased interest in PSOs.

21. **Troop and Financial Constraints**. Closely related to political will are the challenges posed by troop availability and financial constraints. Troop availability and financial support are crucial elements of a peacekeeping deployment, without which a PSO mission cannot assume its full range of capabilities. The risk from Developing Countries in increasing their roles in PSOs stems from their lack of capacity. While there have been many good contingents from developing countries, some of these contingents are under-funded and lack training and/or appropriate equipment. Wider and more challenging mandates not only require more money but also more specialized capacities, for example, Army Engineers and Logisticians, heavy-lift aircraft, proper command-and-control, intelligence gathering capability, etc. The UN requires each member state to voluntarily contribute Peacekeepers because the demand for them is on the increase putting more pressure on Member States. The budget for 2020 is currently $6.5 billion.[13] With the global recession engendered by the pandemic, monetary constraints are one of the current challenges to PSOs.

22. **Rapid Deployment and Standing Capacity**.[14] Rapid response to crises and post-conflict areas remain difficult to achieve, and as such constitute a considerable obstacle to the effectiveness of UNPSOs. It is increasingly recognized that to respond to the challenges posed by contemporary conflicts, forces must be mobile, flexible, effective and sustainable. As the UN does not have a standing peace support operation capacity, it must rely on voluntary contributions from members

[13] https://peacekeeping.un.org/en/how-we-are-funded.

[14] Improving United Nations Capacity for Rapid Deployment by HP LANGILLE 2014.

states, causing the process of planning, authorizing and deploying a peace support operation to be extremely complex. The UN Secretariat in recognition of this fact has been developing tools to support rapid deployment. This has led to the recent establishment of the Strategic Force Generation and Capability Planning Cell. This Cell oversaw the replacement of the flawed UN Standby Arrangements System (UNSAS) with a new Peacekeeping Capability Readiness System (PCRS) in July 2015.[15] UNSAS had become outdated and ineffective, with many member states making commitments that were not available when called upon to deploy to a UN peacekeeping mission. The PCRS is intended to provide greater readiness and predictability to generate military and police contributions, with clearly defined criteria and steps to identifying actual commitments.

23. **Rules of engagement and the use of force**. The fundamental principles of UN peacekeeping-consent, impartiality and the non-use of force except in self-defence have, in specific cases, become obstacles to the deployment and success of UN peacekeeping missions. In particular, respect for the non-use of force has, in many cases, proven to be impractical in the face of large-scale massacre and detrimental to the mission both morally and physically. Rwanda, Bosnia, Somalia and East Timor are stark examples of the consequences of the non-use of force. In response to the new strategic environment, today's missions are for the most part deployed under Chapter VII of the UN charter, authorizing peacekeeping to use "all necessary means" to protect themselves and threatened civilians. However, this use of force raises a number of questions, such as the level of force at which it becomes too much and the extent to which peacekeepers should protect civilians if such protection can jeopardize a mission's objective. It is absolutely necessary for military peacekeepers to have clear rules of engagement that are suited to the particular mission to avoid repeating situations where peacekeepers lacked both capacity and mandate. Indeed, it is crucial that when a force is deployed, the mandate under which it will operate matches the needs on the ground. Experts have even argued for the UN to create a fourth principle of "credibility of force" to compliment the three basic principles already in place.

[15] Prioritizing the Protection of Civilians in UN Peace Operations: ANALYZING THE RECOMMENDATIONS OF THE HIPPO REPORT Aditi Gorur Lisa Sharland.

Emerging Threats (Terrorism, Organized Crime and Narcotics)

24. It has been noted that there are asymmetric threats to peacekeeping operations. These threats from terrorism or organized transnational crime have been growing in severity and should be taken into consideration by the Security Council in the configuration and deployment of UN Peace Support Operations.

The Emerging Threat from Drug Trafficking

25. The UN Office on Drugs and Crime (UNODC) has noted that in recent years West Africa has emerged as a key transit point for illicit drugs, in particular cocaine and heroin, from Latin American countries to Europe.[16] Tightening enforcement and interdiction along the traditional trafficking routes to North America has made drug traffickers to turn their attention to West Africa as a transit zone for conveying a range of illicit drugs to Europe and the US. The impact of the illicit trade on the local economy can sometimes be dramatic. For example, UNODC estimated in 2008 that in Guinea-Bissau the value of cocaine transported through the country may have been greater than the entire national income. Consequently, the drug traders' have developed the capacity to exploit and further undermine National Security of the countries in the regions thus impeding development and reigniting smouldering conflicts.

The consequence is reflected in the instability of States in the Sahel region and some West African Countries, a good example is Mali. The impact of this development on PSOs must be factored into the planning and execution of future PSO missions.

Thoughts on Future PSOs

26. In resonance with observations made in the reports of Brahimi (2000) and Santa Cruz (2017) as well as my personal experiences, the continued relevance of UNPSOs would require that:

a. Peace Support Operations on the basis of UN Security Council Mandates should be configured to have the capacity and capability to attract deterrence from belligerents so that they can execute their mandates.

[16] https://www.unodc.org/unodc/en/drug-trafficking/index.html.

b. Member States should place UN Peace Support Operations on the same pedestal as their National Security Structures as both serve a common goal—peace, security and the well-being of humanity which is a cardinal principle of the United Nations charter.

Appendix Two: Remarks of the Vice-Chancellor at Opening of UN75 International Conference by Professor Akan Williams—October 22, 2020

Acting Vice-Chancellor's Opening Remarks at UN75 International Conference

It is my pleasure to give these remarks at the United Nations at 75 Virtual conference with the theme, "*The Future We Want; the UN We Need: Reaffirming Our Collective Commitment to Multilateralism*". I am delighted to welcome all the distinguished guests, speakers, facilitators and participants. I wish to acknowledge the partnership of the United Nations Information Centre, Lagos, in organizing this conference.

Globalization has generated a variety of problems with global tentacles, which demands multilateral response. Since its inception 75 years ago, the United Nations has focussed on fostering international cooperation in resolving global socio-economic problems and promoted respect for human rights. Under the UN's auspices, the global community has initiated the sustainable development goals (SDGs) as a roadmap to achieve a better and more sustainable future for all, by addressing global challenges related to poverty, climate change, environmental degradation, inequality, peace and justice among others.

However, recent developments at the international level suggest that multilateralism is being undermined and endangered by withdrawals from vital global treaties and institutions, budget cuts and disregard for international law. Disenchantment with formal multilateralism has led to

S. Folarin et al. (eds.), *The United Nations and Sustainable Development Goals*, https://doi.org/10.1007/978-3-030-95971-5

recourse to alternatives, such as parallel bilateral arrangements or cooperation. However, none of these alternatives has the prospect of completely replacing multilateralism.

The prevailing realities of the digital economy and rapid technological advancement require steadfast collaborative actions to address the emergent challenges. As we commemorate the 75th anniversary of the United Nations, it behoves on the international community to celebrate past achievements and to acknowledge the urgent need to retool the Organization to strengthen its capacity to mobilize multilateral systems to act more cohesively. In recent times, it has been widely recognized that the current multilateral system is out of tune with the rapid changes in the economic, demographic and political weight of advanced and emerging economies. There is an overarching need for an inclusive multilateral system that involves the full participation of key stakeholders, including the civil society and youths.

The global community looks forward to a new multilateral system that enhances citizen and national empowerment with the United Nations as the nucleus of a global governance framework, which provides the guidance, leadership and decisions required to ensure sustainable development in our interdependent world.

Covenant is actively involved in research efforts aimed at evolving innovative solutions in facilitating the achievement of the SDGs. The recent ranking of the University in the 401–600 bracket of the 2020 Impact Ranking of Times Higher Education (THE), attests to our contributions in this direction. This conference is one of our contributory platforms to encourage multidisciplinary partnerships in research efforts aimed at achieving the SDGs as the future we want. Our doors are open to opportunities of research collaboration with universities, research institutes, and other stakeholders.

Appendix Three: Closing Remarks by Director, United Nations Information Centre, Mr. Ronald Kayanja, Director UNIC for Nigeria—October 24, 2020

UNIC Director's Closing Remarks at UN75 International Conference

I would like to thank Almighty God who has enabled us to achieve this feat. This year, we mark 75 years of the United Nations, and there have been many events already around the world, but none like this conference, which has examined the theme through an intellectual discourse of a multidisciplinary nature.

I extend gratitude to the Chancellor and Vice-Chancellor of Covenant University; to Prof. Sheriff Folarin, who has been chair of the organizing committee and all the committee members. You have all performed with the excellence always associated with Covenant University.

To the keynote speakers during all the plenary sessions, we also extend gratitude. They handled their topics so well and brought out the content of their valuable experience to share with us.

Thanks to all distinguished scholars who researched, wrote and presented very insightful papers, which will eventually be part of a publication on UN75. Thank you very much.

The stimulating discussions from this conference will continue to resonate for many years to come, guiding future generations. We are honoured to have been part of this exciting experience.

We are ending this conference on a special day. Today, 24th October marks the 75th anniversary of the United Nations. It is the day on which the UN Charter was ratified in 1945, and the United Nations officially came into being.

S. Folarin et al. (eds.), *The United Nations and Sustainable Development Goals*, https://doi.org/10.1007/978-3-030-95971-5

This anniversary comes in a time of great disruption for the world, compounded by an unprecedented global health crisis due to the COVID-19 pandemic, with severe economic and social impacts. But it is also a reminder that times of struggle can become an opportunity for positive change and transformation. The papers presented during this conference are a great testimony to the opportunities that exist ahead of this world if we all commit to working together.

Let me wish all of us a happy United Nations Day commemoration because the organization was established for “we the peoples”.

I wish all of you greater success in all your continuing endeavours.

May God reward all of you greatly.

Appendix Four: Address of the UN Resident and Humanitarian Coordinator in Nigeria, Mr. Edward Kallon—October 22, 2020

UN Resident and Humanitarian Coordinator's Address UN75 International Conference

It is an honour for me to be here today at this virtual conference on UN @ 75. Let me start by thanking the organizers and all of you for this important intellectual exchange on the theme of UN 75 "***The future we want, the United Nations we need: reaffirming our collective commitment to multilateralism***". This is a critical moment for us to look to the future, as we see everywhere around the world our young people demanding a better future for themselves.

And yet the foundations of our world have been shaken to the core by COVID-19. The pandemic has pushed us towards the worst recession in decades, with terrible consequences for the most vulnerable. Societies and citizens are reeling from widespread disruption.

After many years of progress, poverty and hunger are on the rise. Children are suffering from a lack of schooling, debt is skyrocketing and fiscal resources are plunging.

Even before the virus, inequalities were growing. The benefits of globalization and growth had failed to reach millions upon millions of destitute people, deepening their already profound despair. Biodiversity was also disappearing, greenhouse gases were at record levels.

We need a path that brings health to all, revives economies, brings people in from the margins of society and builds long-term resilience, sustainability, opportunity and peace.

S. Folarin et al. (eds.), *The United Nations and Sustainable Development Goals*, https://doi.org/10.1007/978-3-030-95971-5

It was in view of these and other global challenges that the UN General Assembly passed the resolution "***Transforming our World: the Agenda for sustainable development***" in 2015. This ambitious agenda aims to free the human race from the indignity of poverty and heal and secure our planet. As the Brundtland Report "**Our Common Future**" of 1987 says, we are working towards development that meets the needs of the current generations without compromising those of the future. In this agenda, with the 17 sustainable development goals, we focus on the key areas of economic development to promote prosperity; ensure social inclusion and eliminate inequalities; protect and regenerate our environment and build governance institutions.

This Agenda 2030 is transformational. We are working towards a world free of poverty, hunger, disease and want, where all life can thrive. A world with equitable and universal access to quality education at all levels, to health care and social protection, where physical, mental and social well-being are assured. A world where we reaffirm our commitments regarding the human right to safe drinking water and sanitation and where there is improved hygiene; and where food is sufficient, safe, affordable and nutritious. A world where human habitats are safe, resilient and sustainable and where there is universal access to affordable, reliable and sustainable energy. And indeed a world of universal respect for human rights and human dignity, the rule of law, justice, equality and non-discrimination. That world is possible if we all work together.

The UN Secretary-General early this year launched the decade of action for the world to move even faster towards meeting the 17 sustainable development goals. During this decade of action we want to mobilize everyone, everywhere to take action on Agenda 2030; we want to demand urgency and ambition from leaders and to shine a light on those solutions and innovations that are making a difference around the world as we work towards achieving these goals. I hope all of us know how this is now even more critical after seeing the vulnerabilities that COVID-19 has exposed in our societies.

Distinguished participants, allow me to speak about the young people.

According to the World Youth Report 2020, young people between 15 and 24 years of age number 1.21 billion and account for 15.5 per cent of the global population. Close to 90 per cent of them live in developing countries, where they constitute a large proportion of the population.

Connected to each other like never before, young people want to and already contribute to the resilience of their communities, proposing innovative solutions, driving social progress and inspiring political change, in urban as well as rural contexts. Young people constitute a tremendous and essential asset worth investing in, opening the door to an unparalleled multiplier effect. At the same time, young people are also facing incredible challenges and even life-threatening risks, disproportionately carried by girls and young women in many parts of the world.

These arise when accessing their rights, including to quality education, healthcare or decent work. They also arise in situations of conflict, or when young people flee home in search of survival or move for better opportunities. With this large and increasing number of young people across the globe, it is abundantly clear that it is only by engaging and working with them, supporting them in standing up for their rights and creating the conditions allowing them to progress and play an active role, that we will be able to achieve peace, security, justice, climate resilience and sustainable development for all.

The UN wants to see a world in which the human rights of every young person are realized; that ensures every young person is empowered to achieve their full potential and that recognizes young people as agents of change.

The UN Secretary-General has, therefore, developed a strategy to engage young people globally through our various entities operating at national, regional and global levels. We have identified five priorities:

1. **Engagement, Participation and Advocacy**—Amplify youth voices for the promotion of a peaceful, just and sustainable world
2. **Human Capital Development**—Support young people's greater access to quality education and health services
3. **Economic Empowerment through Decent Work**—Support young people's greater access to decent work and productive employment
4. **Youth and Human Rights**—Protect and promote the rights of young people and support their civic and political engagement
5. **Youth, Peace and Security**—Support young people as catalysts for Peace and Security and Humanitarian Action

I hope we can all work together to ensure more inclusiveness for the young people in all our development endeavours because this is part of what sustainability is about. It is my hope that many of these issues will be discussed by our distinguished scholars during this conference.

As I conclude, please allow me to present to you the message of the UN Secretary-General for this International Conference.

Appendix Five: Remarks by National Information Officer, United Nations Information Centre-Nigeria by Dr. Oluseyi Soremekun—October 24, 2020

Remarks by UNIC National Information Officer at UN75 International Conference

I am delighted for this opportunity to speak at this landmark multidisciplinary conference, arguably and probably the only academic conference on UN@75 in the world. It really gladdens our hearts that this is happening in Nigeria. Congratulations to the management and staff of CU and UNIC.

The past three days had been instructive, insightful and intellectually rewarding. It has been three days of knowledge sharing and academic discourse on critical issues that are dear to the United Nations: So far, this conference has interrogated issues bordering on terrorism, diplomacy, peacekeeping operations, multilateralism, human rights, justice, fake news and hate speech and implications on peace and security, science and technology, among others.

These past 75 years had witnessed series of events, interventions and visions that have shaped the world we have got today. The world is dynamic and evolving. People and planet are under pressure. Technology is getting more advanced at a blistering speed. Demography is rapidly changing, and more young people are asking questions and interrogating the status quo. Will we emerge stronger and better equipped to work together? Or will distrust and isolation grow further? These are research questions for the academia. I trust many of the papers presented at this conference have addressed or answered a few of the questions. No doubt,

S. Folarin et al. (eds.), *The United Nations and Sustainable Development Goals*, https://doi.org/10.1007/978-3-030-95971-5

the answers provided today would form the foundation of tomorrow's questions. Engagement and intellectual discourse must continue beyond this conference.

Through these engagements and discourses, as we are having today, the UN aims to build a global vision of 2045—its centenary, increase understanding of the threats to that future, and support enhanced international cooperation to realize that vision.

As you all know, the theme for the UN75 is *The future we want, the UN we need: Reaffirming our collective commitment to multilateralism*'. In reflecting on this theme, the next ten years are critical if we must shape the "future we want" as Nigerians and the UN we need in the context of the Nigerian society. Agenda 2030 for sustainable development explains our present and defines our future.

The year 2020 technically marks the beginning of the Decade of Action to achieve the Sustainable Development Goals (SDGs) by 2030. This is our present and our future. We must be active players in driving the present conversation to shape our future and that of Nigeria. I am glad that this conference covers a wide spectrum of fields as reflected in the SDGs: Arts, social sciences, sciences including engineering, among others.

The Decade of Action calls on governments, businesses, civil society, the academia and individuals everywhere to create an unstoppable force to reach the Goals by 2030. This unstoppable action is hinged on a tripod:

- Let's mobilize everyone, everywhere to take action—individually and collectively, locally and globally
- Let's demand urgency and ambition—hold leaders to account
- Let's supercharge ideas to solutions—shine a light on success stories and drive sustainable innovation, investments and technology

Despite the coronavirus-induced disruption in people's lifestyle, socioeconomic activities and interventions by development partners, we must mobilize and engage to demonstrate our shared ability to deliver the Sustainable Development Goals for people and for the planet.

I call on the academics to be more aggressive in their contributions to the implementation of the SDGs in Nigeria. Not all contributions require funds as some studies have established. However, I also understand that time is money. Contribute your time and talent. Be familiar with not only the 17 goals of the Agenda 2030 but also the 169 targets and the specific

232 indicators for measuring the 169 SDG targets. This knowledge would guide deeper understanding of the salient issues and enhance measuring results and holding government to account.

2030 is just around the corner. Let's cover more grounds in this decade of action towards realizing the 2030 agenda for sustainable development.

Index

S. Folarin et al. (eds.), *The United Nations and Sustainable Development Goals*, https://doi.org/10.1007/978-3-030-95971-5

The manufacturer's authorised representative in the EU is Springer Nature Customer Service Centre GmbH, Europaplatz 3, 69115 Heidelberg, Germany. If you have any concerns regarding our products, please contact ProductSafety@springernature.com

Printed and bound by CPI Group (UK) Ltd, Croydon, CR0 4YY
30/09/2026
02225492-0007